ENERGY RISK MANAGEMENT

ENERGY RISK MANAGEMENT

HEDGING STRATEGIES AND INSTRUMENTS FOR THE INTERNATIONAL ENERGY MARKETS

Peter C. Fusaro

McGraw-Hill

New York San Francisco Washington, D.C. Auckland Bogotá
Caracas Lisbon London Madrid Mexico City Milan
Montreal New Delhi San Juan Singapore
Sydney Tokyo Toronto

Library of Congress Cataloging-in-Publication Data

Fusaro, Peter C.
    Energy risk management: hedging strategies and instruments for the inter-
national energy markets/by Peter C. Fusaro
        p. cm.
        ISBN 0-7863-1184-3
1. Power resources—Prices. 2. Petroleum products—Prices. 3. Energy industries.
I. Title.
HD9502.A2F87 1998
621.042'068'1—dc21

                                                                    97-34906
                                                                        CIP

McGraw-Hill

A Division of The McGraw-Hill Companies

4 5 6 7 8 9 0 DOC/DOC 0 2 1

The sponsoring editor for this book was *Stephen Issacs*, the editing supervisor was
John M. Morriss, and the production supervisor was *Suzanne W. B. Rapcavage*. It
was set in 11 point Palatino by *PageMasters & Company*.

Printed and bound by R.R. Donnelley & Sons Company.

McGraw-Hill books are available at special quantity discounts to use as premiums and sales promotions, or for use in corporate training programs. For more
information, please write to the Director of Special Sales, McGraw-Hill, Professional Publishing, Two Penn Plaza, New York, NY 10121-2298. Or contact your
local bookstore.

 This books is printed on recycled, acid-free paper containing a minimum of 50% recycled de-inked fiber.

This book is dedicated to Martha and Laura, who had to put up with travel and work plans over family holidays, and who all the time were supportive.

CONTENTS

CONTRIBUTORS IX

PREFACE XI

INTRODUCTION XIII

Chapter 1

Why Use These Financial Tools?   1
Peter C. Fusaro

Chapter 2

The ABCs of Energy Financial Instruments   9
Peter C. Fusaro

Chapter 3

European Energy Markets Developments   37
Seana Lanigan

Chapter 4

Asian Market Developments   53
Paul Horsnell

Chapter 5

Risk Management in North American Natural Gas   71
Patricia Hemsworth

Chapter 6

The Evolution of US Electricity Markets   89
Dr. Antoine Eustache

Chapter 7

European Electricity Trading Markets   107
Jeremy Wilcox

Chapter 8

The Development of Coal Futures   119
Jay L. Gottlieb

Chapter 9

Options Theory and Its Application to Energy   133
Dr. Nedia Miller

Chapter 10

Value at Risk for Power Markets   157
Kenneth Leong and Riaz Siddiqi

Chapter 11

Technical Analysis in Energy Trading   179
Henry Lichtenstein

Chapter 12

Credit Issues and Counterparty Risk   195
Robert Maxant and George Travers

Chapter 13

Future of Energy Price Risk Management   217
Peter C. Fusaro

Glossary

Peter C. Fusaro   239

Index   245

CONTRIBUTORS

Editor: Peter C. Fusaro, Senior Vice President, Energy Consulting, ABB Financial Consulting

Dr. Antoine Eustache, Senior Research Manager, Dow Jones Markets.

Jay L. Gottlieb, Senior Research Manager, New York Mercantile Exchange.

Patricia Hemsworth, Marketing Manager Energy, Dow Jones Markets.

Paul Horsnell, Assistant Director for Research, Oxford Institute for Energy Studies.

Seana Lanigan, Press Officer, International Petroleum Exchange.

Kenneth Leong and Riaz Siddiqi, Risk Management, Cinergy Corporation.

Henry Lichtenstein, Managing Director, Institutional Sales—Energy, FIMAT Futures USA.

Robert Maxant and George Travers, Power & Energy Group, Deloitte Touche LLP

Dr. Nedia Miller, CTA & Independent Consultant.

Jeremy Wilcox, Editor, PH Energy Analysis Ltd.

PREFACE

Any book on a new subject requires much foresight as to why it is valuable and whether the work will make a contribution to the field from both an academic and a business standpoint. Energy risk management is still emerging as an academic discipline as well as taking place in a dynamic marketplace that requires only a snapshot of where we are today be sufficient to where we will be tomorrow.

Over the past six years, I have spoken, lectured, and been interviewed on the subject of energy risk management and its evolution in North America, Europe, and Asia. Each market is continuing to undergo changes unique to the energy industry in that region of the world. Yet, I am often asked whether there is a book I can read on the globalization of energy risk management. In the past, the answer was no, with referrals made to magazine articles if much was written at all. This is the first book to capture the worldwide trends of energy commoditization that are accelerating at lightning speed. Financial engineering has entered the lexicon as one means of trying to capture this business discipline.

This book is written deliberately as an overview and introduction to the complex field of energy derivatives. It is hoped that the reader will be able to grasp the intensity of how much the financial world has invaded and coopted the energy world. Management thinking has always been oriented toward risk, but competition drives the need to utilize the financial tools available. This book is just the first chapter on the transformation of energy companies to multiple commodity warehouses.

Peter C. Fusaro

INTRODUCTION

Energy price risk management is still in its early stages of development compared to the more developed paper markets in interest rates and foreign currencies. An innate industry conservatism coupled with highly profitable years sowed the seeds of complacency despite the two oil price shocks of the 1970s. But the world oil price collapse of 1986 and the constant restructuring of the US oil and gas industry during the past decade coupled with the beginning of electric utility deregulation and privatization throughout the world are continuing to drive change in energy commodity markets. Moreover, we are still early in the process of energy commoditization. Oil futures began trading on the New York Mercantile Exchange (NYMEX) only in 1978, and the first oil price swap was introduced in 1986. Natural gas futures and over-the-counter (OTC) instruments began in 1990. And electricity futures contracts began in Norway in 1995 followed by the United States and New Zealand in 1996. Thus, the tools of financial markets have taken time to gestate and take hold in this extremely volatile and capital-intensive energy industry. The key fact is that in less than 20 years world oil markets have become integrated and are using financial instruments as part of their daily trade. Gas and electricity are now accelerating the change process of liquid trading and cross-energy commodity arbitrage. In effect, a conservative industry is continuing to be transformed through financial engineering and the development of competitive markets globally.

Crude oil and petroleum products are now traded globally 24 hours per day every business day in both the physical and the paper markets. With the daily physical consumption of oil at over 70 million barrels and annual trade valued at more than $400 billion, the growth in paper trading seems assured, with new financial products evolving to meet the needs of producers, refiners, marketers, and consumers. Paper trading for oil has grown on established futures exchanges in the United States and Europe to more than 200 million barrels per day with commensurate growth on the forward and OTC markets. The Asian oil markets are now being transformed by deregulation, privatization, and the rise of competition. Moreover, because major oil companies must now buy and trade on the spot markets to meet more of their supply needs that were previously met by their own production, their active involvement in paper trading will be increasing over time throughout the world. These changes, coupled with periods of supply tightness and higher prices predicted for the late 1990s and beyond, signaled that oil price volatility must be increasingly managed by a wide variety of existing and emerging financial instruments for the longer term. Similarly, rapid changes taking place in the natural gas markets in North America and Europe with the advent of futures trading have made it imperative to utilize risk management tools to manage natural gas price volatility.

Electricity risk management is in its infancy, but over the next 5 to 10 years, electricity trading will grow to dwarf natural gas and vie for oil's dominance in paper markets. Electric power generation is the last industry to be deregulated in the United States, and partial deregulation has already occurred in the United Kingdom. As of January 1998, Norway, Sweden, Finland, New Zealand, Australia, and the U.S. have had futures contracts for electricity. Deregulation and privatization efforts are pushing generators and end users to use risk management tools. Emerging competition has changed the dynamic in power markets from cost-of-service monopolistic control to incentive-based rates and multicompetitors.

Because of the great price volatility endured by the energy business during the past decade, the industry adopted short-term hedging tools, such as forward and futures contracts, as a means of conducting business and is now positioned to utilize longer-dated instruments including price swaps and OTC options. Changes in management thinking are occurring because it has become unacceptable in today's volatile price environment (as underscored by the Gulf War) to remain unhedged and acceptable to use the financial tools available to manage price risk. The use of these instruments represents one more step in the continued process of industry restructuring and reintegration which began during the mid-1980s and still continues during the 1990s. These financial tools cannot be used only as a means to hedge price risk but are beginning to be employed to effectively manage corporate assets for the longer term including project finance applications. Thus, energy companies can utilize their corporate assets and extract their present value rather than wait for earnings through future production and sales.

The evolutionary process of risk management that occurred in the oil and gas markets presages the growth of electricity risk management usage globally. Major oil companies now buy and trade on the spot markets to meet supply needs that were previously met by their own production, and their involvement in paper trading has continued to increase over time. Similarly, rapid changes took place in the North American natural gas markets during the 1990s with the advent of futures trading by the NYMEX, making it imperative to utilize risk management tools to manage natural gas price volatility. The same is now true of electric utilities and end users.

Price volatility will increasingly be managed through a wide variety of existing and emerging financial instruments for the short and longer term. Annualized price volatility for crude oil is 25 percent per year. For natural gas, it is 40 percent, the highest of any commodity. Electricity promises to show similar volatility to natural gas, with some analysts predicting 40–50 percent price volatility. It is also a more complex commodity.

Because risk management tools are now more widely accepted and available as a means to reduce financial risk in the commodities markets, their application in the energy markets will only accelerate over time. Risk management tools provide a degree of certainty for oil and gas producers, refiners, electric and gas utilities, airlines, shipping companies, and manufacturers who use them. The energy OTC instruments allow custom tailoring of agreements to meet the needs of the user while the financial intermediaries, oil companies, banks, or insurance companies, assume the risk. Moreover, the agreement arranges fixed price deals for the energy producer or consumer for 6 months or 1, 2, 5, or 10 years forward. These advantages over the shorter-term futures and forward contracts show swaps and OTC options to be not only complementary to futures in meeting different needs for their users but also competitive to standardized exchange-traded contracts.

These financial tools are not new. What is new is the application of tools and technologies of the financial markets to the energy markets in a wide variety of strategies. It has now become necessary to think of oil, gas, and electricity as money. Oil has been stripped of its physical delivery and has become the province of financial specialists, oil traders, and some oil companies who can now assist the industry to tap into their corporate assets more efficiently. Natural gas in the North American market has increasingly become commoditized in the 1990s with an active futures market and the concurrent growth of a robust derivatives market in North America. And electricity is beginning the commoditization process in North America, Europe, and Australasia. The selective use of financial instruments ranging from forwards, futures, and options to price swaps and oil-linked debentures not only aids in managing price risk but also protects cash flow, meets operational needs, finances prospective projects, and services debt obligations for producers, refiners, marketers, and end users. These parties now face economic, political, and environmental uncertainties that impact on how they conduct business under present market conditions and in the future. The use of currency trading tools and techniques might just signal that the energy commodity is a substitute for money.

The maturation of the energy swaps and OTC options market has brought the fundamental concern of credit risk to the fore. Credit risk concerns the ability of swaps counterparties to perform for the length of the transaction. It has become a leading issue in the natural gas swaps market as some swaps market makers will not enter into long-term agreements (beyond 5 years) with otherwise financially healthy companies, and it is beginning to emerge in the electric power markets. This factor has been true of all swaps markets as the pressure to preserve capital and reduce risk are preeminent factors among many market makers especially in light of the highly publicized financial debacles of the 1990s.

This book contains the best available information on the global changes under way in energy commodity markets from knowledgeable experts well versed in energy commodity trading and price risk management. It covers oil, gas, and electricity commoditization in the United States and Europe and offers insights into the development of an Asian paper market for oil, gas, and electric power. The book also offers a wide variety of views on the application of price risk management to the energy industry. It is meant as a primer so that the reader can become familiar with the energy markets and the growing use of the financial tools used in these markets.

GROWTH OF RISK MANAGEMENT TOOLS

Risk management tools are a form of price insurance given at a relatively small fixed cost to protect parties against adverse price movements. These instruments are the necessary tools of the energy trade in today's uncertain and volatile energy markets. As short-term hedging brought futures trading and its strategies into oil markets to protect profits and positions in the physical market, the use of longer-dated instruments is now becoming equally applicable for both short- and long-term risk. Interestingly, the development of active and liquid spot markets for oil following the price shocks of the 1970s presaged the development and success of the futures markets. The two supply disruptions during the 1970s heightened price volatility, and this rising tide of price fluctuation in the oil markets underscored the need to use energy futures. The Gulf War reaffirmed that price volatility continues to be an uncertain and unexpected component of energy markets. Today, the tools of the risk management culture that are used in other commodity markets have permeated the energy markets and include forwards, futures, swaps, options, and other derivative products.

Traders and financial institutions in oil markets are able to take advantage of inefficiencies in transnational financial markets and, by using synthetic instruments, can create a series of swaps or other derivative product transactions that provide the intermediaries—the market makers—a comparative advantage in fixing similar deals. In fact, it is the replication of the established deals using the same tools that is a means of realizing substantial profits for the intermediaries of the financial energy trade.

The use of financial instruments to manage price risk is a new area of business development for the oil traders, oil and natural gas companies, electric utilities, and banks that are able to establish price protection programs for smaller energy companies that need them but cannot develop these tools internally. These commercial interests can create price swaps regardless of how the market is structured, for the deal makers are inventive enough to take advantage of market anomalies. While positions may have to be rejuggled in rapidly changing markets, over time the markets are righted once again and some equilibrium is reestablished.

Price swaps and OTC options allow producers an assured, fixed price for their production. These instruments enable corporate planners and treasury departments to project revenues for upstream crude oil drilling expenditures and development costs. These costs can now be fixed at least 1 year forward and up to 10–15 years forward in more customized deals providing a significant advantage for companies that use these instruments. And some natural gas cogeneration deals, have gone out 20–30 years forward with appropriate price reopeners built into these long-term agreements.

Swaps and options allow refiners, manufacturers, cogenerators, and other energy end users price hedging capabilities with or without using futures contracts. Generally, these tools allow a fixed price and expenditure for the user. End users active in swaps and OTC options include energy-intensive industries such as commercial airlines, the shipping industry, manufacturers, and petrochemical producers.

The continuing commoditization of crude oil, refined products, natural gas, and more recently, electricity and petrochemicals has brought more players into the OTC markets where the application of price swaps, options, and other derivative financial products are growing in usage and importance. These markets are well positioned for explosive growth in the first decade of the 21st century, as they can be used to lower borrowing costs and minimize risk by laying it off on a third party. Moreover, these financial tools attract capital investment to the energy sector and provide greater liquidity and new trading opportunities for the energy futures exchanges. They are also creating more business in bank lending, as access to capital for the energy industries requires that risk be more astutely managed. Most important, the increasing securitization of oil and gas brings new capital liquidity into the energy sector from institutional investors.

The growing market for energy price risk management has brought new players into the field as intermediaries who provide risk management services. In New York, London, and Singapore, increasing numbers of swaps brokers act as intermediaries between principals. Brokers improve price transparency in the market, and they signal the continued maturation of the off-exchange market.

Crude oil initially dominated the off-exchange market, which then expanded to refined products and natural gas. Now electricity is moving into the picture. Energy risk management also has an important role to play in project finance as continued price volatility increases credit concerns in energy lending.

Price volatility continues to be an inevitable component of energy markets. The tools of risk management that have long been used in other commodity markets, including forwards, swaps, options, and other derivative products, have become part of the energy markets. Over-the-counter, as opposed to exchange-traded, risk management tools are often called "synthetic" financial products because they combine two or more financial instruments to create the equivalent of a new security.

Traders and financial institutions take advantage of inefficiencies in financial markets. Immature markets, such as electricity, attract great interest because of the large arbitrage opportunities that exist at the beginning of market development. By using synthetic instruments, they create a series of swaps or other derivative product transactions that provide the intermediate market makers with a comparative advantage in fixing similar deals. It is the replication of established deals that generates profits for the intermediaries of the financial energy trade, as they leverage their expertise. In the evolving electricity market, little money has yet been made due to the inability, so far, to replicate a series of forward price deals.

Most derivative product transactions are privately executed and managed. The details are known only to the principal parties involved. This privacy is another advantage contributing to the popularity of derivative products. Principals are able to shield the details of their trading strategies from other market participants.

The use of financial instruments to manage price risk offers a new area of business development for traders, oil and natural gas companies, and banks. They are able to develop price protection programs for small energy companies that need these services but cannot dedicate their own resources to price risk management. Electric utilities are beginning to offer risk management products to their customers in the form of options as well as swaps. These deal makers can create price swaps regardless of how the market is structured, for they know how to take advantage of market anomalies. While positions may have to be restructured in rapidly changing markets, over time the markets stabilize and some equilibrium is achieved.

Price swaps and OTC options allow producers to fix a price for their production. Corporate planners and treasury departments can then project revenues for upstream drilling and exploration costs, for crude oil and natural gas, and for generation costs for electricity. Costs can now be fixed at least 1 year forward and as much as 10–12 years forward in customized deals, providing a significant advantage for companies that use these instruments. While some 30-year deals have been written for cogeneration projects, the yield curve for electricity at present goes out about 5 years forward. Longer-term deals don't seem likely because electricity forward prices will be lower in the future.

Swaps and options provide refiners, manufacturers, cogenerators, and electric and gas utilities with price hedging capabilities with or without the use of futures contracts. End users active in swaps and OTC options are energy-intensive industries, such as commercial airlines, the shipping industry, manufacturers, petrochemical producers, and aluminum producers.

The continuing commoditization of crude oil, refined products, natural gas, and electricity has brought more players into the off-exchange markets, where the application of price swaps, options, and other derivative financial products is growing in volume and importance. These markets are positioned for explosive growth in the first decade of the 21st century, as they can provide a means to lower borrowing costs by transferring risk to third parties. Moreover, these financial tools attract capital investment to the oil, gas, and electricity sectors and provide greater liquidity and new trading opportunities for the energy futures exchanges. They also create more opportunities in bank lending, as the capital needs of the energy industry demand that risk be more astutely managed. Most important, the increasing securitization of oil, gas, and electricity brings new capital liquidity into the energy sector from institutional investors. Derivative products are changing how companies are managed and organized as they call into question how assets are valued.

OVERVIEW OF THIS BOOK

This book presents an overview of the new uses and applications of financial instruments to energy markets that are now in a state of ever-present change and continuing uncertainty. It describes why these instruments developed, what some of them are, how they are used, their application in oil, natural gas, and power markets, and where the energy industry is heading in its future use of these tools.

This introduction describes the development of forwards, futures, and OTC derivative contracts for the oil markets, where they first were used by the energy industry. Chapter 1 discusses the development of financial instruments that are used to manage risk and why they are needed. Chapter 2 focuses on explaining what these instruments are for the oil market. Chapter 3 examines developments in the European oil and gas markets. Chapter 4 presents an overview of the dynamics of the Asian oil market. Chapter 5 offers an analysis of North American gas trading during the 1990s.

Chapter 6 explores the evolution of US electricity trading markets. Chapter 7 explains the market drivers for the development of electricity trading in Europe. Chapter 8 presents the arguments for establishing coal futures contracts in North America.

Chapter 9 presents the basics of options theory and its application to energy markets. Chapter 10 explains the significance of the value-at-risk (VaR) technique for power markets. Chapter 11 demonstrates the use of technical analysis in energy trading. Chapter 12 expounds upon the importance of credit and counterparty risk, particularly for the electricity markets.

The final chapter describes some of the future applications and new areas of business development for the energy derivatives markets.

Peter C. Fusaro

ENERGY RISK MANAGEMENT

CHAPTER 1

Why Use These Financial Tools?

By Peter C. Fusaro

WHAT IS RISK?

Commodity producers and consumers are constantly exposed to risk in their buying and selling transactions. This risk can be broken down into three parts: *price risk, basis risk*, and *credit risk*.

Price risk refers to exposure to adverse price moves in the cash market. A producer risks loss if prices move lower in the cash market. The consumer will lose if prices move higher.

Basis risk refers to the difference between the price used as a benchmark in a transaction and the price for the actual goods changing hands. The difference is a function of location, quality, and supply/demand for each. If the difference between the benchmark price and the actual price does not remain constant, there will be a gain on one side of the deal and a loss on the other independent of any change in the benchmark. When the actual price is higher than the benchmark, the actual is at a premium to the benchmark; when the actual is lower than the benchmark, it is at a discount.

Credit risk refers to the ability of the parties of a transaction to keep their contractual obligations.

Each facet of risk is a variable in each transaction. This chapter concentrates on strategies for managing price risk, though many of the strategies can also reduce basis risk and credit risk as well.

RISK MANAGEMENT

Risk management and the integration of futures, forwards, swaps, and over-the-counter (OTC) options with the cash markets are now an integral part of an oil company's operations in the global oil markets. A similar process of integration has occurred in North American natural gas since 1990 with the advent of gas futures trading. Now these changes are taking root in the US, UK, Scandinavian, and Australasian markets as electric utility markets deregulate there.

The risk management process reduces financial exposure associated with price volatility by substituting a transaction made now for one that would have been made at a later date. Control over price changes is managed by using these financial instruments. The application of risk management tools allows companies to purchase downside protection, though opportunity for gain is limited, and frees money for other purposes. Some factors for a company to consider in deciding whether to use risk management tools include profit margins, credit exposure, cash flow requirements, debt service obligations, project economics, and planning requirements. All risk management programs must have upper management support and must include set financial limits.

The risk management culture has become part of the behavior of oil producers, refiners, marketers, electric and gas utilities, and end users; the changes now taking place in the global energy industry should not be underestimated. Oil and natural gas are major commodities on the regulated and off-exchange financial markets because of their price volatility. Electricity trading is an emerging market in many parts of the world. The New York Mercantile Exchange (NYMEX) launched electricity futures contracts for the western US market in March 1996. Norway and Sweden have exchange-traded futures which were launched in October 1995.

The development of an energy risk management plan requires knowledge of the specific market and an understanding of the financial nature of the business. Oil and gas company traders now can use the same types of financial instruments to manage risk that currency traders have used for more than 20 years. These are now being adopted to electricity markets. While different units within a company view risk separately and distinctly, it is important to develop an internal consensus on risk management by defining company objectives. Risk management programs should allow for both control over the cost of funds, through budgeted interest expenses, and prevention of unforeseen depletion of capital. Using financial risk management tools is a prudent strategy in an uncertain and volatile economic environment. This is particularly true when resources to finance high-capital cost structures are scarce in cyclical industries such as energy.

A successful risk management program will use hedging strategies that fit a company's culture and involve an educational process for senior management. The program should ultimately incorporate the full range of risk management tools available, taking into account cash flow, tax, and other internal company requirements. The program must be proactive in utilizing company trading expertise to exploit opportunities in the market. The plan should be reviewed periodically to evaluate its effectiveness and to adjust to changing market conditions.

Cultural differences play a role in the development of risk management programs. Some companies delegate foreign currency hedging to their treasury departments. Hedging all exposures to currency risk improves the profitability of commodity transactions. Working with brokers and market makers who know the daily operations of the industry is vital to establishing a practical hedging strategy.

Utilities particularly cannot do this effectively without outside assistance because they have operated for so long as monopolies, insulated from the marketplace.

Companies hedge commodity price risk because they need to meet budget targets, enhance cash flows, and protect project financing economics. They can hedge through forward purchase or sales contracts, exchange-traded futures contracts, or over-the-counter products such as swaps and options. Each instrument offers advantages and disadvantages. It can be argued that OTC swaps and options are the most advantageous because they offer greater flexibility, longer maturities, less basis risk, no margin calls, and lower costs compared to futures or physicals.

HEDGING AND SPECULATION

Risk management tools are used to manage price volatility in order to protect company revenues and profits. In the simplest terms, this is accomplished by *hedging*—establishing a "paper" position opposite to the physical position of the commodity buyer or seller. While speculation may be anathema to some in the industry, they may find the concept more palatable if hedging and speculation are viewed as complementary strategies where one party reduces its risk by transferring it to another who is willing to assume it at a price agreeable to both.

The hedger uses risk management tools to protect a physical position or other financial exposure in the market from adverse price moves which would reduce the value of the position. A seller of the commodity seeks protection against downside price moves; a buyer seeks protection against upside price moves. Hedging protects profit margins and reduces risk. It is a form of insurance in that the hedger pays an up-front cost that is expected to be smaller that what would be lost if the position were not hedged. The hedge position is established to buffer against day-to-day market fluctuations in accordance with strategic company objectives.

The speculator, on the other hand, usually is neither a producer nor a consumer of the physical commodity. What attracts the speculator is the potential for profit. The speculator assumes the hedger's risk and adds liquidity to the market.

EVOLVING ENERGY MARKETS

The oil price shocks of 1973 and 1979 resulted in increased volatility in oil prices, greater trading volume on the spot crude and product markets, and in turn, the evolution of the forward and futures markets for oil. The movement away from fixed long-term contracts in the early 1980s reinforced these trends. Volatile prices fundamentally changed the way the industry conducted business and underscored the need for new ways to control costs and revenues. The Gulf War once again emphasized the volatility of oil prices and their impact on world financial markets. The late 1990s may be another time of oil shocks and natural gas price volatility, and environmental pressures are now beginning to influence price volatility in petroleum products markets as well.

Forward contracts in oil, formal agreements between two parties to make and take delivery at a specific price of a specific quantity of oil at a specific location and future time, developed out of the need to hedge and can be seen as an attempt to reduce price uncertainty in the market. Futures contracts, which are similar to forward contracts but are traded on an exchange, were the next evolutionary step in the commoditization of oil, for now the physical product is effectively separated from its price. The use of forwards and futures and the necessity to actively manage price risk were precursors to the emergence and rapid acceptance of the derivative financial instruments designed to manage risk for the 1990s.

The term "derivative" encompasses a variety of instruments whose value is determined by the price of an underlying instrument or market. The use of off-exchange derivative instruments in the energy markets signals that the application of commodity trading tools and techniques to these markets has become well established. These financial tools may be customized in limitless variations to manage price risk. They should continue to proliferate as oil follows currencies and soft commodities (i.e., coffee, sugar, and cocoa) in the application of risk management tools. The launch of trading in natural gas futures on the NYMEX on April 3, 1990, and the continuing maturation of that contract have contributed to the increased use of derivative instruments in the natural gas industry, especially after the highly volatile prices of 1992 through 1997.

The deregulation of electricity on the retail side in California in 1998 will create greater liquidity for the success of the two NYMEX western region US electricity futures contracts. Then a market for trade from Alberta to Arizona will open up. Price discovery for the electricity futures contract already began in June 1995 with the establishment of the Dow Jones COB Index daily index and the use of McGraw-Hill's Power Markets Week weekly index. And the March 29, 1996, launch of electricity futures is already creating price discovery for the western US markets.

DEVELOPMENT OF
OVER-THE-COUNTER MARKETS

The off-exchange swaps and OTC options markets should be seen as adjuncts to both forward and futures trading. The futures and swaps markets provide complementary trading vehicles to manage risk. Over time, the off-exchange markets will dwarf the futures exchanges and siphon off futures business because of their superior flexibility in customizing risk management contracts and their ability to hedge longer-term energy price risk. Futures markets will continue to provide transparent price quotes that are used as benchmarks for off-exchange transactions, and futures will provide the extra liquidity needed for the swaps market, where market makers offset some of their risk by using futures.

The development of longer-term off-exchange contracts coincided with the need to hedge oil and natural gas price risk exposures for longer periods than futures contracts could provide. The off-exchange markets, through the use of price swaps and over-the-counter options, have allowed the development of longer-term, more complex hedging strategies. These longer-term strategies can be used to provide project finance capital and maintain projected cash flow for one of the world's largest industries.

Projects that can be financed through swaps and over-the-counter options include drilling, refinery upgrades, and cogeneration. Off-exchange instruments are flexible enough to be customized to meet a company's cash flow and internal financing needs. This flexibility has attracted the active participation of banking interests. Large-scale project financing for production, refining, marketing, and large end user consumption will increasingly be tied to these longer-dated instruments. Future power generation projects will use these tools to reduce the cost of capital and fuel costs.

The use of forwards, futures, and swaps reduces price risk, but these instruments cannot nullify all risks associated with commodity price movements. They are financial tools that are developed and applied in line with a company's corporate culture. Despite the aggressive promotion of these instruments by financial and oil trading companies, the nature of a company's business will determine how they are used as part of a corporate strategy to manage price risk and protect assets. Development and implementation of appropriate risk management strategies are important concerns for energy companies to be aware of when contemplating the use of these new financial tools, but they are unique to each company.

CHAPTER 2

The ABCs of Energy Financial Instruments

By Peter C. Fusaro

The energy industry is developing new financial instruments because of the needs of both producers and consumers to manage short- and long-term price risk. These financial tools and techniques have been applied to the currency markets since the 1970s; now they are becoming part of the once heavily regulated electric utility industry. Generally, energy producers are looking for a fixed income stream, and energy consumers are seeking protection from fluctuating market prices. Electric utilities need to manage risk on both the buy and sell sides. Energy financial instruments can serve the needs of both.

This chapter describes the most common financial instruments that are used alone or in combination to hedge price risk. Since this book is a primer, we do not discuss the more exotic instruments and structures available to the energy industry such as roller coaster swaps or rainbow options.

FORWARD MARKETS

A forward market for oil develops because there is a time interval between the day a deal is made and the day it matures (i.e., a client buys now for delivery in the future). Oil on the spot market is priced on a transaction-by-transaction basis. Oil on the paper market is contracted for physical delivery at a specific date in the future; during this time interval, the contract can be bought and sold over and over again. In this way, forward markets are used to hedge forward physical supply.

The success of a forward contract depends on its liquidity and the performance of the market players. *Liquidity* is the ease with which the commodity can be bought and sold in the market. *Performance* refers to the ability of the market players to comply with the terms of the contract. The contract must be satisfied through physical delivery or cash settlement at the time of delivery. A wide range of players actively participate in the forward oil markets, including oil traders, major producers, refiners, investment banks, and major oil companies. These parties all provide liquidity to the market by guaranteeing performance.

Forward markets come and go, but the major active markets are 15-Day Brent for North Sea oil production, open spec naphtha for Japanese and Korean petrochemical producers, and partial Dubai for Dubai crude oil. From time to time, these markets undergo physical squeezes, liquidity crises, and regulatory problems, but they bounce back consistently.

The Brent market, which began trading in 1981, is the oldest forward market in oil. It trades actively 1 to 6 months forward in cargo-size lots and can be traded 2 years forward. The Brent market is the most actively traded forward paper market. Brent trade has been transformed since 1991 as rapidly developing activity in swaps has enhanced its role as the world's leading price marker.

In recent years, the so-called Wall Street Refiners have replaced many oil trading companies that were caught in physical squeezes. These investment houses have helped to preserve liquidity in the Brent market by absorbing some of its risk. They include J. Aron (subsidiary of Goldman Sachs), Phibro Energy (subsidiary of Salomon Brothers), Morgan Stanley, and AIG Trading. Others firms active in Brent trading include Shell, British Petroleum, Conoco, Phillips, Amerada Hess, Lehman Brothers, and AIG Trading.

Often, the development of a forward market for oil is a precursor of the development of a futures market in the same or a similar commodity. This is true in the electricity markets—forward and OTC swaps markets already exist, without a futures contract. Trading between forwards and futures in the same or similar commodities is often used to offset positions. However, there are major differences between the two markets. While both use standardized contracts which are traded regularly, futures contracts are traded on organized and regulated exchanges, while forward contracts trade on the off-exchange, or unregulated, markets. Another important difference is that forward markets depend on market makers who on an informal basis are expected to perform, but future delivery is not guaranteed. The futures market guarantees performance through a clearinghouse and a formal delivery procedure. Also, forward markets often deal in larger trading lots than futures markets. In fact, the ability of the forward markets to absorb larger lots without moving the market represents a significant liquidity advantage over the futures market.

Forward markets generally are used by a relatively small group of well-financed players, in contrast to the wider range of participants in oil futures. Forwards are similar to other off-exchange instruments in this way and have evolved into price benchmarks that are used in 2- to 6-month price swaps or over-the-counter options transactions. This price marker function for setting price differentials for trading other products is particularly important for both Brent and Dubai forward crude oil trading.

In natural gas markets, some analysts feel that the major breakthrough that occurred with gas futures trading for the gas industry was the acceptance of the simple concept of selling natural gas forward. In electricity, it is not the concept of selling electricity forward, which has been going on for many years, but the concept that electricity is now a fungible commodity that is changing that industry's frame of reference.

FUTURES MARKETS

The introduction of *financial futures*—futures on currencies and interest rates—during the 1970s transformed the futures markets, which had been trading agricultural commodities for more than 100 years. Financial futures brought new participants and new strategies to the futures markets, and many more types of risk could now be hedged.

The commodity concept has broadened to include energy, beginning with heating oil futures in 1978, for many of the strategies that were devised for financial futures have been adapted and applied to the energy markets. Energy futures contracts are used by producers, refiners, and consumers to hedge against price fluctuations in these volatile markets. Another function of energy futures contracts has been to protect the inventory value of crude oil, refined products, and natural gas.

The oil futures market developed to allow oil traders to offset some of their risk by taking a position on the futures market opposite their physical position. A producer, who has the physical commodity to sell, hedges by selling futures. The producer's position is then long cash and short futures. A consumer, who needs to buy the commodity, hedges by buying futures. The consumer's position is then short cash and long futures.

A futures contract is an agreement between two parties, a buyer and seller, for delivery of a particular quality and quantity of a commodity at a specified time, place, and price. Futures can be used as a proxy for a transaction in the physical cash market before the actual transaction takes place.

The commodity exchanges set margin requirements for hedgers and speculators. The buyer or seller of a futures contract is required to deposit with the clearinghouse a percentage of the value of the contract as a guarantee of contract fulfillment. The margin deposit made when the position is established is called "original margin." Hedge margins generally are lower than speculative margins. At the end of each trading day, each position is *marked-to-market*—the margin requirement for each account is adjusted based on the day's price changes. If the value of the position has decreased, the holder of the contract will have to make an additional deposit, called "variation margin." This fulfilling of margin requirements on a daily basis means that the extent of default in the futures market is limited to one day's price change.

While futures are a relatively new instrument for the oil markets, they have become firmly established over the past decade. The first viable petroleum futures contract launched was for #2 heating oil on the NYMEX in November 1978. Trade interest in the futures market was slow to develop, but the contract had the elements necessary for success. Heating oil was actively traded on the physical market, the futures contract had an adequate delivery mechanism, and there was good local, trade, and speculative interest. *Locals* are traders on the exchange floor who trade speculatively for their own accounts, providing liquidity.

Most futures contracts do not go to physical delivery. Therefore, futures generally should be used as a price risk management tool, not as a source of physical supply. This basic concept is still a stumbling block to futures trading, as many potential futures players think that physical delivery is a key component of futures trading. In fact, the IPE Brent crude oil is based on cash settlement rather than physical delivery.

The three major energy futures exchanges are the NYMEX, IPE, and SIMEX (Singapore International Monetary Exchange). For electricity and natural gas, only NYMEX and IPE will be significant. Contracts listed on the NYMEX include West Texas Intermediate (WTI) crude oil, sour crude oil, New York Harbor unleaded gasoline, Gulf

Coast unleaded gasoline, #2 heating oil, propane, and three natural gas contracts. The sour crude and Gulf Coast gasoline contracts are not actively traded at this time. A residual fuel oil contract is no longer listed. The IPE trades Brent crude oil, gasoil, and unleaded gasoline futures contracts. The SIMEX trades residual fuel oil (relaunched in April 1997) and has an inactive gasoil futures contract which may be relaunched in the future. In 1995, the SIMEX listed the IPE's Brent crude oil futures contract as a mutual offset contract for the Far East, where it trades much smaller volumes compared to London-based Brent trading.

All three established energy futures exchanges have indicated they will continue to launch futures contracts that conceptually hedge the entire barrel of crude oil as it makes its way from the ground to the consumer, as well as natural gas, electricity, and coal contracts. However, most refiners and end users are more comfortable using other over-the-counter financial instruments to hedge less liquid products such as residual fuel oil, jet fuel, naphtha, and diesel fuel.

The NYMEX trades options on crude oil, New York Harbor unleaded gasoline, #2 heating oil, and natural gas, providing additional tools to manage price risk. Besides launching two electricity futures contracts on March 29, 1996, the NYMEX launched electricity options 1 month later on April 26, 1996. An option gives the holder the right, but not the obligation, to buy or sell an underlying instrument, in this case a futures contract, at a specific price within a specified time period. Options can be used to establish floor and ceiling price protection for commodities and offer a risk management alternative to futures contracts.

There are two types of options: puts and calls. A *put* is an option to sell the futures at a fixed price. A *call* is an option to buy the futures at a fixed price. For hedgers, a put establishes a minimum selling price but does not eliminate the opportunity to receive higher market prices. A call establishes a maximum buying price but does not eliminate the opportunity to buy at lower market prices. Options contracts can be used in combination with futures to form hedging strategies for exchange-traded commodities. They will be widely used in electricity price risk management.

The NYMEX natural gas futures contract, launched on April 3, 1990, has rapidly established itself as an effective instrument for natural gas price discovery in North America. NYMEX launched natural gas options in October 1992, adding another tool to manage risk in that volatile market. Natural gas options have enhanced liquidity in, and can buffer against, price volatility in the rapidly changing North American gas market. A second natural gas futures contract was launched on August 1, 1995, by the Kansas City Board of Trade, which is oriented to the western US market. Two more NYMEX natural gas contracts were launched during 1996: one for the Permian Basin on May 31, 1996, and one for Canada's Alberta market later in the year. These multiple natural gas contracts represent the regional nature of North American natural gas markets, which will also be the case for electricity futures.

In February 1990, the NYMEX initiated long-dated options for the West Texas Intermediate crude oil contract. These options trade 12 months out. Long-dated options were a direct response to the growth of off-exchange markets. They allow users to lock in a fixed price or price range and are useful for refiners and end users entering into long-term supply contracts where crude oil prices are likely to be variable. Since that time, NYMEX has extended the WTI contract out 7 years and its Henry Hub natural gas contract out 3 years forward. The IPE has been particularly successful with its Brent crude oil options and also has a gasoil options contract.

Spread Trading

Spreads are another means to limit price risk in rapidly changing markets. A *spread* is the simultaneous purchase and sale of futures or options contracts in the same or related markets. Intramarket, intermarket, and interexchange arbitrages are commonly used. Purchasing a contract in one expiration of a futures contract while selling a contract in a different expiration would be an *intramarket spread*. This strategy would be useful where there are seasonal variations in demand for a commodity. Crack spreads are *intermarket spreads*—opposite positions are taken in crude and oil products to take into account refining margins. The NYMEX trades options on #2 heating oil/crude and New York Harbor unleaded gasoline/crude crack spreads. *Interexchange arbitrage* would consist of opposite positions in similar contracts on the NYMEX and IPE.

The objective of a spread trade is to profit from a change in the price differential between the contracts, or between futures and options. In natural gas, the wide basis risk of the North American markets has created an active market in spreads trading for different locations, as various locations are priced as a differential to NYMEX. In electricity, it is anticipated that there will be an active market in seasonal spreads and in spreads between contracts covering different delivery points as well as intercommodity spread trading, particularly between natural gas and electricity, called the "spark spread."

Exchange for Physical

Because energy futures are primarily financial management tools, delivery of crude oil, petroleum products, or natural gas is rare. Most futures contracts are liquidated before expiration. However, some contracts do result in delivery. Because futures contracts are standardized as to location and quality, the holders of contracts for delivery usually need to deviate from the terms of the futures contract. To accommodate this, the Exchange for Physical (EFP) has become the preferred method of delivery because it offers more flexibility. It has become an extension of futures and spot market trading.

In an Exchange for Physical, a long futures position held by the buyer of the commodity is transferred to the seller. The firm chooses its trading partner, delivery site, the grade and quality of the product to be delivered, and the timing of the delivery. An Exchange for Physical allows buyers and sellers to negotiate a cash market price, and to adjust the basis, as well as the exact time the physical exchange takes place. They are an important element in the success of the natural gas futures contract because they add greatly to liquidity.

In electricity, a standardized contract has been developed to facilitate electricity trade at locations other than the futures contracts delivery locations of the California-Oregon border and the Palo Verde switchyard.

PRICE SWAP

A *price swap* is an exchange of cash flows, one at a fixed rate and the other at a floating rate. A buyer and a seller agree to exchange the value of the commodity at a given price, quantity, and time period with no physical commodity actually being exchanged. The swap can be short-term (1 to 3 months) or long-term (6 months to 30 years) in duration. The contracting parties agree to pay each other the difference between an agreed-upon fixed price and a price index, that fluctuates. The *price index* is an average market price that will reflect the volatility of the market during the term of the agreement. Payments are made at predetermined times, such as monthly, quarterly, or semiannually. The swaps provider or market maker, either an oil or a gas trading company or financial institution, can match both sides (fixed and floating) of the transaction or assume the price risk itself. Swaps do not require any up-front payment. The cash settlement aspect of price swaps allows energy producers and consumers to make the physical transaction with a party of their own choosing, yet still receive price protection.

There are many components of a swap that must be agreed upon before a binding contract is written. Generally, the following elements are needed to structure a commodity swap: the commodity; the quantity to be swapped each month, quarter, or year; the duration of the swap; the fixed price against which the index (market) price will be evaluated to derive the difference; the index basis such as McGraw-Hill's Power Markets Week, Dow Jones Markets, Gas Daily, NYMEX, or IPE; and settlement procedures regarding payment.

Two parties enter into a swaps contract because they have different price expectations. Each party agrees to pay the other the difference between an agreed-upon fixed price and an index price at agreed-upon intervals in the future. If the index price is above the fixed price, the seller pays the buyer. If the index price is below the fixed price, the buyer pays the seller. No transfer of the physical commodity takes place. By separating pricing from supply, two markets are created, one for the physical commodity and the other for its price.

Electricity rate price swaps are hedging vehicles that allow a participant to fix the price of electricity for a specified time period, ensuring the participant's financial position against adverse price movements during that time. There are no standardized energy risk management swaps. Each agreement is customized to meet the needs of the participants. Unlike futures contracts, there is no concern over liquidity or expiration date. Another way of looking at swaps is to view them as a series of forward contracts that are wrapped into one contractual agreement.

Price swaps agreements can also include provisions to manage credit risk within the transaction. This is an area where banking expertise can be effectively applied. Money center banks can offer structured derivative products (swaps) as a transaction linked to the company's financing in such a way that the market value of the company's assets and the market value of the financing can be positively correlated, reducing asset/liability mismatch. This means that the cost of financing can be lowered by bundling its borrowing with a swaps transaction, creating a commodity-linked security that is not dependent on commodity price swings.

Firms writing swaps hedge their risk by taking a long position in short-term delivery when their contract is appreciating as it nears expiry or by taking a short position if the contract is losing value. The underwriters can run matched books by transferring excess risk to the futures market to balance their portfolios. Or they can run unbalanced books when it is opportune for them; this strategy is used primarily by companies active in derivatives because they possess the physical product and believe they know the market. Unbalanced books can also be run by banks that have the liquidity to do so.

Swaps agreements can be customized to meet the internal cash flow requirements of energy producers and consumers. They are a form of price insurance, for the intermediaries assume most of the risk and are responsible for managing their own books.

These financial arrangements are extremely discreet transactions because of the competitive nature of the energy markets and the necessity to protect the client's positions in the physical and futures markets. The swaps market is by nature a very private business with few deals made public, partially because of low liquidity in the secondary markets, although the recent entrance of swaps brokers as intermediaries has brought greater price transparency by providing more competitive bid/ask price quotes. Also, real-time market electronic news services, such as Reuters, Dow Jones Markets, Bridge News, and Bloomberg, provide swaps quotes for energy commodities.

Price swaps offer both short- and longer-term solutions for energy price risk. They can also be a very effective method of dealing with *basis risk*, the differential between the price of the physical commodity to be bought or sold and the futures or other index price. Basis can vary widely in the oil, natural gas, and electricity markets; therefore, basis risk requires active management by the swaps underwriter.

Price swaps can be viewed as complementary to futures. They allow hedging to go beyond the 6 to 9 months of true liquidity in the futures markets. Some brokers actually consider them "longer-dated" futures contracts. While futures cover only a small number of products, swaps and over-the-counter options offer an almost infinite variety of customized arrangements for different products and time periods. For example, besides exchange-traded oil contracts, swaps can be made for naphtha, jet fuel, non-exchange-traded crudes such as Dubai and Tapis, and vacuum gasoil (VGO), to name a few. And in electricity, price swaps and OTC options have developed initially without a futures contract. Swaps and futures contracts are similar in that the transactions have the same goals, but swaps can be used for longer time periods. Shorter-dated swaps, for 1 to 3 months, are actively written as are longer-dated swaps, from 6 months and to as far out as 10 to 12 years forward for oil, 30 years for natural gas, and up to 20 years for electricity.

Because longer-term instruments are likely to involve wider price movements and can be hedged against a wider variety of swaps agreements than futures, their transaction costs can be higher, although replication of deals and greater competition have begun to bring costs down.

Swaps, options, and other off-exchange financial instruments are considered "hybrid" financial products because they combine hedging strategies of commodities with long-term price risk management. Swaps fill the void left by futures contracts, where liquidity more than 6 months out becomes problematic.

Why Use Energy Swaps?

An energy producer that is constantly selling crude oil or natural gas into the open market is exposing its revenue stream to the volatility of the market. The company's risk can be neutralized by converting the variable market price that it receives on its sales to a fixed price. A swap is then set up in which the company receives fixed payments from the buyer, based on the fixed price, and pays a variable amount to the buyer, based on the index. An energy consumer, who is concerned about rising prices, takes the other side of the swap in order to pay a fixed price and receive a variable price.

For the producer, the swaps agreement provides income stability by eliminating the effects of market price fluctuations on its income stream. Risk is reduced through the swap. While it can be argued that the producer is giving up the opportunity to benefit from rising prices, it is protected from losses due to falling prices. Likewise, the energy consumer, by taking the opposite side of the swaps transaction, insulates itself from rising prices while giving up the opportunity to benefit from declining prices.

Figure 2.1 illustrates a commodity swap. This example shows the relationship between the two sides of a swaps transaction and the role of the intermediary, in this case a bank.

Of course, the natural match between the producer's and consumer's hedging needs could mean that the two parties could simply enter into a series of forward transactions without the services of an intermediary. However, the risk exposures of the producer and consumer usually do not match precisely, and intermediaries can add value by standing in between and assuming the risk.

FIGURE 2.1

Example of a Commodity Swap

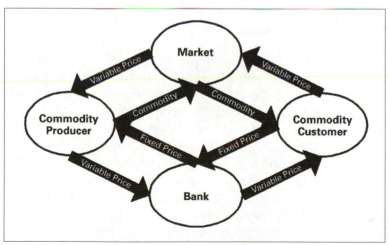

Different Types of Swaps Users

Since most types of energy swaps transactions were originally written for crude oil, a brief review of some of the
variations will be useful before discussing applications to
electricity.

Swaps and options, like futures, can be used to hedge
crude oil production and product prices, carry inventory
costs, and finance projects. Oil price swaps protect the value
of oil in the ground and allow producers to hedge long-
term price risk for their assets while selling production at
market prices. Producers receive a fixed payment based on
the contracted price with the third party. The transaction is
made for an agreed-upon period of time. Banks also can
arrange oil producer swaps to pay down debt and tie in
interest rate and currency risk as well. Oil price swaps are
particularly good instruments for exploration and production companies. These companies need to incorporate price
floors into their development loans to mitigate their repay-
ment risk by assuring that cash flow requirements are met.
This same concept can be applied to utility generating
capacity. The swap maximizes borrowing capacity by
ensuring a future cash flow, protected from falling prices,
that will cover loan payments.

Caps and Floors

Caps and floors are similar to swaps but offer price protection in a different manner. First, an up-front cash premium
must be paid. Second, one side will always benefit from a
change in prices: Consumers benefit from falling prices,
and producers benefit from rising prices.

Caps and floors are complementary trading strategies.
A *cap* sets a maximum or ceiling price for energy consumers
seeking full protection from rising prices with no loss of
benefit if prices decline. Airlines are natural users of caps
because of the price volatility of jet fuel and the need to
limit fuel costs. A *floor* sets a minimum or bottom price and
is used by energy producers seeking full protection from

falling prices with no loss of benefit if prices rise. Oil, natural gas, and electricity producers are natural users of price floors.

Price Protection Programs

Large industrial electricity consumers are interested in protecting themselves from unanticipated price spikes. Their goal is to fix electricity acquisition costs, which are variable, to lock in future profits for their products. A swaps agreement puts production costs under control and locks in price margins. The financial intermediary takes positions on guaranteed differentials between natural gas and electricity to hedge the risk it has assumed. Since natural gas is a growing input to power generation, it also makes it an effective hedge for electricity transactions at the present time because there is little liquidity for electricity futures.

Natural Gas Swaps

Because of the high volatility of North American natural gas prices (40 percent annualized price volatility) and the increasing use of natural gas futures to manage short-term price risk, the natural gas swaps market took off during 1992 and continued to grow through 1997. Both natural gas producers and consumers, such as utilities and cogenerators, are becoming involved in swaps to protect themselves from adverse price movements. The emergence and growth of natural gas swaps brokers during the latter half of 1992 only confirmed the high level of activity in this market. Electricity swaps brokers emerged significantly during 1995 to further market price transparency.

New Types of Energy Swaps Developing Rapidly

Rapid development and adoption of interest rate and currency financial tools have, in turn, brought new swaps instruments to the energy markets. These instruments include basis swaps, location swaps, and calendar swaps. *Basis* and *location swaps* allow positions in different energy markets to be hedged and are very popular in the natural gas market. *Calendar swaps* allow prices to be locked in for seasonal or annual periods. Swaps have become more price transparent as real-time market news services, such as Dow Jones Markets, post bid and ask quotes for energy swaps deals. Also, a new swaps product has been developed that includes the right to extend or shorten the duration of the original agreement, creating volume flexibility.

OPTIONS

Two classes of options are increasingly used in the energy trade. Exchange-traded options were discussed in Chapter 1. OTC options are traded outside the regulated exchanges.

The buyer of an option has the right, but not the obligation, to buy or sell an underlying commodity at a fixed price, called the "strike price." All options have expiration dates that define the time in which this right can be exercised. A *put* is an option to sell at a fixed price. A *call* is an option to buy at a fixed price. The buyer of a put has the right to sell the underlying commodity. The buyer of a call has the right to buy the underlying commodity. The seller of a put must stand ready to buy the underlying commodity. The seller of a call must stand ready to sell the underlying commodity.

Over-the-counter options offer a distinct advantage over forwards, futures, and swaps in that the need to arrange back-to-back transactions is eliminated. There is no need to match buyer or seller. This offers a particular advantage to producers and consumers because there is little chance of doing back-to-back transactions due to mismatched cash flow of the market makers. This greater flexibility makes over-the-counter options easier to market than the other instruments.

While options have an up-front cost, or premium, these costs can often be built into the transaction when it is used for longer-term project finance. Longer-term options can range in length from 1 to 5 years. Most options deals are written for 3 years or less, however. Options can be used to set floor prices for producers, making them ideally suited to long-term project finance since they lock in cash flow.

Options premiums have two components: intrinsic value and time value. *Intrinsic value* is the difference between the strike price and the price of the underlying commodity. It cannot be less than zero. A put has positive intrinsic value, or is in the money, when the market price is less than the strike price—exercise will be profitable. It is at the money when the market price equals the strike price. It is out of the money when the market price is greater than the strike price. A call is in the money when the market price is greater than the strike price. It is at the money when the market price equals the strike price. It is out of the money when the market price is less than the strike price.

Time value is a function of time to expiration and the volatility of the price of the underlying commodity. The value of an option declines each day until expiration because as time to expiration diminishes, the probability of the option expiring in the money also diminishes.

Greater volatility will increase the price of an option because it increases the probability that the option will expire in the money. Volatility is a measure of how much prices fluctuate. Past volatility can be measured and used as a gauge, but future volatility cannot be predicted with certainty. However, if the market is operating efficiently, the prices of active, at-the-money options can be considered fair. Because the strike price, the price of the underlying commodity, and the time to expiration are known, an implied volatility value can be derived from the price of the option.

Market sentiment will affect how the actual price of the option compares to the theoretical price: The expectations of buyers and sellers will make some options relatively more valuable than others.

As a rule, the less liquid the commodity, the higher the options premium because the seller is assuming more risk.

Energy options prices are very volatile, reflecting the nature of the underlying energy markets. Options volatility comes in when there is more certainty in the energy markets. Because of this high price volatility, options would help to smooth some of the erratic price movements that occur with pricing due to seasonality and unexpected events in energy markets. In structuring longer-term risk management agreements, options are used to reduce risk and smooth volatility for energy producers and users.

Options portfolios require active management to adjust to changing market conditions. Options also can be used to structure indexed deals, which should gain in popularity in coming years. Indexed deals are transactions that use an agreed-upon index such as in trade publications, McGraw-Hill's Power Markets Week, NYMEX, Dow Jones's COB Index, or any other agreed-upon index.

The dynamism of options can be illustrated by a trading technique called "stacking and rolling." In this strategy, a portfolio manager buys options to hedge a swaps agreement as far forward as possible, usually 6 months to 3 years, and then rolls over the hedge each month to adjust the portfolio. Options can be bought on a daily basis for shorter-term deals to further fine-tune the portfolio. Sophisticated computer software for modeling options pricing is employed to optimize the series of transactions. This constant management factor, with its additional transaction costs, makes stacking and rolling with over-the-counter options more expensive than hedging with futures, but costs often can be embedded in the deal. If not properly managed, this strategy can lead to disastrous results, as was evidenced by the Metallgesellschaft oil trading fiasco in December 1993.

Average Price Options

Asian options, or average price options, are increasingly being used by oil and gas underwriters. Asian options may be exercised only at expiration, and the strike price represents an average of prices over a specified time period; the strike price is not known until the time period is complete. This is in contrast to American options, which can be exercised at any time up to expiration and whose strike price is fixed, and European options, which also have a fixed strike price but can be exercised only at expiration.

The average price component of Asian options allows the hedge to be based on the average forward price for a particular delivery month or specified period of time. The time interval is negotiable; for example, the exercise price may be a 10- or 30-day or 3-month moving average. Average price options are cheaper than either European or American options because averaging smoothes price volatility. While risk is concentrated at the beginning of the option's term, with uncertainty being highest at that time, average price options allow risk to be dampened over the life of the option. These options offer additional flexibility as they can be used to hedge a daily flow of crude oil or refined products, rather than cargo-size lots where other options are usually applied. Thus, the same size option can be viewed as a series of small deliveries instead of one big one.

Average price options have a settlement period that more closely follows real-life transactions, as suppliers and consumers buy and sell crude oil or products in the spot month over the course of the option's term. Average price options are used to hedge oil production because production coming out of the ground and used by refiners is somewhat constant. Average price options are also used in jet fuel swaps to reduce basis risk. Basis risk is of great concern in the jet fuel market because of the widespread locational demands of the airline industry.

Swaptions

As energy trading instruments continue to become more sophisticated, swaptions are being used to structure swaps deals in ways that increasingly protect borrowers.

Swaptions are options on swaps that allow the writer of the swap the option of either increasing or decreasing the swap volume or increasing the period of the swap. They are written as part of an options portfolio which must be managed actively to limit credit exposure and keep the books balanced. Options on swaps are used because they limit risk factors and add more certainty to the market. Thus, an option's price volatility is lessened.

Participation Hedge or Participating Swap

Another tool that is increasingly being applied to energy swaps transactions is the participation hedge. The *participation hedge* gives a swaps participant the opportunity to benefit from favorable price moves. For example, a producer or owner of oil gets a price floor, as well as a portion of the benefit of any price increase. A consumer would get a price cap, as well as a portion of the benefit of any price decline. Puts and calls are used in combination in the hedge position. Participation hedges are extremely flexible and can be structured with floor and cap prices having varying expiration dates. Participation hedges are a response to increasing competitiveness in the underwriting market. Previously, the market makers took all of the benefit of changing prices. Now they must share a portion of the gain.

THE DEALER'S BOOK

The *dealer's book* is the record of all cash market positions, along with associated futures hedges. Dates of futures and cash positions never exactly match, but they are usually close enough so that liquidity is not a problem. Positions in distant months, which are less liquid, are later switched to more active positions in near months, and as distant months become near as time goes by, their positions in near months are switched as they expire. Because futures and cash are not perfectly matched, a gap exposure is always present. Often, dealers manage this risk by using other hedges. "Rebalancing the book" transfers excess risk from the intermediaries. The dealer's book may be thought of as a dynamic document that is actively managed and continually modified to meet changing market conditions.

Companies active in the physical and paper markets are often comfortable running unbalanced books because they are capable of supplying the underlying physical commodity. And since most electricity deals are still physical, some paper players are inactive at present. Banks are now more likely to run unbalanced books due to increased liquidity in the markets. The book gradually increases in size as more commodity-indexed business is added. Swaps transactions add complexity and result in more active trading because such arrangements are for longer time periods, use more financial tools, and are customized to each client's needs. For these reasons, swaps can require higher transaction fees than futures trading, although replication of transactions and increased underwriting competition are driving down the costs to participants.

DEFAULT OR NONPERFORMANCE PROBLEMS

All off-exchange transactions, including swaps underwriting, must address the question of default or nonperformance by the parties involved in the transaction. The creditworthiness and capital adequacy of swaps providers have come into question during 1997 due to financial problems at some investment banks, energy trading companies, and other parties active in these markets. It has become a sensitive issue in longer-term natural gas deals (more than 3 to 4 years), and has also emerged as an issue in longer-term transactions in electric power markets. Some counterparties are willing to enter into deals only with certain financial and energy trading institutions. Performance must be considered in choosing trading partners. In a swaps transaction, a position could be created that could not be closed at any price. This has happened in the jet fuel swaps market.

Regulated exchanges have clearinghouses which guarantee performance. Since swaps transactions are not traded on regulated exchanges, counterparty risk is an important consideration that effectively limits who can participate. The US Commodity Futures Trading Commission ruled in 1989 that it would take no action to regulate swaps transactions. In that ruling, the agency set forth certain guidelines that defined transactions it would not regulate. Swaps cannot be marketed to the general public, they cannot be standardized agreements, they must have counterparty consent, and they cannot be supported by a clearing organization. The Commodity Futures Trading Commission tried to clearly distinguish swaps from any instrument traded on a regulated futures exchange. The counterparties involved in the swap should be able to assume the risks involved. Most important, the agency continues to monitor the development of the off-exchange market to prevent fundability, or interchangeability, among swaps—that is, to ensure that each transaction is unique and cannot be readily transferred or resold in a secondary market.

There was increased regulatory interest in public disclosure of derivatives transactions during 1997 in the wake of several well-publicized scandals in which risk managers went beyond the bounds of prudent hedging with disastrous results when the market moved the wrong way. In fact, several New York investment banks voluntarily disclosed more information about their swaps positions to regulators in 1995.

The futures exchanges, on the other hand, provide financial integrity to the commodity markets and guarantee the performance of their contracts. This is not an unimportant point, for in the United States no energy futures contract has ever defaulted. Performance is guaranteed by brokers, the clearinghouse, and the exchange. All transactions are matched and offset at settlement. Although there is a perception among the public that futures exchanges exist primarily for speculation, hedging is their true function. The creditworthiness of the exchanges and their standardized, fungible contracts are essential to off-exchange trading, where counterparty performance is a key component of swaps agreements. In off-exchange transactions, the market maker assumes the functions of an exchange. If a transaction unravels, the market maker must perform. Large banks, major oil companies, and large traders not only can make a market, but because of their creditworthiness and performance capability, their customers have confidence in their ability to stand behind their transactions. In the evolving electricity markets, electric utilities are starting to assume the market making function.

Cash settlement, rather than physical delivery, is an obvious advantage of OTC markets over physical or forward markets for electricity in terms of performance. No one can "squeeze" a cash-settled contract, as sometimes occurs in the physical market. Cash settlement also offers a better hedging vehicle, since physical delivery alters supply and demand. Physical delivery at contract expiration can be a recurring problem. These problems do not exist in derivative products because they are cash settled. This enhances their performance function.

THE MARKET MAKERS

Swaps agreements should be viewed as long-dated futures transactions that derive their liquidity from intermediaries who act as market makers. These intermediaries match party and counterparty or run unbalanced books, offset some of their risk on futures exchanges, and generally assume the risk associated with these transactions. In effect, they create a market where none previously existed, for they are able to trade products not listed on exchanges. In the future, electric utilities will perform this market making function as well because they know their customers' needs.

A financial intermediary in a swaps arrangement allows both the buyer and seller of the commodity to be protected on the downside, while curbing opportunity for upside gain. The intermediaries assume price risk and, in some cases, credit risk as well, and they can also assume basis risk for the physical commodity.

Oil trading companies, banks, and some natural gas companies are the principal writers of swaps, options, and other synthetic instruments in the over-the-counter markets. Each has a specific orientation. The oil trading entities, such as British Petroleum, Elf Trading, J. Aron, Texaco, and Shell, to name a few, not only assume price risk for crude oil and petroleum products but also are active in the physical markets for these commodities. Oil traders can assume basis risk for diverse locations because of their activity in the physical markets. Enron and Natural Gas Clearinghouse perform a similar function in the gas markets. Most banks, on the other hand, prefer to transfer basis risk to third parties.

While oil companies do act as market makers in the over-the-counter markets, a large part of the longer-term commodity swaps business is becoming the preserve of large banks specializing in this business. Banks have the ability to assume credit risk as well as price risk. Large banks are able to build on their presence in project finance and futures trading to form commodity-index units that structure longer-term deals to manage the strategic risks of their clients. As these large banks take positions on their own books, they are able to create a market in swaps as part of other bank underwriting and can offset swaps through paper hedging using the underlying commodity as its offset. In effect, the financial institution offers energy and financial brokering. This type of swaps transaction is also used in other commodities such as metals. Those banks that cannot assume price risk transfer it by using market makers to find a counterparty. Banks are becoming subordinate in swaps underwriting. They need to replicate deals many times to create the volumes necessary to cover their costs through fees rather than participation.

Many banks, investment houses, and commodity trading firms are involved in interest rate and foreign exchange risk management. Sometimes these elements are built into energy deals. The longer-term risk is then more fully hedged. The deal can be syndicated to other institutions. Firms active in off-exchange instruments include Chase Manhattan, Banque Paribas, Bankers Trust, Barclay's Bank, Citibank, ING Bank, J. P. Morgan, Merrill Lynch, Morgan Stanley, and Koch Cargill.

Because multinational banks have commercial lending activities throughout the world, their movement into commodity-financed lending with the less-developed countries (LDCs) should skyrocket during the first decade of the 21st century. These countries, in fact, are exposed to far more risk from commodity price movements than from changes in interest and foreign exchange rates. There is the need, therefore, to manage their commodity price risk. Multinational banks are best able to perform this function because of their local presence and their knowledge of both the commodity and lending markets. These banks will be able to tie commodity-backed transactions to new lending for many of the state-owned energy companies (particularly OPEC producers) that provide much of their countries' foreign exchange. In fact, even political risk can be bundled in some of these loans to the developing world and Eastern Europe through the US Overseas Private Investment Corporation (OPIC), a government agency. This opportunity has not been missed by many of the more commodity-oriented banks, but it is definitely an emerging business opportunity.

RISE OF SWAPS BROKERS

The introduction of brokerage firms into the energy swaps markets since 1990 signals the maturation of these markets. The role of the broker is to negotiate financial arrangements between parties with differing views. Brokers bring a more definable marketplace and pricing system to the market as prices become more visible. Swaps brokers in New York and Houston have captured a large portion of the business in the maturing natural gas derivatives market, and some entered the electricity broker business during 1997. They have become active in London and Singapore for oil and in London for electricity and gas.

In the Far East, the rise of swaps brokers has facilitated paper trading. Prior to the launch of residual fuel oil futures trading on the SIMEX in 1989, oil brokers did not exist there. Now there are many active brokers in Singapore, a sign of a healthy market, and they boosted the naphtha, gasoline, and Tapis crude oil swaps business there.

RELATIONSHIP BANKING REEMERGING

Multinational banks and energy companies have always had a strong business relationship due to the large capital needs and worldwide operations of the oil industry. Banks have provided services related to taxation, cash management, and foreign exchange and interest rate risk management. Many energy transactions are not new business, but merely renewals of funding for existing facilities; these capital requirements are high and provide profitable margins for lending banks. Moreover, relationship banks can offer cross-border financial services, including currency swaps, as part of any commodity-linked transaction.

Because the oil and gas industries are cyclical and have high price volatility, price risk management is an element that will increasingly be incorporated into new energy lending. While many energy companies have not yet utilized these tools due to unfamiliarity, the benefits of customized risk management, including interest rate and currency risk reduction, are becoming apparent. Hedging will, at a minimum, allow the industry more flexibility through better cash flow management.

Banks are becoming more involved in oil and gas swaps as part of overall debt management strategies for their clients. Because of the high transaction costs of writing swaps and options, costs will be embedded in more deals as part of project prefinancings. This is a major area of new business development in the natural gas utilities market in

North America. Commodity price swaps will be applied as a tool for other areas of project finance. Electric utilities have high financial and lending needs. As electricity becomes a commodity, more of these deals will include a commodity financing component.

CHAPTER 3

European Energy Markets Developments

By Seana Lanigan

INTRODUCTION

The sophisticated and mature western European energy market provides the backdrop for the International Petroleum Exchange's (IPE) highly successful energy futures contracts for gasoil and Brent crude oil. Representatives from 28 countries agreed to set up the exchange in late 1980, and the first contract to be listed was gasoil futures in April 1981. The current Brent crude oil contract began trading in 1988 and, like gasoil, has an accompanying options market. Traded volumes have grown exponentially since 1981, with almost 16 million contracts traded in 1996, a record for the 11th consecutive year. And both the Brent and gasoil contracts have become important industry benchmarks, meaning that their influence extends far wider than the futures market. Brent, for example, is used as a price marker for two-thirds of the world's internationally traded crude oil supplies.

IPE Annual Futures Volumes 1991–1996

January 1991–December 1991	8,409,060
January 1992–December 1992	9,758,371
January 1993–December 1993	12,531,552
January 1994–December 1994	13,184,152
January 1995–December 1995	13,510,279
January 1996–December 1996	13,827,069

All of these oil futures and options contracts are trad-ed in pits on the market floor using the open outcry system. This mechanism involves all orders being shouted out in public, resulting in fully transparent price movements and trades, as well as clear indications of the latest bids and offers. The open outcry system, although often appearing strange to outsiders, is one of the most efficient ways of developing price discovery and ensuring that all relevant information and news are immediately and fully reflected in the market.

Despite the advantages of open outcry markets, the IPE moved away from tradition when launching its natural gas contract on January 31, 1997. This new contract is Europe's first natural gas futures market, and it is traded through an automated energy trading system (ETS) located within company offices. The ETS is a state-of-the-art elec-tronic trading system and was developed by the IPE's tech-nology department. The ETS is a quick and low-cost way of introducing new contracts, particularly those with multiple delivery points and other variations as may ultimately be the case for natural gas. The early stage of development of the competitive UK natural gas market and the fact that many companies involved in the physical market had lim-ited, if any, experience trading futures were some of the fac-tors behind the decision to use the ETS rather than the traditional open outcry system.

BENCHMARKING

The IPE's two main oil contracts—Brent crude oil and gasoil—are used extensively as international benchmarks.

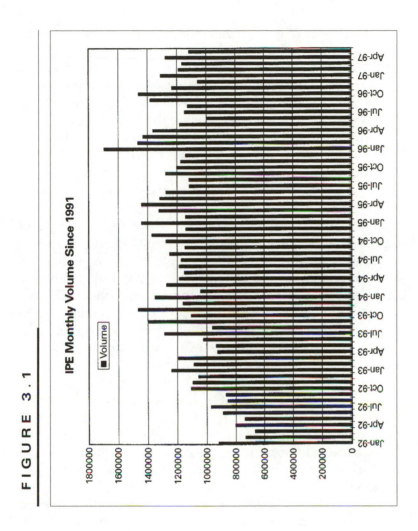

FIGURE 3.1

IPE Monthly Volume Since 1991

This means that many different types of crude oil and middle distillates are priced at a differential to the relevant IPE contract rather than at an outright level. Brent futures, for example, help to provide the base price for two-thirds of the world's internationally traded crude oil supplies. IPE gasoil is a key price benchmark for physical trade within Europe and beyond.

The principle of benchmarking is simple. Energy prices are extremely volatile and can change significantly in a fraction of a second. Rather than negotiate an individual price for each of the many different grades of crude oil or gasoil that are available, traders will use a reputable index such as the IPE contracts to provide the basis for price fluctuation and concentrate on establishing a suitable differential to the chosen benchmark. This is particularly important for long-term contracts, where agreeing on an absolute price for a year ahead or more can be extremely difficult, if not impossible.

Benchmarking helps to separate out the two types of factors that influence prices. The first group of factors includes news and information that affect prices in general. This could include political unrest in a major oil-producing state for crude or forecasts of sharply colder weather in a key consuming area for gasoil. If production is disrupted in the Middle East, for example, all oil prices will tend to rise. The second group of factors influences the difference in value between the specific oil being bought or sold and that of the benchmark. Examples could include whether demand for oil products is for gasoil or gasoline, output of which is related to the individual quality of different crudes. For example, gasoil rich crudes such as Nigerian Forcados would be more expensive compared to the benchmark Brent in the peak winter demand season than in the summer.

The value of specific types of oil in relation to each other tends to be far less volatile than the outright price of oil. Benchmarking allows traders to link to an index that will reflect any news and information that affect prices in general on a second-by-second basis. The appropriate differential to the benchmark can be negotiated on a more long-term basis.

BRENT

The IPE's most liquid futures market is for North Sea Brent blend crude oil. This contract regularly trades volume equivalent to 50 million b/d (barrels per day)or two-thirds of daily world oil consumption. Open interest is typically about 180 million bbls, or two and a half times more than daily world oil demand. This compares to a physical base of less than 800,000 b/d of Brent Blend production. The standardized contract size is for 1000 barrels. Most traders with open positions at the end of the month elect to settle against the IPE's 15-day index, which is derived from deals and assessments listed by the mainstream physical oil price reporting services. But positions may also be taken to physical delivery through the Exchange for Physical (EFP) mechanism discussed in Chapter 2.

Unprecedented structural change in the world's oil markets during the late 1970s and early 1980s stimulated the rapid development of a framework for the forward trade of crude oils. Only a limited number of crudes have emerged as benchmarks against which other grades may be priced because only a small number satisfy eligibility criteria relating to liquidity, transparency, diversity of ownership and participation, as well as international "tradeability."

The Brent forward market became an international benchmark in the early 1980s for over-the-counter trading of oil. Its almost universal adoption as a pricing tool came about due to a unique combination of circumstances. First, production of Brent was high relative to other grades, and ownership was divided among a large number of players, helping to keep the spot market liquid and ensuring that no single company had a dominant influence on price formation. The strategic position of the North Sea also helped develop Brent as a price benchmark. North Sea crudes move into all major markets, including North and South America, the Asia-Pacific region, and Africa as well as Europe. This is not the case for all crudes. US grades, for example, could not legally be exported until recently. And West Texas Intermediate (WTI), the basis of the NYMEX crude futures contract, is a landlocked grade which never appears on the world market and only competes with other international supplies when they are imported into the United States. Production of Brent and North Sea crudes has been historically free from government interference; this contrasts with other key crudes including those produced from OPEC (Organization of Petroleum Exporting Countries) member states. But it was the Gulf War that became the catalyst for securing IPE Brent's position as an international marker as liquidity developed in the contract.

The price of Brent has become a benchmark for crude destined for all major consuming regions including Europe, North America, and the Asia Pacific, and it is used to price directly or indirectly 65–70 percent of traded world oil supplies. The specific benchmark used by the industry is "dated" Brent, but the price of dated Brent is critically linked to two other markets: the 15-day forward market and the IPE Brent futures contract.

DATED BRENT

Dated Brent is the spot physical market for specific cargoes of crude oil for which the loading dates are known. Trade can be for cargoes that have either been loaded or allocated a specific 3-day loading range at the Sullom Voe terminal. Prices for such cargoes tend to be based on a differential to the forward market known as "15-day Brent." In the physical market, about 45 to 50 500,000 barrel cargoes are produced per month.

15-DAY BRENT

This is essentially a forward market, normally trading between 1 and 4 months ahead. It was established in the late 1970s and has developed into the largest and most important crude oil forward market in the world. The 15-day market remains informal in that it is not subject to formal regulation mechanisms other than those relating to the English law of contracts. Instead it relies on self-regulation, using a set of standard procedures. Contracts are based on a 500,000-barrel cargo, with a 5 percent tolerance.

Most of the trade in 15-day Brent is cleared by "book-out," when participants agree to cancel mutual contracts by cash settlement. Participants not wishing or unable to enter a bookout are served with a 15-day notice to take delivery of a specific cargo at Sullom Voe, the North Sea port, during a nominated 3-day loading window which may either be accepted or passed on to the next buyer in the contract sequence.

Spread trades have become dominant in this market, with price differentials established against Brent futures.

The rapid development of this forward market, particularly in the early to mid-1980s, clearly demonstrated that the industry felt the need to hedge and to secure prices for forward supplies and requirements. This in turn helped to justify and ensure the success of the IPE's Brent futures contract, which was launched in its present format in 1988.

The Brent market is unique in that the different constituents of the benchmark price are still thriving. Often, forward markets wither away and die as futures markets take over their functions, as was the case for the Russian gasoil forward market that existed in the 1980s. But this has not happened for Brent, and each of the three elements retains a vital role in price formation.

IPE BRENT

The Brent crude contract listed on the IPE provides the visible and liquid baseline underlying physical markets and attracts a broader cross section of participants than do either the dated or 15-day Brent markets. It was launched in 1988. Prices are established by open outcry on the IPE's trading floor. This means that all deals and prices are completely transparent, and any trade is public the instant it has taken place.

GASOIL

Gasoil is a middle distillate which can be either heating oil or diesel fuel. In western Europe, gasoil is the biggest single product market, with daily consumption of about 4.5mn bl. Currently, demand is split roughly half and half between diesel and heating oil. Germany is the largest single market, accounting for about 30 percent of total European gasoil consumption and over a third of heating oil consumption.

The gasoil contract was the basis for the IPE's foundation and was launched on August 19, 1981. Originally, the contract was a hybrid between heating oil and diesel, but since tighter transport fuel environmental restrictions were adopted across the European Union in 1996, the IPE specifications have reflected heating oil.

When a contract month expires, traders have the option of taking or making physical delivery of any positions left open. Delivery is based on the barge market in the Amsterdam, Rotterdam, and Antwerp (ARA) area, which contains the key ports feeding the enormous German market. The physical delivery options mean that IPE gasoil prices are closely linked to spot physical market conditions and have helped to develop use of the contract as a benchmark.

Varying temperature conditions and environmental regulations across Europe mean that there are wide quality and price differences between national grades of heating oil and diesel. Scandinavian countries, for example, tend to impose much tighter sulfur limits on gasoil than do other European nations such as the United Kingdom, France, or Germany. Specifications also vary depending on the season or local area.

The IPE gasoil contract has been almost universally accepted as the industry benchmark for Europe and has a dominant influence on the physical market price. Almost every trade in northwest Europe is priced at a differential to IPE gasoil. Although the differentials for the various grades of heating oil and diesel will change from time to time, by far the biggest single component in the outright price and the daily changes will be the IPE gasoil settlement level, or its trading range. In the Mediterranean, pricing formulas are slightly different, with most trades based on Platt's published price assessments, but these in turn are heavily influenced by daily movements in futures markets. The high levels of liquidity seen on gasoil futures show that traders see it as a reliable price marker that cannot easily be influenced by an individual trader.

The IPE gasoil contract is supplemented as a hedging tool by various over-the-counter instruments, including active swaps markets for heating oil and diesel and a declining but still traded forward physical market. But even these alternative hedging mechanisms tend to rely on quality-specific needs of the European markets. Diesel purchasers would typically hedge some of their risk using the IPE and then use swaps to lock in an acceptable differential between the physical price of diesel as reported by one of the main assessment services and futures prices on the IPE. The French forward gasoil market can involve physical delivery of cargoes, and this too trades at a premium or discount to prompt IPE futures.

NATURAL GAS

Natural gas was initially an unwanted by-product of oil production, but it is now an increasingly important energy source in its own right. Its main uses are in heating, in power generation, as a household fuel, and as a chemical feedstock. Natural gas has enormous growth potential in Europe. In 1995, gas consumption in OECD Europe was 280.3 tonnes of oil equivalent (mtoe). And its share of primary energy consumption in Europe, currently standing at 20 percent, is predicted to rise dramatically over the first decade of the 21st century.

Electricity and natural gas are intimately linked. In the UK market, a combination of electricity liberalization and new combined-cycle gas turbine technology boosted gas usage in power generation from less than 1 percent in 1990 to 23 percent in 1996. This growth is expected to reach 30 percent in 2000. A similar switch to gas-fired power generation can be expected on the European continent due to the European Union's Electricity Directive and environmental pressures to reduce carbon dioxide emissions from coal-fired plants.

UK deregulation provided the IPE with an opportunity to launch a UK natural gas futures contract, the first such contract in Europe. It was launched on January 31, 1997. Although the contract was introduced at an early stage of the development of a spot gas market, its launch was the culmination of 2 years of development by the exchange, the UK gas industry, and Ofgas, the UK gas regulatory body. Liquid natural gas futures are perceived as key to the evolution of a competitive market in the United Kingdom by government officials.

The UK natural gas market has been transformed from an industry dominated by a state-owned monopoly, the British Gas Corporation, to an evolving competitive market with a diverse cross section of players. Ofgas is in the process of finalizing competition in gas supply in the domestic UK retail market by April 1998.

In a process mirroring the development of natural gas markets in North America, new entrants, such as gas marketers and shippers, have entered the supply chain previously controlled by British Gas. The introduction of competition in supply meant that individual companies were no longer able to match their own supply exactly to demand, resulting in the development of a short-term or spot market for these supply imbalances. Moreover, the development of a spot market has begun the important function of price discovery, which is reported by several daily price reporting services.

The National Balancing Point (NBP) of the National Transmission System (NTS) has emerged as the focus of spot trading in the UK gas market. The NBP is the notional location at which TransCo carries out daily balancing of supply and demand for the gas pipeline system. The continuing growth of this spot market together with the related increase in gas price volatility led the IPE to develop and launch a monthly gas futures contract with physical delivery at the NBP.

The commoditization of natural gas is overturning traditional business culture in the UK gas industry. More important, businesses are now learning about price exposure and how best to manage their new price risks. Companies that were previously involved in protracted long-term contract negotiation spanning months must now acquire new skills and new resources to deal with a real-time trading environment. Competition will also bring new entrants into the market, attracted by the potential of providing new services such as price risk management to the industry. One key to this brave new world is the existence of a liquid gas futures contract as a means to manage price risk.

The natural gas contract is expected to quickly assume broad European importance with the completion of the UK-continental interconnector in October 1998 and the ongoing liberalization of the European gas industry. The interconnector is giving those companies active in the UK market the opportunity to apply their skills and experience on the continent. A number of deals between UK producers and shippers with Dutch and German purchasers, amounting to 5 billion cubic meters of gas, have already been concluded.

The EU Gas Directive, due to be agreed upon during 1997, is unlikely to be effective in promoting competition in continental Europe. Competition is more likely to evolve as a consequence of commercial pressures from gas consumers and gas suppliers as well as from governments such as Germany and Holland that are pushing for gas competition. On the demand side, large European industrial consumers wish to be able to purchase gas on the same terms and enjoy the same price reductions as their UK competitors. Electricity liberalization and environmental pressures may result in a "dash for gas" by existing and new gas-fired power plants that would also want competitively priced gas supplies. On the supply side, Europe is also faced with gas-on-gas competition as sellers such as Gazprom, Sonatach, and Norway have a surplus deliverable gas supply and a desire to increase market share.

ELECTRICITY

The IPE is also actively researching the possibility of developing an electricity futures contract, noting increased electricity growth, deregulation efforts, and a $110 billion electric power market in OECD Europe. Most European electric utilities have a vertically integrated structure for generation and distribution, but state control is lessening due to progressive privatization efforts in some countries. Moreover, the EU Electricity Directive was agreed upon in June 1996 and will progressively open markets to competition. This directive began to take effect in 1997, will eventually require third party access to all grids, and mandates competition in generation.

The IPE is examining a number of issues regarding nascent electricity and gas futures contracts. First, is there the sufficient critical mass of industry players in any individual country in Europe or grouping of countries to support the development of successful futures contracts? The IPE feels that for an electricity or gas futures contract to be successful in the long term it must be European in scope. Second, how effective will the arbitrage mechanisms be in the future European gas and electricity markets? Effective arbitrage depends on the existence of adequate transmission infrastructure and legislation that allow competition through third party access. If arbitrage mechanisms are weak, then Europe will consist of a number of regional electricity and gas markets which may each require their own futures contracts. With effective arbitrage, we may see a situation similar to the one that has evolved in the North American market, where a single contract, the NYMEX Henry Hub futures contract, is the focus of the majority of risk management activities.

With the launch of natural gas futures during 1997, the IPE has made a long-term commitment to be an integral part of the UK and European power sector. The overall goal of the exchange is to offer a complex of energy products which should mutually reinforce the individual contract. However the markets evolve, the IPE intends to work with the European oil, gas, and power industries to develop the trading instruments they require.

FUTURE DEVELOPMENTS

The IPE has ambitious plans to increase its business by promoting its existing contracts, launching new contracts, and helping to lower transaction costs for users and potential users. The performance of existing contracts is regularly evaluated to ensure that they are meeting the needs of the market. Working groups have been set up for Brent, gasoil, and natural gas to assess each market and to suggest alterations to specifications if and when necessary. The IPE is planning to extend the number of forward periods listed for the Brent contract, and a review of the gasoil contract completed in March 1997 has resulted in major changes to enhance the contract as a hedging vehicle.[1]

The scope of the natural gas futures contract is likely to expand dramatically. The contract currently available is based on the notional National Balancing Point (NBP) within the UK transmission system, which is also the focus of physical market activity. But the NBP-based contract was always conceived as the starting point for a wider pan-European market. The interconnector pipeline is due to link the United Kingdom to continental Europe by October 1998, and different delivery locations together with daily as well as monthly contracts may develop in time. The pace of change will depend on how quickly competition extends across Europe.

While maintaining its independence, the IPE has not been afraid to pioneer cooperation with other exchanges to increase volumes of trade and lower costs for users. A Mutual Offset arrangement launched in June 1995 enables companies to trade Brent futures on the floor of the Singapore International Monetary Exchange (SIMEX). Positions opened up in Singapore can be closed in London, or vice versa. The Brent futures trading day is now up to 17 hours long. The IPE is also discussing various issues with the New York Mercantile Exchange including the possibilities of cooperation on systems and electronic trading. Other plans including the Automated Brokerage project, which the IPE is working on in cooperation with the London International Financial Futures and Options Exchange (LIFFE) and the London Clearing House (LCH), will also help to reduce costs for members.

---

1 Editor's Note: Futures contracts in commodity markets must be adjusted periodically to reflect the changes in the physical underlying markets.

TABLE 3.1

Futures Contract Specifications

	Brent Crude Oil	Gasoil	Natural Gas
Unit of Trading	1000 barrels (42,000 US gallons) of Brent blend crude oil	100 metric tonnes of gasoil with delivery by volume	1000 therms of natural gas per day during the delivery month traded in rights in natural gas of 1000 therms with delivery in kilowatt hours and traded in multiples of five contracts.
Delivery Months	12 consecutive months	12 consecutive months and then quarterly out to a maximum of 18 months	Monthly contract: 12 consecutive months. Balance of the month contract: a single contact tradeable upon expiry of the related monthly contract.
Last Trading Day	Trading shall cease at the close of business on the business day immediately preceding the 15th day prior to the first day of the delivery day in London. If the 15th day is a nonbanking day, trading shall cease on the business day immediately preceding the next business day prior to the 15th day.	Trading shall cease at 12:00 hours two business days prior to the 14th calendar day of the delivery month.	Trading in the monthly contract shall cease at the close of business on the second business day immediately prior to the day on which delivery commences. Trading shall cease in the balance of the month contract at the close of business two business days prior to the penultimate calendar day of the month.

TABLE 3.1 *Continued*

Futures Contract Specifications

	Brent Crude Oil	Gasoil	Natural Gas
Quotation	The contract price is in US dollars and cents per barrel	The contact price is in US dollars and cents per tonne on an EC import duty paid basis	The contract price is in Sterling pence per therm
Minimum Price Movement	One cent per barrel equivalent to a tick value of $10.00	25 cents per tonne equivalent to a tick value of $25.00	0.01p per therm.
Maximum Price Movement	There are no limits	There are no limits	There are no limits
Trading Hours (Local Time)	10:02–20:13 hours	09:15–17:27 hours	10:00–17:00 hours
Settlement Method	Delivery via the EFP mechanism with an option to cash settle against IPE daily published Brent Index	Physical delivery within the ARA area between 16th and last calendar day of the delivery month	Physical delivery by the transfer of rights to natural gas at the National Balancing Point within the National Transmission System

Further ahead, the IPE is considering the introduction of new contracts, many of which will be energy rather than purely petroleum based. An electricity futures contract could have strong potential, and interest has also been expressed in other possible markets such as fuel oil, coal, and unleaded gasoline.

TABLE 3.2

IPE Traded Option Contracts Specifications

	Brent Crude Oil	**Gasoil**
Unit of Trading	One lot of Brent crude oil futures	One lot of IPE's gasoil futures
Expiry Months	As per futures contract 6 months out into the future. New month added following expiry of near month such that 6 months are always displayed.	As per futures contract 6 months out into the future. New month added following expiry of near month such that 6 months are always displayed.
Expiry Day	Trading ceases at the close of business on the third day prior to the cessation of trading in the underlying futures contract	Trading ceases at the close of business on the third day prior to the cessation of trading in in the underlying futures contract
Quotation	The price is in US cents per barrel	The price is in US cents per tonne
Minimum Price Movement	One cent per barrel	Five cents per tonne
Exercise Price Intervals	Set at 50-cent intervals	Set at $5 intervals
Trading Hours	10:02–20:13 hours	09:15–17:27 hours
Exercise Style	American	American

These specifications will change from time to time. Please refer to current IPE literature for updates.

CHAPTER 4

Asian Market Developments

By Paul Horsnell

INTRODUCTION

A key feature of the Asian energy derivatives market is that it has evolved differently from the energy trading complexes of Europe and the United States. There can be no supposition that Asia is merely lagging behind the developmental path of Western markets. While Asia is certainly lagging in its development of an energy complex that was started much later and whose market is still very immature, the path taken is a unique one and bears few of the hallmarks of the progress of Western developments.

The first question to be addressed is why Asia should be a separate case. Consider a generalization of the route that Western trading has taken. In both Europe and the United States, spot oil trading emerged first, followed by the development of informal forward markets. After this, futures markets emerged, in some cases (e.g., NYMEX light sweet crude oil) almost completely supplanting the informal market, and in others (e.g., IPE Brent) grafting themselves onto the existing informal structure. Following this, higher-order and longer-term derivatives were established,

and derivatives were established for other forms of energy
such as natural gas and electricity in the 1990s. By contrast,
only one informal forward market (open spec naphtha)
with physical delivery has emerged in Asia, and to date,
futures markets contracts have failed to establish themselves firmly. Instead, the major growth area over the 1990s
has been in informal over-the-counter (OTC) swap trades,
an area that emerged relatively late in the Western energy
derivative complexes.

To understand why Asian energy trading has emerged
later and in a different form than trading in Western markets, we can begin by considering the conditions that led to
oil trading being established in the West during the 1970s
and 1980s. Market structure matters in that, if oil moves
through integrated channels or along a chain where there is
a high degree of market power on either the buying or selling side of the market, then price setting spot markets will
tend not to emerge. The growth of markets will also be
stalled by government price regulation or by taxation systems based on official prices rather than on prices actually
realized through third party sales. Likewise, if price rises
can simply be passed on to final consumers, or if companies face regulated input and output prices, then the incentives to hedge are removed.

The changes in the oil market during the 1970s,
including those wrought by the two oil price shocks,
moved Western and Eastern markets in opposite directions. Nationalizations in many OPEC countries destroyed
the integrated structure of the market, leaving the major
companies crude oil short. In Europe, the scope for the
development of the market was further increased by the
development of independent refining in northwest Europe
and later by the development of North Sea oil production.
Throughout the West, a whole raft of price regulation and
market controls was lifted, increasing competition and
exposing companies to the force of market prices. With
integration reduced, along with many elements of market
power, and price regulation removed, the stage was set for
the growth of first spot and then hedging markets for oil.

While the West was moving toward an industrial structure that facilitated markets, in Asia the oil price shocks created a legacy of concentration on the issue of supply security. A move was made toward greater state control of oil and toward greater insulation of the economy from swings in international prices. Private capital fared badly in the 1970s, with full or partial nationalizations most notably in India, Thailand, and the Philippines. National oil companies were created, and the power and reach of existing state companies were extended. Even in economies that had previously been fairly liberal, rafts of new price regulation were introduced. Government controls over industry operations were extended, and competition was reduced or removed, given the reliance on the strategic implications of energy above the efficiency of the energy sector itself.

What emerged in Asia (with the notable exception of Singapore) was then in general highly regulated and immune to price signals. Derivatives were slow to emerge because throughout most of Asia there was simply no demand for price risk management. Industry participants were either state companies operating in a highly uncommercialized environment or private companies in regulated markets facing little exposure to movements in world prices. The structure of state oil company management was not one that encouraged independent trading, even at the simplest possible level of spot transactions. Instead, a reliance on tender operations and long-term supply contracts was fostered, with no incentive to handle any associated risks.

The tardiness of Asian derivatives then needs to be seen in the light of what until at least the late 1980s was a highly ossified competitive structure. Until the movement began to roll back some of the 1970s' legacy of state control and regulation, and also to liberalize and commercialize in countries where government control had always been total, the basis for any derivatives complex would have been very flimsy.

That process of liberalization began in the 1990s, and the idea of an Asian energy derivatives complex has started to become meaningful. We begin by reviewing the first set of derivatives to emerge. Of necessity, the discussion centers on oil derivatives, since there has been little development of derivatives for other forms of energy. The scope for nonoil derivatives is considered in our conclusions. To date, two liquid derivative markets have emerged, a swaps market in Singapore and a physically delivered forward market for naphtha deliveries into East Asia (the open specification naphtha market). We consider these two markets in the next section. The main issue concerning energy futures in Asia is their lack of success to date, and we examine this in the third section. A final section offers some conclusions and pointers to the future.

SINGAPORE SWAPS AND FORWARD NAPHTHA MARKETS

The major growth in Asian derivatives during the 1990s has come in the form of OTC derivatives. A swaps market has developed in Singapore, primarily for gasoil and fuel oil. What has emerged is a very precise form of standardized swaps, which mimics all the functions of a forward market, bar that of physical delivery. These swaps occur in three main forms. First, there is the swap of a monthly average price, with that average being the assessment of the spot market made by a price agency, in almost every case the Platt's quote. There is one cash settlement of the difference between the swap price and the assessed average. In virtually all cases, these swaps will be for a volume of 50,000 barrels for gasoil and of 5000 tonnes (i.e., about 33,000 barrels) for fuel oil, or for an exact multiple thereof. Second, there is the swap of a quarterly average, normally for the next full quarter, and finally the rollover swap which is for the differential between the averages of successive months.

The key feature of these trades is their standardization. A tailor-made swap between a swaps provider and a client company is by its nature flexible. It can be defined for any particular time period, specific grade of oil, delivery location, and volume. While such swaps, which tend to be for longer time periods, are sold in Singapore, they only make up a small minority of trades. By contrast, the key feature of the Singapore swaps market is the standardization of trade, using the same volume (or multiple thereof), and the same price assessment relating to the same specific quality at the same delivery point. The inherent flexibility of a swap is thus forgone to enable the use of a portfolio of homogeneous swaps as a trading instrument.

The identity of the major traders of gasoil and fuel oil swaps is shown in Table 4.1. These lists combine companies with oil refining operations in Singapore, notably BP, Caltex, and Mobil, with Wall Street finance houses and their oil trading overshoots, as well as international oil trading companies. The most notable absentees from Table 4.1 are Asian national oil companies, with the sole exception of Sinochem, the Chinese state oil trader. Indeed, Asian capital overall is underrepresented in the market, with only a handful of active Japanese and Korean firms and the Singapore-based trader Hin Leong (one of the major traders of physical gasoil and fuel oil).

Table 4.1 also shows the number of firms recorded as being active in the market over the first 8 months of 1996 and the concentration of trading (expressed as an inverse Herfindahl index). Both markets have a large participant base, and the concentration statistics are characteristic of a dispersed market with little effective market power present. In terms of inverse Herfindahl indexes, the market is more dispersed than most major oil derivatives markets.

Quantification of the volumes traded in the swaps market causes some difficulties. Only a minority of trades are reported to price assessment agencies, and companies are of course guarded about revealing the scale of their involvement. Brokers are in a strong position to judge the overall volumes, but do have a tendency to overstate their own share of trades. In addition, the volume of trade can swing very sharply on a week-to-week basis, and perceptions tend to be more heavily influenced by the highs than by the average. However, from a variety of sources and cross-checks, we can identify some broad trends. While a few trades were made previously, it was in 1990 and 1991 that volumes began to build, and the market then reached a peak in 1994. At this point, the average daily volume of trade was about 2 million b/d, with about half of this in gasoil. Volumes declined in 1995 and 1996 to reach perhaps half the peak levels. In addition, what had been active markets for jet fuel, gasoline, naphtha, and Tapis crude oil had all contracted sharply by the end of 1996, leaving liquidity heavily biased toward gasoil and fuel oil.

TABLE 4.1

Major Participants in Singapore Gasoil and Fuel Oil Swaps Markets, 1996, Rank with Market Shares in Percentages

Rank	Gasoil		Fuel Oil	
1	Elf	12.3	BP	12.3
2	J Aron	8.1	Vitol	8.1
3	BP	6.9	Mobil	6.9
4	Sinochem	6.4	Shell	6.4
5	Shell	5.7	Hin Leong	5.7
6	IPG	4.9	Elf	4.9
7	Vitol	4.7	Sinochem	4.7
8	Hin Leong	4.2	IPG	4.2
9	Morgan Stanley	4.2	Morgan Stanley	4.2
10	Phibro	3.7	BB Energy	3.7
11	Cargill	2.9	Caltex	2.9
12	Banker's Trust	2.7	Stinnes	2.7
13	Mabanaft	2.7	Idemitsu	2.7
14	Mobil	2.7	Neste	2.7
15	Hyundai	2.2	Mabanaft	2.2
Number of Firms		55		46
Concentration		16.2		18.3

Note: The table is based on trades reported to the price assessment agency Petroleum Argus in the first 8 months of 1996.
Source: Paul Horsnell, *Oil in Asia: Markets, Trading, Refining and Deregulation*, Oxford, England: Oxford University Press, 1997.

The Singapore swaps market raises a series of questions as to why it took the form it did, why it grew when it grew, and why its growth stalled after 1994. We address these issues in turn.

The form that trading evolved into is very much a function of the logistics of the market. First, the location had to be Singapore, the only Asian market at the end of the 1980s where there was first significant production beyond that needed for internal company transfers, where prices and trade did not fall under heavy regulation, and where there was a dispersion of market power across both the buying and selling sides of the market. In Europe and the United States, forward markets with physical delivery and then futures markets could evolve. In the United States, trading took place along pipelines, with trade of small parcels possible. Likewise, Europe had the Rhine barge trade, again providing a base of transactions with small volumes.

Singapore has no parallel, with the export market being for cargoes, typically for 20,000 or 30,000 tonnes (i.e., for gasoil 150,000 or 225,000 barrels). The ratio of the number of possible physical deals to the physical base is very high in the United States and Rotterdam, but extremely small in Singapore. The ratio is shrunk even more drastically by the high proportion of Singapore exports that move under tender or through integrated channels. In short, the conditions that enabled the development of small parcel size and high trading volume forward markets in the West were not replicated in Singapore. What evolved as a parallel to those forward markets could not then be based on physical delivery, but instead on cash settlement.

Forward markets in the West needed to trade standardized terms to facilitate the clearing process that resulted in physical delivery. That standardization also helped their use as a trading instrument, allowing the use of a portfolio of fungible contracts to take positions and to hedge. Singapore swaps do not need to be standardized to facilitate delivery, given that they are cash settled. However, they do need standardization in order to be used as a trading instrument, since nonstandardization would create a series of basis risks.

Swaps have then enabled the Asian market to achieve the same trading possibilities as forward markets, without the need for clumsy delivery procedures. Indeed, every trading operation that a forward market can achieve, bar actual supply, can be replicated by a standardized swaps market. Thus, swaps developed the way they did in Singapore because of the difficulties of basing a forward market on physical delivery.

The second question we posed was that of why the market began its major expansion in the early 1990s. There was a series of contributory factors. First, the Singapore government provided direct incentives in a bid to expand oil trading in Singapore and to benefit the service industries (legal, accounting, etc.) that trading utilizes. This was encapsulated in the Approved Oil Trader (AOT) scheme introduced in 1989, which confers a preferential tax rate for oil trading activity. As of 1997, the AOT scheme had about 55 members, including virtually all of the companies shown in Table 4.1. The launch of the AOT scheme coincided with when many international oil and Wall Street trading firms were seeking to expand into Asia, and it certainly helped provide a general prod toward centralizing their expanded activities in Singapore. A rapid influx of traders ensued, mainly with a background in Western markets, and the swaps market provided a focus for activity, especially when the difficulties of creating physical forward markets were fully gauged.

The early 1990s also saw some significant changes in the international oil trade. The end of the Gulf War left Asian oil product prices significantly higher than those in the West, not the least due to the removal from the market of the output of Kuwaiti refineries and their hydrocracking units. The AOT scheme had brought in traders who wished to think in terms of global trading, and now relative prices meant that arbitrage from Europe into Asia (primarily for gasoil) was facilitated. Using a combination of European futures and Singapore gasoil swaps, differentials could be locked in. The appearance and then rapid growth of significant Chinese oil product imports (especially for gasoil and fuel oil) provided another spur, with swaps again providing instruments to support physical trading.

After 1994, some of the foregoing factors went into reverse, and the swaps market declined in volume. The imposition of import controls in March 1994 greatly reduced the scope for trading into China. The scope for arbitrage trading from Europe was also reduced, with the Kuwaiti refineries coming back on stream. In addition, a general overexpansion of Asian refinery capacity relative to the rate of demand growth also reduced arbitrage trade. The Singapore market has become highly competitive, with trading margins extremely thin. In some senses, it may have expanded too quickly, with the profit opportunities not living up to the initial expectations of some of the early 1990s influx of traders. In line with a more global downscaling of activity, a significant retrenchment began.

Some markets for individual oil product swaps were hit by special factors. In 1994, active swap markets existed for gasoil, fuel oil, naphtha, gasoline, jet fuel, and Tapis crude oil. All but the first two of these have now either greatly contracted or effectively disappeared (at least in terms of a high-volume market of standardized short-term swaps). To give but one example, naphtha swaps were effective negatively by what, de facto, amounted to manipulation by one major trader, which led to a drain of confidence in the market.

Swaps are still the central component of the Asian oil derivatives market, and their apparent decline after 1994 is more symptomatic of market conditions than any longer-term malaise. We noted earlier that derivatives growth has been stalled across Asia by regulation and market structure. To some degree, the availability of derivatives instruments has run ahead of the speed of liberalization and the growth of indigenous Asian demand for derivatives. While that remains the case, the development of swaps in Singapore is more likely to follow market cycles than any remorseless linear growth.

Although forward markets have not emerged in Singapore primarily as a result of logistics, there is one forward market in Asia based on physical delivery. This is the

open specification naphtha market. While greatly reduced
in size from its peak in 1991, it is still an important part of
Asian oil trading. The market began in 1986 primarily due
to the dislocation caused by the collapse of official Middle
East pricing systems.

Naphtha has been the major oil product import into
Japan, sourced primarily from the Middle East. The collapse of official pricing systems combined with the high
levels of price volatility in 1986 left Japanese firms with
price risk that they were not exposed to either in their
domestic activities (due to regulation) or in their crude oil
imports (due to the monthly average formulas used by
Middle East producers for crude oil). The open specification market emerged in part as a response to that sudden
immersion in risk.

TABLE 4.2

Major Participants in Open Specification Naphtha Forward Market, 1988 and 1996, Rank with Market Shares in Percentages

Rank	1988		1996	
1	Marubeni	18.9	Itochu	18.1
2	Nissho Iwai	13.7	Samsung	14.1
3	Shell	9.0	Vitol	10.9
4	Mitsubishi	7.0	J Aron	7.5
5	C Itoh	6.2	Mitsui	6.2
6	Mitsui	5.2	Glencore	5.4
7	Nippon Oil	4.1	Kanematsu	5.2
8	Kanematsu	3.4	BP	4.4
9	Phibro	3.1	Yukong	4.4
10	Sumitomo	3.1	Shell	4.0
11	BP	2.3	Cargill	3.6
12	Asahi	2.1	Honchu	3.2
13	Tonen	2.1	Marubeni	3.0
14	Toyo Menka	2.1	Elf	2.6
15	Idemitsu	1.8	Showa Shell	2.6
Number of Firms		36		21
Concentration		12.1		11.1

Source: Paul Horsnell, op. cit.

The major traders in the naphtha forward market are shown in Table 4.2, together with their market shares for both 1988 and 1996. Note that this is a more concentrated market than Singapore swaps (as evidenced by the lower inverse Herfindahl statistic), and it also has fewer participants. Over time, the composition of trade has changed. As shown in Table 4.2, Japanese firms dominated trade in 1988 (indeed they represented 75 percent of the liquidity). By 1996, the share of Japanese companies had fallen to 43 percent, with a significant share accounted for by Korean companies and international traders. The forward naphtha market is perhaps a special case. However, as a pointer to the future, it does show that the emergence of significant price risk in the Asian context can give rise to a derivatives market.

ENERGY FUTURES MARKETS IN ASIA

A key feature of Asian energy derivatives has been the failure of energy futures markets to take root. Even those contracts that have managed to gain some initial liquidity have been unable to sustain growth and eventually faded away. The most concerted attempts to launch an energy futures complex in Asia have been carried by the Singapore International Monetary Exchange (SIMEX). The first contract to be launched was for High Sulphur Fuel Oil (HSFO), which began trading in February 1989. This was a success in that it survived for a considerable time, but it was a failure in that the liquidity of trade stagnated. During 1993, the contract's peak year over the 1990s, trade averaged 1266 contracts per day. To put this into context, that represented less than one-half of 1 percent of global oil futures trading in that year. After 1993, volumes of trade fell continuously, until liquidity effectively disappeared completely in the autumn of 1995. A few trades were registered in late 1996, but the average for the year equated to only half a contract per day. While still listed by the exchange, the contract (at least in its original form) was effectively dead. It was relaunched in April 1997 with a changed sulfur specification, but has died again.

The other contracts launched by SIMEX have tended to fail rather faster. Dubai crude oil was launched in June 1990 and stopped trading in 1991. A contract for gasoil was introduced in June 1991, relaunched in June 1992, and finally delisted in November 1993. As of early 1997, the only active SIMEX contract is for Brent blend crude oil, which we consider further below.

The failure of the early SIMEX contracts was due to several factors. First, there was an absence of any informal market for futures to grow off. Oil futures in New York and London have grown by either taking over or adding to the functions of existing liquid informal markets. There was no such base in Singapore. The informal fuel oil swaps markets grew after the launch of the SIMEX contract and tended to bleed liquidity away from SIMEX rather than act as a base. Second, there was the problem of physical delivery, the same problem that, as noted earlier, had stalled the development of forward markets. This was a fatal problem in the case of the gasoil contract, and it also posed a problem for the HSFO fuel oil contract. The fuel oil contract had the advantage that, as the world's leading ship refueling port, Singapore had a high-volume market in bunker grade fuel oil. Even here, however, the delivery procedures were complex and potentially involved tankers having to load small parcels of oil at different terminals, all to clear the same futures position.

The failure of the Dubai contract came from the features of the Dubai market. This is the only forward market for a Middle East crude oil, but primarily it always been traded out of London. The bulk of Middle East exports to Asia have been priced on the monthly Dubai/Oman average (very difficult to hedge using the Dubai market itself) or have gone to end users who have preferred to buy on tenders. In total, Singapore futures could not build on a London-based forward market, especially when Asian crude users had no demand for hedging a daily Dubai price.

Despite the failure with Dubai, crude oil futures are currently the major source of development in the Asian derivatives market. No viable forward market for any Asian crude oil has ever emerged on which an indigenous contract could be based. This has been ruled out by combinations of low spot availabilities, monopoly or dominant sellers, fiscal regimes based on retrospective official prices, and again, the preference of most Asian refiners to buy on a term or tender basis.

Given the difficulties of creating a futures market for indigenous Asian or Middle East crude oil, the focus has fallen on importing already successful contracts from other regions. In particular, the two crude oil contracts now available in Asia are those for UK Brent blend, as traded on the International Petroleum Exchange (IPE) of London, and the light sweet crude oil contract as traded on the New York Mercantile Exchange (NYMEX). A Brent crude oil contract was launched on SIMEX in June 1995, with a mutual offset of SIMEX positions with the IPE (i.e., a position opened on one exchange can be closed out on the other). NYMEX launched a deal with the Sydney Futures Exchange (SFE) in September 1995 to enable the trading of NYMEX contracts on the SFE through electronic, rather than open outcry, trading systems. A similar deal was concluded between NYMEX and the Hong Kong Futures Exchange (HKFE), which began operation on June 13, 1997.

The bulk of trading activity in Asia seems to have gone to SIMEX Brent, although a full comparison is difficult given that figures for NYMEX's electronic system are not broken down by country of origin. Overall volumes of trade have been reasonably steady, but not spectacular. In the 12 months to February 1997, monthly trading volumes for SIMEX Brent had ranged from a low of just over 2 million barrels (June 1996) to a high of nearly 8 million barrels (January 1997). On the IPE, Brent regularly trades between 30 million and 40 million barrels on a daily basis, although the differences in market structure and trading culture between Europe and Asia are so extreme as to make the comparison an unfair one. In our opinion, it would have been unrealistic to expect much more from the first 2 years of Asia's links with the Western futures exchanges.

The future for crude oil futures trading in Asia still remains potentially bright, particularly for Brent. Since 1995, world trade patterns in crude oil have changed, brought on by a mismatch between the location of most incremental supply (non-OPEC producers in the West) and the greatest of incremental demand (i.e., Asia). A significant flow of Brent-related crude oil has appeared at the margin of the Asian market. In the absence of any indigenous Asian or other candidates, Brent currently appears best placed to serve as the long-missing marker crude oil for Asia.

Beyond the attempts to launch oil futures in Singapore, and the NYMEX tie-ins with Sydney and Hong Kong, there have been other markets in Asia. In Japan, gasoline or crude oil futures trading in Tokyo has been long discussed, and recent deregulation has improved the chances, but to date progress has been very limited. However, it is in China where futures trading has made a fleeting, but nonetheless spectacular, appearance. We have already noted that futures markets development in Asia has been very slow. It might then come as a surprise that in fact, during the 1990s, Asia has had more exchanges trading oil, and more different oil contracts, than the rest of the world put together. To be precise, China alone has had the plurality of world exchanges, with at one point in early 1994 no fewer than six trading crude oil or oil products. China had a brief flourish of oil derivatives beginning in March 1993 with the launch of a gasoil contract in Nanjing, followed by other exchanges in Beijing, Shanghai, Daqing, Guangzhou, and Hunan. The leading exchange was the Shanghai Petroleum Exchange, accounting for about 80 percent of total volume, trading some 1.7 billion barrels per oil in the year from May 1993.

This extremely fast growth and profusion of exchanges and contracts were brought to an end by a State Council directive in spring 1994 (known as the "rectification program"), which banned futures trading in strategic commodities, including oil. The reimposition of price controls on oil also rendered trading fairly pointless, and domestic

Chinese oil futures effectively came to an end, at least temporarily. The exchanges were (unfairly) being blamed for adding to inflationary pressures, in addition to which their regulatory structure could only be described at best as being rather loose. The extremely brief flowering demonstrates the potential for futures in the domestic Chinese context, and it can be expected that oil futures markets will reemerge, but with fewer exchanges and a far greater level of regulation.

Overall, Asian futures markets for oil have struggled in comparison with both Western markets and Asian financial futures. However, the shell of a futures complex has begun to form, and it awaits the future developments to which we now turn.

FUTURE OF ASIAN DERIVATIVES

While the development of an energy derivative complex has been slow in Asia, there are factors in play that will over time encourage that development. In the context of oil, these factors are primarily deregulation, globalization, and energy balances.

Deregulation processes are generally at work throughout Asia, albeit at different speeds and with different priorities. Overall, companies are beginning to be faced with more competitive pressures and with more exposure to price risk. Generally, the scope for derivatives development is emerging, although three key provisos need to be made. The first is management structures and accounting procedures, which to date have not been conducive to the successful use of derivatives. This is not a function of economic development; for example, Japanese companies have a particularly poor track record in the use of derivatives. It is solely a function of organizational form and what can be loosely termed "trading culture." For derivatives use to reach its full potential, these management deficiencies will need to be addressed, or else the preference for physical operations using almost exclusively term contracts and tenders will survive the onset of exposure to risk.

The second proviso is that energy liberalization is not normally an instant process. The United Kingdom, often held up as a role model, is as of 1997 in the 16th year of the process, with a significant timetable still to go. The current Japanese deregulation process began in earnest in 1986, while China arguably began in 1979 and has been through several cycles of liberalization followed by partial retrenchment. Finally, it would be naive to suggest that energy has been depoliticized in Asia. While the degree of deadweight efficiency loss that governments are prepared to accept for notions of supply security has been reduced, strategic considerations are still in play for many Asian governments, particularly those faced with the fastest rate of growth of the absolute level of energy import dependence.

Globalization is helping the growth of derivatives, as Asia combined with the Middle East can no longer be seen as an insulated system. We noted earlier that arbitrage trading of gasoil from Europe helped the development of Singapore swaps, and while that flow has been reduced in physical terms, it still impacts on prices and on swap market activity. Likewise, we have also noted the growth since 1995 of significant volumes of Brent-related crude oil into Asia, primarily from West Africa. Asia is no longer a crude oil system governed solely by unhedgeable retrospective or monthly average pricing, and the growth of spot oil trading from the Atlantic basin represents a significant source of new (and more hedgeable) absolute and relative price risks.

Globalization is also related to our third factor, that of energy balances. Asia is becoming more dependent on other regions to bridge its deficit. International trade flows are increasing, bringing new directions of trade, new arbitrage possibilities, and a greater volume of energy bought at fluctuating international prices. Relative price risk is also increasing, with a fractionation of the markets across for specific oil products due to more heterogeneous environmental specifications.

Deregulation processes and the increases in energy deficits do not only encourage development of oil derivatives. Natural gas demand is expanding fast, and gas mar-

kets are also subject to deregulation together with privatization and commercialization of gas concerns. The longer
term will see the continued development of international
pipeline systems, particularly in Southeast Asia, with the
emergence of hubs. Gas derivatives are well established in
the United States and relatively new in Europe, and Asia is
again lagging far behind, but it is evolving in a way that
will facilitate gas derivatives. Electricity is also a potential
source of derivative growth. Deregulation is again a strong
force, most notably in Japan, and market structures across
Asia are becoming less integrated with the growth of
Independent Power Producers (IPPs). Perhaps more immediate than the use of derivatives based on functioning markets in gas and electricity are the financial implications of
the rapid expansion of gas and power industries. This is
creating the need for large capital investments in infra-
structural projects. With a growing reliance in Asia on private capital, rather than the public purse, comes the scope
for the use of derivatives as part of a financing package.

The structure of Asian energy markets is undergoing a
profound change. Having headed in a direction opposite to
that of the West in the 1970s, changes in government policy
and in the fundamentals of the market are now encouraging the growth of markets. The energy derivatives complex
may have started late and has still only reached an early
stage, but the scope for expansion is now very real.

CHAPTER 5

Risk Management in North American Natural Gas

By Patricia Hemsworth

INTRODUCTION

The deregulation of the natural gas industry was a gradual process which began in 1978 and ended in November 1993 with US FERC (Federal Energy Regulatory Commission) Order 636. This process was matched lockstep by the evolution of a deregulated physical and financial natural gas marketplace. This marketplace gradually changed from one dominated by fixed long-term contracts provided by pipeline companies to include a fledgling spot market and then a liquid forward market. This forward market provided the foundation for the development of a successful futures market, whose stability and liquidity supported other over-the-counter (OTC) markets in basis swaps, options on futures, OTC options, and finally, a plethora of complex derivative structures that combine elements of all of the instruments.

As the market itself evolved into a fully deregulated environment, the practical need for these instruments to solve a number of gas marketing and risk management needs grew. Derivative tools which were developed in the crude oil and petroleum products markets were adapted to the particular needs of the physical marketplace for natural gas. Full deregulation of natural gas involved evolution not only of a new marketplace, but of the physical infrastructure of pipelines and storage facilities for natural gas.

Open price discovery allowed for the development of the most economically efficient infrastructure, and the instruments themselves adapted to the idiosyncrasies of moving gas through the nation's pipelines and in and out of storage facilities to end users. As marketing tools, risk management instruments allowed for increasingly flexible methods of selling physical natural gas, blending seamlessly the physical and financial markets. Forwards, futures, swing swaps, basis swaps, options on futures, and OTC options allow for the efficient marketing of natural gas and the mitigation of risk associated with price volatility. Liquid, stable derivative markets enable market participants to change their risk profiles to those more in tune with their tolerance for risk. They also afford traders the choice of how much counterparty risk to assume in the process. These derivative markets, which have served to promote overall market efficiency, continue to adapt to new market conditions, including the dramatic changes in the energy markets brought on by the deregulation of the electric power markets. Today, the beginning of deregulation of electric power has served to integrate the energy marketplace into one large Btu energy trading marketplace. Risk management instruments used in the marketing of natural gas are being integrated with transactions for electric power in new and creative ways.

The first piece of the puzzle in the evolution of the natural gas market was the development of a spot market and then a forward market. The partial decontrol of natural gas wellhead prices and separation of the merchant and transportation function in the marketplace led to the development of both spot and forward markets in different trading locations during the 1980s. Gas trade gradually shifted away from long-term fixed-price contracts to a greater concentration of spot transactions, which in turn evolved into a forward market. The gas forward market involves the physical purchase or sale for some future date with specifications as to date of delivery, location, and price or price formula. These forward contracts in physical gas laid the groundwork for price discovery in the early stages of deregulation. Trading was dominated by marketers who assumed the merchant roles once held by the pipelines, buying gas from producers and selling the gas to end users and local distribution companies (LDCs). Through early trading in the forward markets, standardized trading practices and conventions emerged, supporting the development of a futures contract. The gas forward market, in contrast, is one which is purely physical, limiting activity solely to traders of the physical commodity, a natural limitation to the development of liquidity.

NYMEX FUTURES

The development of the spot and forward market laid the groundwork for the development of the very successful New York Mercantile Exchange (NYMEX) Henry Hub futures contract, which began trading in April 1990. In contrast to the forward market, a futures market does not require physical delivery of the commodity, but may be offset prior to the physical delivery period. Initially, the contract called for 12 months of futures delivery at any time, was expanded to 18 months, and now allows for trading up to 3 years forward, accommodating long-dated swap business which is hedged on the exchange. Standardized specifications were made for the contract size (10,000 MMBtu of natural gas), which was deliverable at Henry Hub, Louisiana, according to a strict set of delivery specifications. The fact that all futures trades can be settled with physical delivery of the natural gas in accordance with standard industry practices strengthens the appeal of the contract to commercial users, although fewer than 5 percent of all futures transactions are settled by physical delivery.

The futures market helped to change the trading practices of a physical market that maintained certain legacy trading arrangements from a regulated market. Often, gas end users contracted with pipelines for gas, but exited from them if their needs changed, thereby reneging on contracts. However, the delivery mechanism on NYMEX—which included exchange delivery in which buyers and sellers were matched by the exchange, ADPs where exchange-matched buyers and sellers made alternative arrangements, and the Exchange for Physical (EFP)—all required firm commitments to take or make delivery of gas with penalties for nonperformance. This contractual firmness helped to standardize trading practices and to enforce contract performance, creating a stable, reliable marketplace for physical gas traders.

While trading in the forward market is a principal-to-principal market, NYMEX trades are executed by open outcry on the floor of the NYMEX through the clearinghouse function of the exchange. The other side of every transaction is the exchange. Every buyer and seller of a futures contract is required to do so through a clearing member and is required to post original margin for each trade, a good faith deposit that must be maintained. Futures positions are marked to the market on a daily basis, with settlement based on daily settlement prices determined at the end of the trading day. Losses on futures positions must be paid on a daily basis with the clearing member, or the clearing member is required by the exchange to forcibly liquidate the losing trade. Should a customer default on a futures contract, the clearing member, often a financial institution, is required to cover its customer's losses. If the resources of the corporation are exhausted, a special clearing fund to which all 80 members have contributed $500,000 is tapped. The next step is a pro rata assessment to each member corporation to make good for the loss.

Thus, the key characteristic of the futures market is its stability, which comes from its guarantee of contract performance. The standardization of terms, relatively small contract size, fungibility, lack of requirement for physical delivery, and rigorous performance requirements serve to attract large amounts of financial capital to this market. The participants include not only natural gas producers, marketers, processors, utilities, and end users, but also a host of other speculative market participants. Exchange members, local floor traders, small speculators, and large investment and commodity hedge funds provide the liquidity to enable natural gas traders and the financial institutions that provide specialized OTC hedging services for the industry to transfer or shift risk. An additional benefit to the hedging community is the ability to maintain anonymity in the marketplace.

The attraction of risk capital to the marketplace is critical to the efficient transfer of risk. The extraordinary success of the natural gas futures contract during the 1990s enables the industry to engage in a series of efficient risk management transactions, such as EFPs, ADPs, storage hedging activities, strip trading, swing swaps, and OTC basis trading. The virtual elimination of counterparty credit risk provides a stable foundation for all other forms of OTC transactions to take place. The futures market successfully adapted itself to the trading practices of the industry, improving them in the process. In turn, the successful futures market then became the foundation for many other forms of derivative trade.

BASIS RISK

While a hedge on the NYMEX will allow the trader easy, anonymous entrance and exit from trades as well as the virtual elimination of counterparty credit risk, it cannot eliminate geographic basis risk. A natural gas producer in Alberta, Canada, for example, may wish to hedge part of its production on NYMEX, but the hedge will only be effective to the extent that there is a reliable, high level of price correlation between Alberta and Henry Hub, the active NYMEX contract delivery point. The natural gas production, pipeline, and storage infrastructure in North America, however, creates distinctive patterns of trade by geographic area. There are limitations and constrictions on natural gas transportation that tend to regionalize trade, in some areas more than others. Market conditions in Alberta, for instance, are affected by such local factors as the level of snowfall in the Canadian Rockies which will be utilized to produce hydropower, potentially displacing gas-fired electric power generation in the Northwest. Transportation limitations localize this trade, isolating it to some extent from the Henry Hub delivery area. These issues serve to create different price relationships between geographic areas, with varying degrees of correlation depending on local demand patterns, the integration of the local pipelines with other trading hubs, available storage facilities, and local production.

Several distinct geographic areas can be identified in North America. The Henry Hub, delivery point for the futures contract, located in Louisiana, is a major transfer point through which enormous volumes of gas move. Although there is little storage in its vicinity, it is a huge transfer point with great accessibility to major consuming markets in the US East and Midwest. Another is the Iroquois pipeline system near the US/Canadian border which serves the large space-heating market in New England, which has very little storage. Katy Hub in the Houston Ship Channel is another major center of trading activity and a major east Texas transfer point, through which vast amounts of gas move. This area, which has large amounts of production, pipeline access, and storage, often shows relative price stability during extreme weather conditions compared to the Henry Hub, which has less storage and serves the space-heating markets.

Appalachia is another key hub area dominated by the Columbia Gas Transmission system with excellent storage, serving heating markets of Pennsylvania, Ohio, and West Virginia. Permian Basin and San Juan Basin mainly serve western markets, particularly California. While there are pipeline limitations in moving gas east, there is good correlation with the Northwest market export point, Sumas, in the state of Washington, since both of these hubs are well connected by pipeline to the California gas market, where they compete for gas sales. Alberta, Canada, at AECO-C is another distinct region with pipelines into the United States. Fairly isolated are the Rockies with limited pipeline accessibility east. While gas deregulation has resulted in increased investment in pipelines and storage facilities that integrate markets, each area has its own production, markets, weather patterns, storage and pipeline, and its own unique locational basis relationship to NYMEX.

To accommodate this risk management need, a vibrant OTC basis market developed concurrently to NYMEX futures in which OTC dealers and brokers facilitate basis hedging. Alberta producers needing to hedge forward gas production for 3 months forward will sell NYMEX futures. This will leave them at risk, however, that Alberta gas might drop in price at a greater rate than NYMEX gas. To hedge this basis risk, producers would go to OTC brokers or dealers who would arrange for them to sell the basis in a swap 3 months forward. In this way, the producers would lock in current differentials so that, if Alberta prices dropped faster than NYMEX, they would have covered their risk. The OTC brokers may also have helped to hedge their currency risk because all hedges would be executed in US dollars. Unlike a trade done on NYMEX, the OTC deal is done on a principal-to-principal basis, so care has to be taken about the creditworthiness and reliability of one's trading counterparty. Counterparties agree to swap payments on the relationship between NYMEX and Alberta. For example, if the Alberta weakens relative to NYMEX, the producer will receive periodic payments from the buyer of the basis swap, and vice versa.

Another issue to deal with is that the pool of basis market participants may shrink under certain market conditions. If the producers decide to exit the trade under certain market conditions, they may be unable to find a counterparty to trade off their swap or might only be able to do so at unfavorable bid/ask spreads. This kind of locational basis trading described for Alberta, Canada, takes place in the different market hubs mentioned earlier. Each region has its own particular pattern of trade versus Henry Hub, including overall level of correlation with seasonal patterns.

REGIONAL GAS MARKETS

Because NYMEX has been extremely successful at developing a Henry Hub futures contract, why wouldn't it be able to provide the same services to the industry in the form of other futures contracts with different delivery specifications? Futures exchanges saw this need, and in 1995, the Kansas City Board of Trade (KCBT) launched a Western Gas Futures Contract mimicking the size and specifications of the NYMEX Henry Hub contract with the Waha Hub as a delivery point. This contract, called the Western Natural Gas Contract, has drawn modest attention from its local market participants, with daily volumes of about 400 contracts, or about 1 percent of the NYMEX Henry Hub contracts. In 1996, the NYMEX launched two new futures contracts in natural gas: the Permian Basin futures contract, which competes directly with the Kansas City Board of Trade contract, and the Alberta Natural Gas futures contract, a dollar-denominated natural gas contract with an AECO-C delivery point.

While the idea of creating futures contracts for these market hubs seems to make sense, it is extremely difficult in practice to maintain more than one futures contract of the same class, particularly on the same exchange. Several futures contract choices compete for the investment and speculative capital that provide the lifeblood of a successful futures market. The KCBT's very modest success might be accounted for by the fact that it is sponsored by a different exchange with separate local participants and members and meets the needs of a market that is highly distinctive, being isolated from the eastern part of the United States by pipeline limitations. Yet in the case of the NYMEX, multiple contracts have proved consistently unsuccessful. Multiple futures contracts for the same commodity compete for speculative capital, limiting the potential for liquidity. Practical economic considerations in maintaining these smaller contracts further limit development. Local floor brokers, who either execute orders for brokerage houses or trade for themselves, are looking to maximize expensive trading privileges and want to trade liquid contracts, which offer more moneymaking potential for them. Clearing financial institutions with floor brokers, are also unwilling to dilute their resources for contracts which have limited appeal. The contracts were also launched too late; OTC markets had already developed depth and liquidity. Well-established electronic exchanges for natural gas in Canada, such as the Natural Gas Exchange and the Quick Trade/Energy Exchange, have also made it difficult for the successful launch of a Canadian futures contract. To date, the Alberta and Permian Basin futures contracts have virtually no volume or open interest and are in danger of being delisted. It appears that there will continue to be good demand for active OTC market services in basis swap trading as an adjunct market to the broadly active Henry Hub futures contract.

EFPS

One way the OTC basis market converges with the futures contract to provide flexible risk management tools for the industry is in the Exchange for Physical (EFP) market. The EFP market integrates the OTC basis market, the physical market, and the futures market. It is a mechanism allowed by the NYMEX, permitting futures trading off the floor of the exchange as part of a physical gas transaction. It comprises 97 percent of all deliveries done on the NYMEX and has greatly facilitated price discovery in basis and risk management. While there are many creative permutations, essentially this arrangement allows for the off-exchange swap of futures positions between two physical traders as part of a physical deal between the two. It links seamlessly the futures market and the physical market, making the futures market an integral part of marketing the physical commodity.

For example, a marketer may arrange to sell gas for delivery in 3 months to a northeastern LDC at a certain premium over NYMEX with the price to be fixed at the choice of the LDC. The parties may negotiate this premium based on quotations in the OTC basis market. To hedge a potential drop in prices and a loss in revenue, the marketer sells NYMEX. The LDC buys NYMEX when it wishes to price its gas, and when the gas is actually delivered, the two parties exchange futures positions: The LDC sells futures to the marketer at the agreed premium to NYMEX, liquidating futures transactions on both sides and consummating the physical deal.

These kinds of transactions are not unique to energy, but have been used extensively in other commodity markets, such as grains and soft commodities in the form of Against Actuals (AAs). They offer a number of advantages for both parties. The flexibility in offering the ability to choose the time to fix prices presents a distinct marketing advantage to the marketing organization. The LDC gets to choose the flexibility in pricing. And the mechanism allows for both parties to liquidate their futures positions at the same price, which becomes their invoice price, without having to go to the floor of the exchange to liquidate futures. Having to do so often results in execution risk, or slippage due to market trading conditions.

Price discovery provided by the futures markets and its derivatives allows for the development of a fully transparent yield curve, extending to 3 years. Just as fixed income markets reflect the distribution of cost of money at different points on the yield curve, the commodity markets allow for the same mechanism. The forward curve reflects the cost of money involved in owning the commodity, costs of storage and insurance, or the "carrying charges" associated with owning, storing, and insuring a commodity. It also reflects the existing storage levels and the perception of future supply and demand. Supply and demand dislocations such as spikes in demand or sharp reductions in supply caused by weather-related factors can override the natural carrying charge fundamentals or contango, skewing this relationship to show sharp premiums in front months over back. Skillful use of these relationships can allow natural gas traders to lock in favorable differentials on costs associated with storage or to exploit these differentials for profit, particularly for inventory management of natural gas supplies. For example, if the carrying charges implied in the forward curve exceed the actual cost of interest, insurance, and storage, one might buy spot natural gas, store it, and sell forward on NYMEX, "EFPing" the physical gas at the time of delivery. On the other hand, if the market is trading in a backwardation, with front months at a premium to back months, one might exploit this situation by selling excess inventory by selling nearby NYMEX contract months, delivering the natural gas on NYMEX through an EFP mechanism, and buying cheaper gas in the deferred contract months.

STORAGE

Inventory management in natural gas storage has gone through dramatic changes since FERC Order 636, when it was determined that storage services be unbundled and that customers be offered greater access to storage space as well as the right to use space sublease capacity. Patterns of gas injection into storage and withdrawal from storage changed to become more efficient. The development of the futures market and full price transparency allowed customers to inject gas into storage from April through September and leave it there until the heating season, when gas would be withdrawn from October through March. Now, however, gas is injected or withdrawn not just according to this seasonal pattern but by market conditions. The frequency of injections and withdrawals has increased dramatically since the deregulation of the natural gas markets and trading natural gas futures.

One way that marketers might use the futures market to lock in storage costs plus a profit is to look at the spread relationships between futures months. If the cost to store natural gas between April and October is 35 cents per MMBtu and the differential between April and October in futures is 50 cents, then a marketer can buy April and sell October at the 50-cent differential. One can take delivery of the April gas and then liquidate the October short position by doing an EFP later for October delivery, thereby locking in a 15-cent profit. Because of the increase in the amount of natural gas storage facilities in the United States, as well as the more economic use of this storage, natural gas injections and withdrawals are now being done more frequently. Rather than having an asset stored as disaster insurance, as was done before deregulation, inventories are being dynamically managed in a more nimble way than ever before. Option strategies can also be used to hedge or maximize revenues connected with owning inventory.

OPTIONS

All of the risk management activities described so far with forwards, futures, or swaps involve what could be called "symmetric hedges" or ones in which the associated risk is transferred on a one-to-one basis. If an owner of storage wants to hedge gas supplies by selling NYMEX futures, assuming the cash prices correlate perfectly, a loss in the value of inventory will be offset evenly by a profit in futures. The Alberta producer who sells NYMEX as a hedge and then sells the basis between NYMEX and Alberta will have hedged on an even basis outright price movement on NYMEX and locational basis on the OTC market. Options, on the other hand, allow traders to place asymmetric hedges or hedges in which the risk profile assumed by a position is not offset on a one-to-one basis by an equal and opposite transaction.

In 1993, after FERC Order 636, options trading was launched on the NYMEX. These are American-style options on the Henry Hub futures contract, which allow for exercise of the options prior to expiration. The success and liquidity of the futures, as well as the freer marketplace, were the necessary conditions for these to work. Essentially, the use of options allows a trader to transfer risk, but with a different risk profile than with futures and forwards. Producers who hedge inventory on NYMEX with futures gives up the ability to participate in an up move in price when selling futures. But if they buy puts, they have the right, but not the obligation, to assume a short position at a certain strike price. If the price of futures declines, they have hedged themselves against a declines, but if prices go higher, the puts expire worthless and allow them to enjoy the appreciation of their inventories. Their risk associated with the hedge is limited to the cost of a premium, but their potential reward is unlimited. Likewise, an industrial consumer might hedge against a price rise in supplies by buying a call, or the right, but not the obligation, to assume a long position at a certain price.

Traders might find that the price of the premiums, which is determined by maturity, strike price, and volatility of the marketplace, could be prohibitively expensive, and since options premiums are a wasting asset, producers might buy puts, selling them at a lower strike (a vertical spread) to provide price protection within the price band. Or they may decide to buy puts and sell calls above the market, called a "fence," to partially finance the cost of the puts, giving them downside protection, but locking in a sales price above the market for another risk profile.

Sales of options are excellent methods of revenue maximization. A marketer might be maintaining large inventories in storage. One strategy to maximize revenues might be to sell out-of-the-money calls to raise revenue. The choice of strike price should correspond to levels above the market at which the marketer would be comfortable selling inventory. If the marketer is "exercised" or the strike price of the calls makes it profitable for the buyers of the calls to assume a long position, the marketer assumes a short position in futures, but can use the EFP mechanism to deliver inventory out of storage. The best timing for this kind of strategy is when the market is very strong, looks close to a top, and volatility is high, yielding good premiums. The same strategy, in reverse, might be used for a buyer of natural gas. After a steep decline in the market, the buyer might sell puts. In the case of selling options, the risk profile is the reverse of buying (i.e., reward is limited to the premium, risk unlimited). Other combinations—strangles (buying or selling two different strike prices) or straddles (buying a put and call at the same strike price or selling a put or call at the same strike price)—yield different risk profiles and can be used for different market situations.

Options that trade on NYMEX enjoy all the advantages and disadvantages of the NYMEX futures contract. They are standardized, they require margining (on short positions) which helps to assure performance, and they are liquid. The standardization that encourages the depth of liquidity limits flexibility and leaves the user open to geographic risk. Just as dealers have created OTC basis swaps, there is a plethora of customized OTC options products that meet the special needs of natural gas traders.

For example, dealers and brokers dealing in basis swaps are willing to make markets in options on basis relationships, or the difference in price between different geographic areas. In addition to the exchange-traded American price options, which can be exercised at any time, European options, which can only be exercised at the time of expiration, are actively traded. Asian options, or average price options, are options whose strike prices are set at the expiration date to be the average rate of the underlying instrument compared with its final value at expiration are actively traded. They are calculated on predetermined fixing of an agreed reference rate. These can be exercised for physical delivery, and because volatility of average options is lower, they are often lower than American-style options or European-style options.

Like the bundled use of futures, OTC basis swaps, and EFPs, many of the risk management products incorporate several forms of swaps, options, and physical transactions to mitigate risk. Swing swaps are an example. *Swing swaps* are contractual agreements which ensure that the buyer will be able to take delivery of a certain amount of natural gas, the nominated amount, at fixed prices to be delivered over a certain period of time. In the swap are embedded call options that allow the holder of the contract the option to take delivery of additional amounts of gas up to a certain number of additional swings. Gas purchases, once contracted for monthly packages at "bid week," or the last 3 days of the last week of the month, can now be augmented by additional purchases at the buyer's option, should the buyer need additional supplies or wish to take the gas into storage if conditions are favorable.

RECENT DEVELOPMENTS

Swing swaps have been combined with some unique arrangements to take advantage of relationships between natural gas and electricity prices. As the electric power market peels away layers of regulation, the marketplace for electricity is evolving from a cost-plus pricing model to a market-driven one. As a result, natural gas, a key feedstock for electric power generation, and electricity pricing have shown greater convergence. Astute traders are watching the price relationships between natural gas and power closely for arbitrage opportunities. The relationship between the price of natural gas and electric power is referred to as the "spark spread," and it is actively monitored by gas marketers and power marketers for trading opportunities. Toll processing is an good example of this increased power/fuel arbitrage. In a declining market, a gas broker may elect to take delivery of more swing gas and then contract with a utility to generate electricity if market rates for electricity are high. In a declining natural gas market, utilities will sometimes hesitate to burn natural gas inventories bought at higher rates. If electricity rates are high and natural gas prices are declining, the gas marketer might elect to buy additional swing gas and contract with the utility to utilize the idle capacity to generate power. The gas marketer will then market the promised power at a profit. However, under certain market conditions, the utility might want the option to purchase this electricity for its own needs. The marketer might sell embedded call options to the utility, which would give the utility the right to purchase the electricity under certain market conditions. The marketer would receive a premium for granting this right to the utility, thereby earning additional revenue.

If market conditions for natural gas are very strong, utilities might go to the marketplace to sell their gas inventories at a profit and purchase power generated by a cheap-er fuel source such as hydropower or coal-fired generation. Using market instruments can give utilities freedom in choosing the source of their generation and in managing their fuel inventories for greatest efficiency.

Certain industrial processes will allow for inter-changeability in sources of energy, and trading based on Btu content is one way that marketers can guarantee the most inexpensive energy packages to clients. Yet with the use of creative pricing deals, this switching can be done in the financial markets by dealers who agree to price energy at the cost of the lowest Btu price. An industrial customer, for instance, might be able to use heating oil or natural gas for its operations and contracts with a gas marketer to pur-chase natural gas at the price per Btu of the cheaper fuel. The marketer will then lock in the differential or Btu rela-tionship between heating oil and natural gas, hedging the possibility that natural gas prices will rise in relationship to heating oil. The use of the futures markets allows maxi-mum flexibility to both the marketer and the end user.

CONCLUSION

The evolution of the physical natural gas market from a highly regulated environment to a fully competitive one was matched by a gradual development of derivative finan-cial markets which promoted market efficiency in the pro-duction, marketing, and consumption of natural gas. Physical market development from a simple spot market to a forward market provided the foundation for the develop-ment of financial markets of depth and liquidity. The estab-lishment of a broad, liquid futures market for natural gas was a key element for the efficient transfer of price risk, and it enabled the creation of other sophisticated OTC financial markets to address a number of marketing and risk man-agement needs.

Price transparency brought about by these financial markets for natural gas has also resulted in the creation of a more efficient infrastructure, including exploration and production for natural gas and the building of pipeline and storage assets. The freely competitive markets have also allowed for use of financial instruments to provide flexible marketing arrangements and to hedge risk exposure caused by price volatility. The instruments promote the economically efficient use of fuel inventories, allowing owners to monetize these assets.

The deregulation of the natural gas markets and subsequent market development form part of a larger process of energy deregulation in the United States. As the electricity markets continue with their evolution from a monopolistic environment to a freely competitive one, the markets will continue to develop and integrate into a larger Btu marketplace. As the market continues to mature and integrate with the electricity markets, the forms will change and offer new opportunities to those who use them.

CHAPTER 6

The Evolution of US Electricity Markets

By Dr. Antoine Eustache

INTRODUCTION

The deregulation of the electricity industry is giving way to a global trend toward the commoditization of electric energy. This trend has recently intensified in North America, where market forces have forced legislators to begin to remove artificial entry barriers that once shielded electric utilities from competition. The end result has been a major explosion in the number of nontraditional power suppliers and financial engineers marketing electricity and financial products in the wholesale power markets. With this explosion emerged a pressing demand for price transparency across the nation. It first began on the West Coast, where the Western Systems Power Pool (WSPP) had already taken the lead in setting the mechanism for a competitive wholesale power market. It then gradually spread across the continental United States to the point where, 5 years following the enactment of the US Energy Policy Act (EPACT) in 1992, electric utilities have begun to price electricity sold to wholesale and large industrial customers based on market indexes currently published in major newspapers and trade publications. This chapter looks at the structural changes that sparked the growth of the power market in the continental United States and explores some of their early ramifications.

CHANGING REGULATORY STRUCTURE

Until recently, businesses involved in the production of electric energy were believed to be natural monopolies whose operation would result in severe productive ineffi-ciencies if left to the vagaries of the marketplace. This belief was and still is rooted in a number of factors. First, it was widely understood that the electricity supply process is governed by certain characteristics that set it apart from most commodities. Economies of scale in supply and demand meant that larger generating units serving very large markets would result in lower production costs. Utilities have been seen as playing a special role in society in the sense that the type of service they provide is a neces-sity. For the most part, these services are essential in the day-to-day living of the individual to the point that even a temporary disruption can result in highly damaging conse-quences to society.[1] In general, these conditions meant that not only the single firm serving an entire market was preferable over a large number of small utilities, but also that the vertically integrated firm providing a unified set of generation, transmission, and distribution services was desirable over any other means of production.

The enormous production economies that resulted from the consolidation of the small isolated systems typical of the early 1900s reinforced these beliefs and further con-vinced regulators that competition could only increase costs and, therefore, was socially undesirable. However, in the absence of the corrective forces of the markets, utilities' enormous monopoly power could, if left unchecked, lead

---

1 See Bonbright et al., *Principles of Public Utility Rates*. Arlington, VA: Public Utilities Report Inc., 1992.

to price discrimination and other coercive practices detrimental to consumers. To limit that power, federal and state governments demanded that utilities provided just and reasonable services to the public at prescribed and regulated prices.

Over the years, however, efficiency improvements in productive technology led to a worldwide acknowledgment that electricity generation was no longer a natural monopoly. Improved gas turbine technology gave birth to a new breed of small electricity producers, while advances in information technology made it even easier to interconnect with these producers without any loss in system reliability. Coupled with mounting economic and political pressure, these developments forced the US Congress to first allow limited (though imperfect) competition in the US power industry in 1978. The successes of this experiment and those of several European countries further convinced the US government of the feasibility of outright competition in the continental United States. In 1992, Congress enacted legislation that removed the remaining barriers to wholesale competition. Since then, the industry has seen a major escalation in market activities that has astounded even the most ardent proponents of deregulation.

PURPA AND THE RISE OF INDEPENDENT POWER PRODUCERS

The US Public Utility Regulatory Act (PURA) of 1978 was one of the most sweeping pieces of legislation that marked the transition to a wholesale competitive power market in the United States. Designed as a set of incentives for improving fuel use efficiency through cogeneration and the use of renewable resources, it required electric utilities to interconnect with and purchase power from certain small producers known as qualifying facilities (QFs). To qualify as a QF, less than 50 percent of a small producer's equity could be owned by an electric utility. It could not exceed 80 MW in size. At least 75 percent of the feedstock used in power generation must come from renewable resources.

Cogenerators—that is, producers who jointly produce electricity and another form of thermal energy from a single energy source—had no size limitation provided they met minimum efficiency criteria. Because of a provision that allowed these small producers to sell power to electric utilities at a set price known as "avoided cost" and because of exemptions from rate and accounting regulation by the US Federal Energy Regulatory Commission (FERC), there emerged, de facto, a guaranteed market for any nonutilities wishing to abide by FERC's criteria. In the years immediately following PURA, the growth of nonutility generation was slow due to economic uncertainty and legal challenges. However, through the 1980s, nonutility generation became one of the fastest-growing segments of the industry, and by 1992, their combined sale was reported at over 166 billion kW,[2] a number that far exceeded wholesale purchases by investor-owned utilities in the entire Western System Coordinating Council (WSCC).

FROM AVOIDED COST TO COMPETITIVE BIDDING

PURPA's phenomenal attempt to open the wholesale power market to nonutilities was not without its limitations. First, it was seen as a limited step toward meeting the greater social demand for more competition. More important, in requiring utilities to buy electricity from the independent producers at their own *incremental cost*—that is, the cost avoided in making these transactions as opposed to generating additional electricity, it forced some to buy capacity they did not need. Furthermore, while the avoided-cost formula guaranteed the qualifying facilities unlimited profits in the short term, it did not address the long-term uncertainties resulting from tariff revisions. Although some states accounted for long-term capacity planning, in many cases these uncertainties created negative consequences for

---

2 DOE/EIA, *Electric Trade in the United States 1992*. Washington, DC: Energy Information Administration, 1994.

the QFs that needed some form of assurance about prices in order to secure long-term financing.[3] Finally, avoided-cost pricing was seen as being grossly inefficient in the sense that the savings that may have resulted from the experiment were absorbed by the QFs.[4] A more efficient pricing mechanism was needed.

By the early 1980s, many states had begun to revise the avoided-cost formula and concluded that competitive bidding could achieve PURA's objectives with a greater level of efficiency.[5] It did not take long before this idea caught on across the continental United States. By the late 1980s, many states had in place a competitive bidding program allowing QFs and other independent power producers to enter into long-term supply relationships with purchasing utilities. Today, competitive bidding remains a major component in the long-term planning of bulk power supply. However, like the avoided-cost experiment, it also faced a few challenges including a lack of price transparency, and a difficulty in resolving potential conflict of interest stemming from utilities' reluctance to relinquish their traditional roles as electricity suppliers.[6] Finally, it could not address one of the central issues dominating the debate: transmission access. For the proponents of competition, no pricing formula could ever substitute for the unrestricted flow of energy across utilities' transmission lines. Over time, the pressure for wheeling energy from one transmission system to another became a major priority among small producers and those who truly believed in the greater efficiency gains that would result from a fully competitive marketplace.

---

3 Edward Khan, *Electric Utility Planning & Regulation*. Washington, DC: American Council for an Energy Efficient Economy, 1988.
4 Chi-Keung Woo, "Inefficiency of Avoided Cost Pricing of Cogenerated Power." *The Energy Journal*, Vol. 9, No. 1, 1988.
5 In New England, where the QFs had made their earliest penetration, the Maine Public Service Commission and Central Maine Power proceeded with the implementation of the first competitive bidding program in 1984.
6 Charles A. Goldman, John F. Bush, and Edward P. Kahn, "At the Electricity Resource Bazaar: Lessons from Case Studies of Integrated Bidding in New York." *Energy Studies Review*, Vol. 6, No. 2, 1994.

This pressure culminated in the enactment of the US Energy Policy Act of 1992.

EPACT AND THE SHIFT TO A MORE COMPETITIVE MARKET

Widely recognized as the most sweeping reform in the power industry since the enactment of PURA, the Energy Policy Act (EPACT) practically set the tone for removing the remaining barriers to the emergence of an efficient marketplace. First, it removed one of the most restrictive barriers set by the US Public Utility Holding Act (PUHCA) of 1935, which kept holding companies from engaging in businesses that were nonessential to the operation of a single integrated system, and made it extremely difficult for nonutility generators to enter the wholesale power market.[7] In so doing, it created a new category of power producers called "exempt wholesale generators" (EWGs). These new generators were no longer limited in size or in the type of fuel they could use for power generation. On the other hand, they were not guaranteed a market or a set price as had been the case for the QFs. Instead, EPACT gave FERC the authority to ensure that these EWGs had access to the transmission grid as long as their activity was confined to bulk power marketing. EPACT also freed utilities with limited transmission facilities to buy power from sources other than their neighboring suppliers.

Armed with this broad authority, the Federal Energy Regulatory Commission issued a major program for restructuring the wholesale power market in early 1995. In its Notice of Proposed Rulemaking (Mega NOPR) issued on March 29, 1995, FERC recognized that discriminatory access to transmission services could create major impediments to a fully competitive bulk power market.[8] To resolve

---

7 Energy Information Administration, The Changing Structure of the Electric Power Industry 1970–1991. Washington, DC: DOE/EIA,1993.

8 See *Promoting Wholesale Competition Through Open Access, Non-Discriminatory Transmission Services by Public Utilities,* in Notice of Proposed Rulemaking and Supplemental Notice of Proposed Rulemaking, Docket No. RM95-8-000, March 29, 1995.

this problem, FERC made clear its intention to require public utilities that own or control transmission facilities used in the transport of wholesale power across states to file open access transmission tariffs. While stopping short of mandating the vertical deintegration of generation, transmission, and distribution, FERC required public utilities to price separately all wholesale generation and transmission services. To further limit the potential for discriminatory practices, FERC required public utilities to give all transmission users the same access to transmission information as they would give to themselves or their power marketing subsidiaries. This information is posted on a real time information network nationwide called Open Access Same Time Information System (OASIS), which began to operate on January 1, 1997. Judging by the recent explosion in the number of power marketers, the exponential growth in wholesale transactions so far completed by nonutility suppliers, and the ever-increasing number of financial engineers servicing the market for electricity derivatives, it is fair to say that these measures may have already had a profound impact on the way electricity is bought and sold in the United States.

INITIAL RESULTS OF DEREGULATION

It may be too early to produce a yardstick for measuring the full impact of the deregulation. However, there are indications that market forces have not waited for full compliance with FERC's Mega NOPR to change the landscape. Already, the number of power marketers buying and selling energy at market prices has soared from fewer than 5 prior to 1992 to over 350 by the end of 1997. Together, these power marketers have sold over 100 million MWh from 1993 through 1996. This number is growing rapidly at an average rate of nearly 700 percent a year.[9] Electricity exchanges are sprouting throughout the continental United States. Though struggling to win traders' confidence, electronic trading is

---

9 Federal Energy Regulatory Commission.

becoming more and more common. Electricity derivatives, which were almost unheard of in 1993, are setting the standard for financial risk management. This section examines these developments and their benefits.

POWER MARKETERS

A direct consequence of the Energy Policy Act in 1992 was the advent of a whole new generation of businesses created for the purpose of marketing electric power. Commonly known as "power marketers," these businesses have little or no assets tied to the generation and transmission of electric energy. Under the US Federal Powers Act, *a power marketer* is a public utility that is subject to FERC regulation. As a prerequisite for transacting in wholesale energy across state lines, a power marketer must file a market-based rate schedule with the FERC.

Except for a few power marketing companies created at the height of the debate,[10] the first generation of power marketers came, for the most part, from the Natural Gas Industry. With over a decade of experience marketing natural gas to electric utilities, these companies had both the infrastructure and the marketing expertise necessary to face the complexities of the burgeoning electricity markets. Nonetheless, their quest for gaining acceptance among power dispatchers and utility managers proved an almost insurmountable challenge initially. In the view of many power engineers, the complete electrical network could collapse if opened to nontraditional suppliers with limited knowledge of the electricity business. In some quarters, many power marketers were ridiculed for not knowing the basic terminology familiar to power schedulers. For quite a while, these attitudes prevailed despite the many benefits the new marketers were expected to bring to the changing marketplace.

---

10 In August 1989, FERC granted a power marketing license to Citizen Power & Light Corporation, a Boston-based company, which later became Citizen Lehman Power DC Tie Inc. FERC also granted a license to Chicago Energy Exchange Inc. in April 1990.

However, attitudes began to change as the industry finally came to terms with the realities of the new competitive era. Over time, electric utilities came to regard the power marketer as a cornerstone in the new competitive environment. Not only did they begin to invest in the creation of their own marketing arms, they had to live with the realization that the power marketers brought in a level of sophistication that far surpassed anything they were accustomed to. Through their wide network of customers, power marketers offered utilities a convenient outlet for shifting business risks too broad to handle internally. In a relatively short time dealing in bulk power, the marketers developed an unrivaled ability to trade electricity as a commodity. Many utilities found they had to match the sophistication with which the larger marketers handled large electricity transactions. As a result, there emerged a growing trend among utilities to form strategic alliances with some of most success marketers such as ENRON Capital & Trade, Louisville Gas & Electric, and Natural Gas Clearinghouse. In forming these alliances, utilities hoped to better focus on managing the risks associated with electricity distribution, while leaving the supply risks to their more sophisticated allies.

PRICE INDEXES AND
ELECTRICITY DERIVATIVES

The phenomenal growth in power marketing created great demand for price transparency. As competitive pressure forced electric utilities to rethink their traditional approach to buying and selling electric energy, the need to preserve the good neighbor policy, which in some way consisted of buying energy from each other regardless of cost, was replaced by the greater need to maintain financial stability. In many cases, maintaining financial stability meant playing a proactive role in the fledgling power marketing business. This in turn led to the greater need for price discovery and other reliable tools for managing the financial risk that

resulted from these marketing activities. Initially, this need
was particularly strong in the western United States where
the Western Systems Power Pool had laid the foundations
for a competitive marketplace. There, the need for compa-
rability took on a great sense of urgency. Terms such as
"firm" and "nonfirm energy"and "standardized products,"
became entrenched in the basic vocabulary of the typical
dispatcher. The major challenge became one of pricing
these products. Two major developments offered a set of
solutions to these problems. The first was the development
by the New York Mercantile Exchange of two electricity
futures contracts. Launched in the spring of 1996, these contracts now serve as major benchmarks for pricing electricity products up to several months forward at two different
locations on the West Coast. The second was an industry
initiative to develop a market-based electricity price index
at the California and Oregon border (COB), which was
launched in June 1995.

The search for a comprehensive methodology for
designing this index drew attention from a wide spectrum
of financial institutions, trade associations, and power
marketers nationwide. It also brought together investor-
owned electric utilities, municipal utilities, and federal
power agencies from across the WSCC (Western Systems
Coordinating Council). For the utilities involved, the
major obstacle was to define an index that would enhance
the competitiveness and the efficiency of the wholesale
power market in the west. Such an index had to be robust
enough not only to ease the pricing issues in the cash market, but also to facilitate the shifting of risk from buyers
and sellers of electric energy to the financial institutions
willing to assume the risk associated with the volatile
prices in the region.

The thriving market hub at the border between
California and Oregon offered a convenient solution. First,
COB had all the characteristics of a major market hub in the
region. From a physical standpoint, it allowed for easy
transfer of ownership from one control area to another. The
bulk of the transactions is concentrated around three major

transmission lines with a capacity of 500 kV each. COB has a large number of buyers and sellers, with over 40 regular suppliers delivering an average of 17 million MWh a year. This is roughly 13 percent of the wholesale transactions in the WSCC. Competing demand from both the Pacific northwest and the Pacific southwest and the seasonal pattern in production guarantee a continual flow of energy at COB all year round. In the end, this abundant flow of market data provided sufficient resources for the calculation of a series of volume-weighted averages computed for actual transactions occurring at the California-Oregon border. These averages are currently known as the DJ-COB (Dow Jones) Index.

It did not take long before these averages became the benchmark for pricing financial instruments in the over-the-counter markets. Financial instruments such as swaps[11] and options[12] are not new to the electricity industry. Their growth has been stifled by the lack of transparent and reliable prices. The DJ-COB Index removed that impediment by providing electricity traders with a barometer that enabled them to gauge the dynamism of the cash market on the West Coast.

Designed to help simplify risk management practices in the power market, electricity price indexes have been at the core of a recent explosion in the growth of electricity derivatives nationwide. For instance, less than 3 months after Dow Jones began publishing the DJ-COB Index, Prebon Financial Products, a New Jersey–based subsidiary of Prebon Yamane, brokered the first index-based derivative in the market. Since then, the number of swaps and options

---

11 Swaps are private agreements between two parties to exchange cash flows in the future based on a prearranged formula. (See John C. Hull. *Options, Futures, and Other Derivative Securities*, Prentice Hall, Upper Saddle River, N.J., 1993.)

12 An *option* is a financial instrument that gives the buyer the right to purchase or sell a security at a predetermined price. In some ways, it works like an insurance policy. The buyers pay a premium to minimize the risk of paying a larger sum of money in the future should they be affected by some adverse conditions. Like buyers of insurance, electricity buyers who fear the impact of a major price hike may contract to buy power at a price negotiated well ahead of the time they actually need it. In financial terms, the price negotiated by the parties involved is called the "strike price."

tied to these indexes has grown at an average rate of over 200 a month. For the most part, these transactions are short-term swaps ranging from 25 to 50 MW in size. Because these deals are tied to the nonfirm on-peak index, the terms of the contracts usually include a delivery period of 16 hours a day Monday through Saturday. In the case of COB, the size of the derivatives market could be estimated at 2 million to 4 million MWh a month less than 6 months following the publication of the first price index. Compared to the monthly peak delivery of less than 2 million MWh at COB, these numbers suggest that some parts of the derivatives market have already surpassed the physical market in size.[13]

To appreciate the significance of price transparency on the growth of the power market, it suffices to look at the way utilities managed risk prior to the publication of these indexes. Traditionally, electric utilities bought options through the issuance of requests for proposals (RFPs) inviting companies with opposing needs to bid for the right (or the obligation) to buy or sell power at a predetermined price and at a predetermined time in the future. For example, a company seeking the right, but not the obligation, to buy energy under certain predefined conditions could issue an RFP for a call option. Most likely, the company with the most favorable response would assume the responsibility to supply that energy.

Not only lengthy and complicated, the process involved in completing these transactions was further limited by the lack of a benchmark for pricing these options. Most of the time, the premium paid on the options was based on sketchy information and was not governed by market forces. As a result, the number of transactions completed through this mechanism was very small and rarely exceeded two in any given year.

The success of the electricity price indexes in solving the price transparency problem in the WSCC generated an

---

13 Antoine Eustache, "DJ-COB Electricity Price Index Explodes onto
   Commodities Markets with a Bang," *Energy Marketing: A Supplement* of
   PennWell Publishing Co., June 1996.

unprecedented demand for more price indexes elsewhere in the country. Today, these indexes have become an essential tool used by utilities and power marketers seeking a benchmark for pricing electric energy in the bulk markets, and many more have been developed by both electronic and print journalists. They are also used by government agencies and industry analysts seeking a better understanding of the impact of price deregulation on the power market. In addition, they are adding depth and liquidity to the OTC markets for electricity.

Computerized Trading

The revolution in computer technology has brought tremendous progress in trading practices. The concept of the traditional market revolving around a physical setting has been expanded into virtual markets allowing buyers and sellers to conduct transactions without leaving the office. Energy traders have been quick to profit from this leap in technology. One striking example is the proliferation of the number of operators buying and selling natural gas by means of computerized trading systems. For instance, during the 1990s, electronic trading has given natural gas traders the ability to instantly measure the level of supply and demand, determine the spot market price, and execute point-to-point transactions with complete anonymity in a fraction of the time it would take to complete the same transaction in the traditional marketplace.

In the view of a growing number of electricity traders, this revolution will play a major role in the development of an efficient power market. In fact, several experiments are currently under way in the United States to integrate the computer in the day-to-day activities of the cash and futures trader. So far, close to a dozen attempts, with varying degree of success, have been made in that direction. For the most part, these experiments can be classified under three broad applications: electronic bulletin boards, fully automated computer trading systems, and computer matching systems.

Electronic Bulletin Boards

Since the enactment of EPACT, electronic bulletin boards have played an increasing role in bulk power marketing. Three of the best-known pioneering experiments are the Western Systems Power Pool (WSPP) in the western United States, The International Power Exchange (IPEX) in the Eastern Interconnection, and The Power EX Corporation in British Columbia. The WSPP experiment was an attempt to provide a medium where member utilities could market excess electricity. This includes transmission capacity, unit commitment, and wholesale energy contracts ranging from 1 day forward to several years into the future. The bulletin board was operated by Arizona Public Service and was updated twice a day. IPEX had a similar objective, but unlike the WSPP, it was open to all buyers and sellers of electric power. Subscribers could access IPEX through dial-up technology via the Internet. Power EX, on the other hand, was the result of a growing need for price transparency expressed by the initiatives of legislators in British Columbia and The Power EX Corporation. This resulted in the daily posting of bids and offers ranging from 1 day to 1 month forward on the Dow Jones Telerate information system in 1992.

Like most of the bulletin boards that followed, these experiments faced major resistance from dispatchers and systems operators. First, they were considered too static to meet the needs of an industry that placed a greater premium on real-time information. Second, the utility industry felt a certain malaise in quickly embracing a technology that was too indicative of a new competitive era it was not quite ready for. To address the first problem, those that anticipated the inevitability of change began shifting from the static environment of the bulletin board to the more dynamic interface of the fully automated computer trading systems. The WSPP set in motion the steps for the development of a dynamic electricity trading system; IPEX saw a gradual decline in its clientele; while Power EX, under contractual agreement with Dow Jones Telerate, continued to update its bulletin board on a regular basis.

Fully Automated Computer Trading Systems

Since 1992, the demand for a more dynamic trading environment brought a plethora of computer software and computer trading system providers into the electricity trading arena. Following the WSPP initiative to move to a full-blown electricity trading system in 1993, industry analysts saw a natural fit for the trading system operators who then had a successful track record in helping modernize the natural gas market. Like electricity, natural gas was a regulated industry until 1978. Both shared many of the same legal and business characteristics in production, transportation, and distribution. Both were vertically integrated entities with natural monopoly characteristics in transmission and distribution. But what many failed to understand was that electric utility operators regarded their business as a much more complex operation. As a result, the assumption that the specifications developed for natural gas trading software could easily be expanded to meet the needs of the electricity dispatcher proved quite erroneous.

At the onset, though, electricity traders felt that the computer solution had to come from providers who showed a keen sense of the intricacies inherent to power technology coupled with an even deeper understanding of the markets. This proved to be a tall order to fill, since software providers at the time that truly understood the power industry were perceived to have limited knowledge of the markets. The converse was believed to be true for software providers with a proven record in the financial markets. Whether these arguments were backed by the evidence or engendered by a reluctance to face the inevitable realities of the new competitive era is debatable. Nonetheless, they posed an almost insurmountable obstacle to the early providers of software and trading technology. On one side of the fence were the visionaries who continued to promote the computer solution from the executive desk; on the other side were the operators who proved reluctant to adopt the new technology. In the end, software providers had to face the challenge of building more efficient systems that needed to account for the human element so strongly demanded by traders. Those that could not adapt to these realities quickly went out of business. However, many of those with vast financial resources who were willing to make the leap proved that, with time, electronic trading would become an integral part of the solution.

Despite the early success of some of the leading providers of trading technology at entering the power market, the race for a standard solution is still on. Recent attempts by electric utilities to use the Internet as a vehicle for meeting FERC's requirements of the federally mandated OASIS and the proliferation of new and smarter computer technology suggest that much of the debate will focus on the Internet over the next few years.

COMPUTER MATCHING SYSTEMS

Computer matching technology has had a long and proven track record in the power industry. Unlike the fully computerized trading system, computer matching systems allow very little room for negotiation among traders. They are typically used for economy interchange among utilities and use a set of algorithms for matching the best bids and offers. The most successful is the Energy Broker operated by the Florida Electric Power Coordinating Group. Since its launch in 1978, the system has saved its members nearly $1 billion. Since 1992, several attempts have been made to replicate this experiment across the country. So far, the results have been mixed. However, judging by their popularity among power dispatchers and utility executives, matching services are likely to evolve side by side with the more open computer trading systems currently in the market.

CONCLUSION

Over the past few years, policymakers have grown comfortable with the thought that price regulation is no longer the best way of ensuring efficient utilization of productive resources in power generation. As a result, many have shown great willingness to introduce legislation aimed at promoting full competition in the power market. So far, the experiments resulting from this legislation have been quite successful, proving that far from destroying the electrical system, as many once predicted, competition is likely to infuse new productive energy into an otherwise aging industry.

CHAPTER 7

European Electricity Trading Markets

By Jeremy Wilcox

Unlike the US market, the European electricity market is still in the early stages of growth in terms of market competition and trading. Although the European market in the West is interconnected, with Scandinavian countries being members of Nordel and most of the other grids (with the exception of Great Britain and Ireland) being members of the Union for the Coordination of Production and Transmission of Electricity (UCPTE), less than 10 percent of European consumption is traded between member European countries. And in terms of domestic market trading, there are only three markets, the United Kingdom, Sweden-Norway, and Finland. But a clear route to European competition has been established with agreement on a European Union (EU) directive for electricity competition in 1996.

Under the EU electricity directive, competition will be phased in over three stages, with a third of Europe's total electricity consumption to be opened to competition by the end of the final stage. The first stage will enable competition for customers with an annual consumption in excess of

40 GWh, equivalent to 22 percent of total European consumption. The second stage, to be effective 3 years from the commencement of the first phase, will open up competition to all customers with annual consumption in excess of 20 GWh. The final phase, commencing 3 years after the commencement of phase two, will reduce the threshold for competition to annual consumption in excess of 9 GWh.

Within the EU directive, competition will be implemented either through a negotiated access system or through a single-buyer system. The single-buyer system will allow competition between producers but only one customer, the buyer. In contrast, negotiated access opens competition to more than one customer as well as producers. Clearly, in terms of implementing a fully competitive market, the negotiated access system would be preferable.

But even if member states choose the route of single buyer, it is a step in the right direction. And once the first step toward market liberalization has been introduced, individual market forces should come into play. Those countries that achieve a more competitive market structure will likely force other countries that have a less competitive structure to follow suit. In other words, the market could experience a domino effect with the momentum for change coming from within the individual markets, primarily the large industrial customers and generators, rather than from the individual governments.

Competition will also be influenced by the generation fuel mix of individual countries, particularly those that have a large gas-fired generation percentage, since the European natural gas market is opening up to competition in tandem with the electricity market. It will also be influenced by market structure, since those countries which have a large proportion of consumption dictated by large industrial customers will face external competition from nondomestic generators under the EU directive.

Currently, active trading is limited to the emerging markets of the United Kingdom and Scandinavia. The remainder of this chapter analyzes the current trading framework within these markets and the scope and implementation of risk management practices.

UK POWER MARKET

In 1988, the UK Electricity Act signaled the formal process of electricity market deregulation and with it provided the regulatory framework within which the electricity supply industry now operates. Since 1990, there has been a program of progressive deregulation that is due to be completed by October 1998 (phased in from April 1998) with the provision of full competition in the UK market.

Prior to 1990, most UK generation was provided by the Central Electricity Generating Board, which was also responsible for the national grid transmission system. Ahead of privatization, the electricity pool was created on March 31, 1990, as the wholesale market mechanism for the trading of electricity between generators and suppliers. The pool enables competitive bidding between generators in setting the electricity price for each half-hour period for the following day. It also provides the financial settlement processes required to calculate and ensure payment of bills.

Privatization of the distribution, supply, and generation companies has radically changed the structure of the "old" electricity market. Fossil fuel generation was privatized as National Power and PowerGen, and nuclear power plants were restructured into two companies, British Energy and Magnox. Additional generation is now provided by the vertically integrated Eastern Group and a growing number of independent generators. Interconnectors with the Scottish power companies and Électricité de France also facilitate imports of electricity into England and Wales. Installed UK generating capacity in March 1996 totaled 70,213 MW (of which 65,900 MW is provided by the major generators) and provides for a sufficient margin of surplus capacity.

Electricity distribution via low-voltage power lines is provided by the 12 regional electricity companies (recs) and the two vertically integrated Scottish power companies. The National Grid Company is responsible for high-voltage distribution. As a consequence of deregulation, distribution via the low-voltage transmission line is no longer the captive market of the recs. Any supplier (subject to meeting industry requirements) can contract for the purchase of physical electricity from the wholesale market and then resupply to its customer base.

With the exception of on-site generation and exports of less than 50 MW, all electricity generated in England and Wales must be supplied into the national grid and traded on the electricity pool. In addition, all electricity has to be purchased through the pool. Pool prices are set via a competitive bidding process, with all generators submitting bids for each half-hour period for the following day as well as additional information such as operating constraints. The grid then produces a forecast of demand for each half-hour period and schedules the generators' bids to meet this demand. Finally, via a complicated computer system, the lowest-cost generation schedule is produced for the following day.

A merit order is established which ranks each genset by its price of electricity. The most expensive genset is referred to as the "system marginal price (SMP)." To this is added a capacity payment, which is an incentive payment to ensure that generators meet the declared electricity demand for each half-hour period. Capacity payments can be volatile and are influenced by the margin of declared availability versus forecast demand. When combined, these two components produce the pool purchase price (PPP), which is the price paid to generators. The price paid by suppliers is the pool selling price (PSP), which equates to PPP plus an uplift component, to cover various system costs. Due to the uncertain nature of system costs and supply-demand variances, all day-ahead prices are set on a provisional basis and are fixed approximately 28 days in arrears.

Pool prices are extremely volatile and are influenced by seasonal, economic, weather, capacity, and storage factors. Historically, pool prices have ranged from near zero to in excess of £1000. The volatility associated with pool prices encourages hedging policies as part of a prudent business plan. As with other commoditized markets, there are a number of instruments that can be applied to manage price exposure, although in the nascent UK market there are essentially two instruments used: contracts for difference, cfd's (either one-way or two-way), and electricity forward agreements, efa's (short-term cash-settled swaps).

Traditionally, generators and recs have entered into long-term bilateral cfd's with cover ranging from 1 to 3 years. At the onset of competition, growing concern over the relative inflexibility of cfd's led to the development of the electricity forward agreement, essentially a short-term cfd, in 1991. Similar in structure to forward rate agreements, efa's are settled against the average pool price. Efa's are quoted as four-hourly blocks for both weekdays and weekends, and they act as building blocks that can be traded either individually or as strips.

As market disenfranchisement has progressed, and the need for closer management of contract cover has gathered pace, efa terms have been increasingly incorporated into cfd structures. Contracting rounds have become more competitive as full competition approaches. Most contracts to supply large industrial customers commence in April, July, or October, with the price being fixed against projected customer demand profiles. In this scenario, the risk lies with the supplier. Where customers elect to remain exposed to the pool price, the onus on hedging is with the customer.

Increasingly, additional contract cover periods are being hedged, with summer and winter season contracts gaining in popularity. Rebalancing of cover, involving individual months, either baseload or peaks, is also popular. By employing a combination of cfd's and efa's, players can construct hedges that closely match their projected demand portfolios. While there is some standardization of maturities and shapes, the flexibility afforded by efa's has led to more player-specific hedge portfolios being traded. Currently, most derivative transactions are of the plain vanilla type, with typical profile covers being either base-load or load shape 44 (which represents peak demand between 7 A.M. and 7 P.M.).

At present, hedging in the UK electricity market has been limited to core market participants numbering around 25, consisting primarily of the generators and recs. And with limited involvement from outside interested parties, the market is fairly opaque. However, the opening up of full competition starting in April 1998 will likely act as a cata-lyst to greater participation in hedging. This will be further aided by the end of the coal-backed contracts in March 1998, which will free up additional volume of pool expo-sure that will consequently need to be hedged. It is difficult to quantify the extent of participation, but estimates sug-gest that around 10 percent of pool exposure is currently hedged on the cfd/efa market. These volumes are forecast to grow at 5 percent annually starting in April 1998.

As the market grows, major new entrants into the elec-tricity sector will include banks and other financial institu-tions seeking to capitalize on their recent success in other commodity markets. Natural gas suppliers are also likely to take a more proactive interest as they seek competitive advantages through indexing their gas supplies to electric-ity prices.

In respect of natural gas suppliers, gas tolling agree-ments, already popular in the United States, are now start-ing to find favor in the UK market. In 1997, Eastern Power and Energy Trading, an operating subsidiary of the Eastern Group, entered into a 15-year gas tolling agreement with Rolls Royce Power Ventures for a new open-cycle mode 98-MW plant in the Midlands. Under the agreement, Eastern will provide all the gas and, in return, receive all the pool receipts.

Such agreements represent attractive financing oppor-tunities for new generation plants, with all the fuel risk that is the spread between the gas and electricity price being borne by the fuel supplier. It also necessitates a proactive approach to price risk management in order to manage the fuel risk. The implementation of spark spread trading, however, has yet to materialize within the UK market. Although there is a transparent forward curve for natural gas, assisted by the International Petroleum Exchange's (IPE) natural gas futures contract launched in January 1997, the same degree of transparency is not yet evident in electricity. One factor that could assist this would be the launch of an electricity futures contract.

Both IPE and OMLX, whose parent group OM in Sweden is behind both the Nord Pool and El-Ex electricity exchanges, have signaled their interest in a futures contract. But it is unlikely that a futures contract from either exchange will be launched before the UK market embraces full competition in April 1998. Without a liquid and transparent underlying cash market, it is difficult to envision a futures contract being successful. Another area that needs to be addressed before a contract could be launched with any degree of success is that of pool reform.

Under the current structure of the pool, the marginal cost of generation is largely dictated by the two prominent power generators, National Power and PowerGen. For the market to be more reflective of market forces, additional generation bids are required, including those from IPP's, as well as the introduction of demand side bidding. If such reforms were to be introduced, the electricity price would reflect to a more market-based mechanism. However, even with more competitive and diverse marginal costs of generation being incorporated into the pricing mechanism, the current structure still falls short of reflecting a truly competitive commodity market. To complete the reform would require an amendment to the current process of setting prices 24 hours in advance. Ideally, there should be instant price discovery. With the market now fast approaching its true test of competition, it is hoped that transparency will start to filter through. This should then force regulators to address the aforementioned issues.

NORDIC MARKET

In Scandinavia, there are two traded markets: one for Norway-Sweden and the other for Finland. Each has a regulated exchange as well as an active over-the-counter (OTC) market.

Launched in July 1993, Nord Pool was the first futures contract in electricity. In November 1996, the exchange moved to the Powerclick electronic trading model, and there are now more than 25 members connected to the system.

The futures contracts can be traded against two different load factors: base load, which represents 1 MW of electricity for every hour of the day from Monday to Sunday, giving 168 MW of electricity for the full week; and day load which is for 1 MW of electricity between the hours of 7 A.M. and 9 P.M. Monday to Friday inclusive, giving 72 MW of electricity over the week.

Trading in futures contracts is broken down into three different maturity terms: week contracts, block contracts, and season contracts. Base load trades for all three contract maturities, whereas day load trades only for week and block contracts. The contracts have been designed in a cascading structure whereby each season contract breaks down into block contracts, with block contracts then breaking down into individual week contracts:

> **Season Contracts:** There are three seasons traded on Nord Pool, with the term of each season fixed. Season one runs from calendar week 1 to 16, season two from week 17 to 40, and season three from week 41 to 52. On any given date, there will be a minimum of four and a maximum of six season contracts available for trading. It is only possible to trade season contracts a year out. Therefore, in calendar week one, the season one contract for the following year is broken down into block contracts one to four.
>
> **Block Contracts:** There are 13 block contracts, each representing 4 weeks, with a minimum of 8 and a maximum of 11 block contracts available for trading

at any given time. When a block contract has only 4 weeks left to delivery, it is converted into four individual week contracts.

Week Contracts: These are the lowest-denominator contracts available for trading. This arrangement ensures that it will always be possible to trade a minimum of four and a maximum of seven week contracts on any particular day.

Futures trades are cleared and marked to market on a daily basis against the spot markets' system price, which is calculated for each corresponding hour in the daily market. The system price represents the spot price that would be payable for the Norwegian-Swedish region on the basis of no grid constraints. Margin requirements for futures positions are 10 percent for week contracts, 5 percent for block contracts, and 3 percent for season contracts.

The structure of the futures market ensures that liquidity is concentrated in the lowest-possible-denominator contract. Any maturity up to 2 years out can be traded by constructing strips of week, block, and season contracts. However, by encouraging short-term liquidity in the market, the long-term liquidity has suffered at the expense of the OTC market. Measures to improve long-term liquidity, and to grow volumes in general, have involved the implementation of a market maker scheme, which took effect in April 1997. Under this scheme, the market maker guarantees a spread of 12 kroner for all base load trades with a minimum volume of 10 MW for week contracts and 5 MW for block and season contracts.

On average, Nord Pool trades a daily volume of 400–500 contracts across all contracts. Typically, up to 70–75 percent of volume is seen in the week contracts, 20–25 percent in the block contracts, and about 5 percent in the season contracts. Whereas the futures market is the domain for short-term trades, the OTC market accounts for the volume in the medium- to long-term market where there is reasonable liquidity going out 2 to 3 years.

Due to the severity of weather in the Norwegian-Swedish region, in terms of both temperature and rainfall, and the heavy dependence on hydropower, market volatility can be severe. Since 1991, spot market prices have fluctuated between a low of 10 SEK/MWh and a high in excess of 350 SEK/MWh.

In terms of volume, most trading is predominantly bilateral, accounting for approximately 75 percent of all trade. Derivatives trading on Nord Pool is valued at around £1200mn annually, while the Nord Pool spot market trades about 15 percent of the overall Norwegian and Swedish spot market.

FINLAND

Launched on August 16, 1996, El-Ex is an integrated electronic spot and futures market with physical settlement. As with the Nordic region, trade is heavily skewed toward bilateral, contracts, with only 2–3 percent of total volume traded on the exchange.

The structure of the Finnish El-Ex exchange is similar to that of Nord Pool in that it utilizes a cascading structure. Two load factors are traded: day week (Monday through Friday), which provides for 75 hours of electricity, and night week (Monday through Sunday), which provides for 93 hours of electricity.

Unlike Nord Pool, there are four different maturities: season contracts for summer and winter, 4-week block contracts, base-week contracts, and hour products. Similar to Nord Pool, the cascading structure of the market ensures that there are always 168 hours (1 week) of available contracts. Liquidity is heavily orientated toward the hourly contracts, with most volume being traded in the day-ahead power hour market. Average volume on El-Ex is just under 3000 contracts, with record volume recorded in September 1996 at just under 18,000 contracts. Although Finland has a more diverse generation fuel mix than the Nordic region, its prices are just as volatile.

Given the interconnected nature of the Scandinavian grids via the Nordel model, the incorporation of Denmark into the trading forum is highly likely. This could then facilitate some form of merger of the Nord Pool and El-Ex markets, leading to an integrated Scandinavian market. And the building blocks are already being put into place. Investment by some Swedish power utilities into the Finnish market, mainly for distribution purposes, has been picking up pace, while similar investment by Scandinavian utilities into the German sector, and vice versa, has also taken place. The one factor to be considered in integrating the Nord Pool and El-Ex markets is the different market forces caused by the different generation fuel mixes.

The Scandinavian utility sector has been identified for massive consolidation of the region's distributors within the next 10 years. And combined with expected power shortfalls forecast by the end of the century, due to the commitment of the Swedish government to phase out its nuclear power stations, investment in new generating capacity should encourage a greater emphasis on price risk management.

With the rest of Europe in varying stages of market deregulation—Spain is planning to move to a competitive market structure in 1998, and the Netherlands is planning another tranche of deregulation in the same year—the respective merits of the UK pool structure and the bilateral markets of Scandinavia are being analyzed. The Nord Pool market, in particular, has generated its success based on its diversity of marginal generation and good price discovery. The European electricity market has a lot to learn from developments in the United States, as well as from experiences of current traded markets in the United Kingdom and Scandinavia. But the route to competition, and hence a stronger focus on trading and risk management, has already commenced.

CHAPTER 8

The Development of Coal Futures

By Jay L. Gottlieb

The New York Mercantile Exchange (NYMEX) is currently developing coal futures contracts to be launched in early 1998 because the US coal market is undergoing its most dramatic structural change since the end of World War II, especially due to the deregulation of electricity markets. Other developments, particularly in the area of coal transportation and environmental regulation of coal use, are rapidly moving what was once a highly regionalized and heterogeneous market into a national market with commodity pricing. These changes will expose coal producers and consumers to price risks that will necessitate the use of futures and options contracts to manage these risks. This chapter describes these changes in the coal markets and how NYMEX is working to develop suitable risk management products.

CHANGING US COAL MARKET

The predominant use of coal is in electricity generation, which accounts for 88 percent of all domestic coal consumption.[1] Therefore, electricity markets drive coal markets. Some basic statistics round out the overall picture of US coal production and use in 1995:[2]

- Total US production in 1995   1033 million short tons
- US electricity consumption   829 million short tons
- US industrial consumption   73 million short tons
- US residential consumption   6 million short tons
- US exports   89 million short tons

World coal production in 1995 is estimated to have been 4680 million metric tons.[3] Fuels used to generate US electricity are as follows:[4]

- Coal   55.2%
- Nuclear   22.5%
- Natural gas   10.3%
- Hydro   9.8%
- Petroleum   2.0%
- Other   0.2%

Coal consumption for electricity generation is concentrated in the Midwest and the Southeast. Statistical data on electricity production is organized according to North American Electricity Reliability Coordinator (NERC) regions. The Midwest, the East Central Area Reliability Coordinator (ECAR) region, the Southeast, for the South-eastern Reliability Coordinator (SERC) region account for 51 percent of total coal consumed for US electricity generation.[5] Coal fuels 85 percent of ECAR's gener-

---

1 *Coal Industry Annual 1995*. Washington, DC: Energy Information
    Administration, US Department of Energy, October 1996, p. xi.
2 Ibid.
3 *International Coal: 1996 Edition*. Washington, DC: National Mining Association,
    February 1997, p.i.
4 *Coal Industry Annual 1995*. Washington, DC: Energy Information
    Administration, US Department of Energy, October 1996, p. xi.
5 *Electricity Supply & Demand Database 1995*. Princeton, NJ: North American
    Electric Reliability Council, August 1996.

ation and 55 percent of SERC's. Coal does play a large, but not quite as prominent, role in electricity generation in other NERC regions.

The need for coal futures arises from the increasing exposure to price risk for all coal market participants that is a result of electricity market deregulation and changes in fuel purchasing practices by utilities. A national market for coal commodities has developed due to increasing transportation efficiencies and environmental regulations. How these developments are interacting to create the need for coal futures is described in the following sections.

ELECTRICITY MARKET DEREGULATION

From the end of World War II to the early 1990s, coal's market structure was marked by geographically segregated markets, product heterogeneity, and long-term contracts to highly regulated buyers. Electric utilities have been regulated monopolies that are able to pass on fuel price increases directly to their customers. Their coal purchases were dominated by long-term, fixed-price contracts negotiated directly with the mining company producers. Thus, there appeared to be minimal price risk for either buyers or sellers and no need for risk management tools such as a futures contract. Further, no single futures contract could have served a wide enough segment of the market because of its historical regional fragmentation. Any single standardized set of coal quality specifications and delivery locations would have served only a limited segment of coal buyers and sellers.

Furthermore, state and federal regulation sheltered the utilities from competition for customers and enabled them to pass on fuel price increases if they could be demonstrated to be the result of "prudent" decisions. This minimized incentives for utilities to manage their fuel costs. As a result of industry restructuring, utilities have become increasingly competitive and fuel price conscious. Coal mining companies and utilities are developing alternate ways of arranging and pricing coal sales. Long-term fixed-price contracts are giving way to increased reliance on spot purchases and contracts of much shorter duration and with much greater pricing flexibility. These changes are exposing coal market participants to unaccustomed price risks. Thus, coal futures will be important to manage this risk.

CHANGES IN FUEL PURCHASING PRACTICES BY UTILITIES

Changes in fuel purchasing practices by coal-buying utilities include shorter-term and more price flexible contracts, increasing reliance on spot market purchases, and dramatic reductions in inventory holding levels. Previously, US coal markets were dominated by long-term, fixed-priced contracts between coal producers and utility consumers developed shortly after World War II. By the end of the war, coal was no longer purchased directly to power locomotives or to heat buildings. Rapidly expanding electric utilities became the prime consumers of coal. Both the utility and the coal mining industries required massive financing to open the new mines and build the new power plants demanded by postwar growth. To help obtain this financing, both parties found it beneficial to have long-term coal contracts with fixed prices.

This environment also allowed both plant managers and coal salespeople to share the presumption that coals for creating steam were nonfungible, which thus encouraged the development of niche markets. In general, utility plant management could be simplified by burning the same coal day after day. One set of procedures can be developed for handling the coal from delivery, to the plant, and to burning in the generator's boiler. Neither the managers nor their staffs needed to learn how to adapt flexibly to other coals which can be burned in their plant's boilers. Therefore, utility fuel buyers had been told by the plant managers that only coal of particular types from specific origins would work in their plants. This enabled coal companies to increase their profits by selling a unique niche product rather than a fungible commodity. Coal buyers could deal with a small number of salespeople who could provide that specific coal type rather than aggressively obtaining the cheapest fuel. All this works well for the participants as long as the utility does not have to compete to provide power to its customers and its customers can be forced to pay for fuel price increases.

Even before deregulation of electricity markets began, utilities became increasingly concerned about their fuel costs as spot market prices fell deeply below the fixed contract prices, with spot prices reaching 50 percent of contract prices in many cases. Fuel costs typically represent 75 percent of the operating and maintenance costs of a coal-fired utility and upward of 85 percent for a natural gas-fired plant.[6] Therefore, utility financial managers found it necessary to have plant managers explore the flexibility of their power plants to burn a broader range of coals and coal blends. They found that the physical plant configurations offer a lot more flexibility than originally thought. Electricity market deregulation and competition also contributed to the breakdown of highly regionalized and quality-specific niche markets for coal.

The long-term contracts that were in place from the early 1980s to the mid-1990s were shaped by the energy crises of the 1970s. There was a general consensus in the days of the energy crises that crude oil prices would trend to $100 per barrel, which would raise the value of all other energy commodities including coal. The prudent utility executive established 10- or 20-year coal contracts at prices reflective of petroleum prices at $30 to $35 per barrel. In retrospect, it can be seen that the utilities locked in these contracts at the highest coal prices of the last 30 years.

---

6 *1993 Production Costs of Operating Steam-Electric Plants.* Washington, DC: Utility Data Institute, September 1994, Figure 2.

In spite of the regulated monopoly nature of electric utilities, their largest industrial customers have access to alternative power sources such as cogeneration and other fuels. As coal prices have generally declined since the mid-1980s, the gap between contract coal and spot coal prices has widened considerably. Contract coal prices can be almost twice as high as current market prices. Therefore, utilities increasingly have begun to pressure their coal suppliers on the fine points of contract specifications in order to find grounds for renegotiating the prices or breaking the contracts. This has caused further price decreases. This decline has also led utilities to greater use of the spot market, which has in fact hurt them when prices have risen sharply during times of supply disruption or increased demand due to severe weather. Also, since most of the needed electric generation capacity has been constructed, the utilities no longer need the long-term contracts to bolster capital financing efforts. Both mining companies and utilities recognize that they are entering a new environment where price risk matters. As the utilities must compete to produce the cheapest kilowatt hours, the mining companies must compete to sell them the cheapest Btu's of coal heat.

Many of the classic long-term coal contracts have matured, or will mature shortly, never to be renewed on the same basis. Five-year durations are typical in new long-term contracts. Most significantly, they incorporate much greater pricing flexibility. Resource Data International's recent report on Central Appalachian Coal summarizes the changes in coal contracting practices: "During the past decade, utilities have been moving to contracts of shorter duration, more frequent reopeners, and greater flexibility for buyers. The net effect has been to increase the level of risk on coal producers."[7] The data from their report, shown in Table 8.1, document these changes in contracts.[8]

---

7 Central Appalachia Coal Study, 1996: Challenges and Opportunities. Boulder, CO: Resource Data International, Inc., pp. 1–7.
8 Ibid., pp. 2–39.

TABLE 8.1

Central Appalachian Coal Study

Year Length of Contract	1985 Percentage of CAPP Coal under Contract (Cumulative)	1995 Percentage of CAPP Coal under Contract (Cumulative)
1–3	3	11
4–5	10 (13)	17 (28)
6–10	25 (38)	29 (57)
11–19	33 (71)	18 (75)
20 +	29 (100)	25 (100)

SPOT MARKET PURCHASES AND INVENTORY LEVELS

An increasing reliance on spot purchases of coal will also expose buyers and sellers to greater price risks. Utilities have been reducing their working capital requirements by reducing inventory levels. Whereas utilities often held 45- to 60-day supplies of coal inventories at each plant until the early 1990s, now 14- to 21-day inventories are typical. With a history of declining prices, increased transportation efficiencies, and fewer labor problems, utilities have seen no need to tie up large amounts of capital in coal storage. They also use spot market purchases more often, increasing from a weighted average of 13 percent for the years 1986 through 1988 to 20 percent for the years 1993 to 1995.[9] Interviews with many utility fuel buyers have indicated that they expect spot purchases to reach 30 percent in the near future.

COAL TRANSPORTATION

The Staggers Act deregulation of the railroad industry in 1980 has dramatically changed the US rail system.

---

9 *Cost and Quality of Fuels for Electric Utility Plants.* Washington, DC: Energy Information Administration, US Department of Energy, Annual Reports, Table 3.

Railroads are the major component of coal transportation, accounting for roughly 80 percent of all ton-miles of coal transportation.[10] The resulting consolidation and major efficiency gains in the railroad industry have greatly increased the distances that coal is transported in the United States. Wyoming's Powder River Basin (PRB) has been the greatest beneficiary. This is a coal that was rarely used 15 years ago and now accounts for a fifth of all US coal production. Because the rail infrastructure has been created to meet this demand and because of the low mining costs of these coals, they can now be economically shipped throughout the United States and thus compete with all other US coals.

COMMODITY PRICING FOR COAL

Commodity pricing for coal does not mean that all coals are the same (i.e., a totally homogeneous product). Rather, it means that different coals are being priced in terms of a limited number of variables. These variables are primarily related to quality characteristics and transportation differentials. Very distinctive coals are being evaluated in terms of heat output, sulfur content, transportation cost, and a few other variables. Utilities are no longer wedded to a single coal for each plant, but instead use models, such as the Electric Power Research Institute's (EPRI) Coal Quality Impact Model (CQIM), to compare the value of burning all types of coal at a particular plant.

The first step in commodity pricing for coal began when some buyers moved in the late 1980s to price coal shipments based on total MMBtu's rather than tons. This practice has now become universal.

Next, increasingly stringent pollution control requirements have also contributed to the process of commodity pricing. With the SO_2 (sulfur dioxide) emission allowance trading program administered annually by the Chicago

---

10 *RDI's Coal Transportation Study*. Boulder, CO: Resource Data Incorporated, 1996, ES–4.

Board of Trade, one of the key quality characteristics, sulfur, is now being priced in forward markets. To find alternatives to meet the increasingly stringent federal and state emissions controls, utilities have examined fuel substitution and new coal sources. This helped create a market for low-sulfur, low-heat-content Western fuels, particularly from the PRB. PRB coals are noted for their relatively inexpensive mining costs due to extremely thick seams close to the surface. Transportation competition and efficiencies have made it possible for PRB coals to compete on a delivered MMBtu basis against high-sulfur, high-heat-content Illinois Basin coals. However, in many cases, utilities find that they cannot rely on PRB coals alone. Therefore, they have begun to blend coals to optimize emission control and heat rate. Utilities are also examining the potential economic and environmental benefits of blending coals from other basins. These developments have broken the barriers between niche markets for coal.

PRICE VOLATILITY IN COAL MARKETS

Market participants most exposed to price risk use risk management instruments such as futures. The competitive market for coal described earlier means that the potential for risk exposure is there. However, this potential does not present either the sellers or the buyers with significant actual risk unless the prices are volatile. In analyzing the feasibility of a market for futures contract development, price volatility is a key factor. If the price for the commodity is not volatile, neither potential hedgers nor speculators will have the need to trade futures and options contracts.

Coal prices have been perceived to have low volatility, and previous research has supported this perception. However, previous research has used price streams that were based on the aggregating price paid for both long-term contracts and spot transactions for many companies across all US production regions. This aggregation did not make it possible to examine the volatility in spot prices experienced by particular buyers of coal from different regions. NYMEX performed original research to develop price streams for particular utilities making spot purchases for coal from specific regions to measure the volatility these buyers were exposed to. Analyzing these price streams shows that actual coal price volatility is above 15 percent as shown in Table 8.2. These volatilities compare to other commodities actively traded on futures exchanges, and therefore, coal exhibits sufficient volatility to be considered according to other criteria for futures market development.

In addition, the long period of declining coal prices has led to greater reliance on opportunistic spot purchasing and more pricing flexibility in long-term contracts as has been described. These shifts in market practices could lead to increased price volatility and make the past history of price movements less relevant to predicting future volatility.

POTENTIAL USERS OF COAL FUTURES

The New York Mercantile Exchange is currently developing coal futures contracts for both Central Appalachia (CAPP) and the Powder River Basin (PRB). The exchange's contract development efforts have been actively supported by a Coal Industry Advisory Committee made up of coal-burning utilities, coal mining companies, trading companies, rail and barge lines active in coal transportation, and others. These are potential users of coal futures for their rising risk management needs. In each segment, the committee has

TABLE 8.2

Coal Price Volatilities, Price Delivered to Utility, Weighted Average for Region, Annualized, 1988–1994

Appalachian Region	17%
Interior Region	19%
Western Region	26%

representatives from across the United States and of all different sizes and market positions. These firms are working with NYMEX because they understand how functioning coal futures markets will benefit them in flourishing within competitive electricity markets.

The exchange will introduce a CAPP contract initially. This is because CAPP offers the most developed trading infrastructure and has the most diverse group of mining companies producing, and utilities using, its coal. CAPP is the most closely tied contract to the midwestern and southeastern coal-consuming regions.

The potential benefits of a coal futures contract desired by coal producers, consumers, and other market participants include:

- Price transparency that would enable coal producers to more efficiently develop pricing strategies.
- Hedging opportunities that would enable coal producers and consumers to develop "win-win" supply agreements.
- Information that can be used in coal price forecasting and coal inventory management.

The availability of a coal futures contract would provide a variety of risk management approaches that can be used by both sellers and buyers of coal. First, the futures price would provide the most reliable independent benchmark price to be used in coal supply agreements. Indexes could be developed to provide benchmarks, such as market surveys performed by third parties that are often industry news media. However, other indexes do not provide a benchmark that is the result of a large number of transactions for a specific grade of coal delivered at a specific location. Buyers and sellers can use this futures market benchmark to set the base price of the contract, rather than trying to outdo each other with a winning forecast for coal prices in the future. In using benchmark pricing for supply agreements, the utility and the coal mining company can agree to price each month's delivery based on the average settlement price for the futures contract for that month. This average can be adjusted by a premium or discount fixed in the actual supply agreement to reflect differences between the grade and location of delivery of the actual coal sales versus the NYMEX coal futures specification. This is typical of how futures prices are used in other physical commodity markets.

Furthermore, futures provide flexible and relatively inexpensive approaches for companies to hedge their exposure to movements in the price of a commodity. Consumers of a commodity can hedge against unforeseen price increases, and producers of that commodity can use the markets to hedge against unforeseen price declines. The liquidity of futures markets enables hedgers to easily adjust their risk management positions as markets change. Those using coal supply agreements based on a NYMEX coal futures price could easily take advantage of the risk management methods provided by hedging with futures and options contracts.

INTERNATIONAL COAL MARKETS AND NYMEX COAL FUTURES

A paper was presented at a recent international coal conference that analyzed key developments in the international seaborne (export) coal markets that will support the use of futures:[11]

- **Size:** The international trade in steam coal alone has grown from 20 million tons per year in the early 1970s to 240 million tons per year in the mid-1990s and is projected to grow to over 300 million by the end of the century. At a price estimate for the f.o.b. price at port of origin of $30 per ton, this represents a $7.2 billion market. Over 30 percent of this coal, or over $2.2 billion, is sold on a spot basis. Spot basis in the international market refers to

---

11 Mark Walters, *Futures in the International Coal Industry: An Update.* Tel Aviv, Israel: International Coal & Carbon Club Annual Meeting, 1996.

deals that are done for a specific tonnage at a fixed price. Most of the deals are for under 6 months' duration and can be for single cargo deliveries. Contract deals in international coal markets are fixed supply agreements between producers and consumers, where the price is renegotiated on an annual basis.

- **Price Volatility:** In 1994 , steam coal from South Africa was selling at under $20 per ton, f.o.b. origin port. It had risen to a high in November 1995 of $35, then fallen over 7 months to under $29 in June, and now is back over $32.
- **Competition:** Increasing competition exists on a geographic basis, with the list of producer countries and companies growing.
- **Desire for Risk Management Tools:** As the reliance on coal contracts with fixed prices for long periods into the futures declines throughout the world, lenders are suggesting that coal mining and utility consuming clients consider other means of price risk management such as derivatives.
- **Standardization:** The international trade does refer to benchmarks, such as 6000 kcal NAR (net as received) from South African ports or 1.5 percent sulfur, 11,800 Btu coal from the US Gulf (as this coal is shipped to the Gulf ports by barge from Central Appalachia, it could have a direct pricing relationship to the NYMEX CAPP futures).

CONCLUSION

Coal futures contracts are now desired by coal producers and consumers. The need for price transparency and risk management for this commodity is emerging, with the structural changes in the US coal market dramatically changing. Coal futures will ultimately be of use not only for the domestic US market but also for the world's seaborne coal market.

CHAPTER 9

Options Theory and Its Application to Energy

By Dr. Nedia Miller

During the last 20 years the evolution of financial engineering has gone through tremendous changes, moving beyond academia to become the theoretical foundation for understanding today's financial/commodity markets. Physical scientists and engineers, as well as mathematicians, have brought with them a high level of understanding of mathematics, statistics, and physics to financial engineering. These disciplines have been applied to create valuable complex financial products, such as exchange-traded or synthetic instruments, which allocate risk more effectively in the financial/commodity markets.

The most explicit example of this transition in the way financial markets are interpreted today is reflected in the options markets and the understanding of derivative instruments. It should be mentioned that the importance of options goes well beyond the profit-motivated trading that is most visible to the public. Today, options research has advanced in step with the exploding options market.

Scholars have found that there is an options way of thinking in the financial decision-making process through the
use of an options framework.

The transition in the markets just described moved
traders from traditional trading, which was mostly intuitively traded through a technical analysis phase where
traders used manually prepared charts of the markets and
read the underlying fundamentals using accounting methods and internal financial information. The first indications
of the use of financial engineering in the financial community date back to use of the capital market theory (CAPM)
and the arbitrage pricing theory (APT). The latter became
the basis of options theory.[1]

---

1 Both CAPM and APT indicate that the required equilibrium or the required
   expected return is a linear equation as indicated below, where E is
   expected return, R is risk-free rate, E_m is expected market return, and ß is
   risk:

   CAPM equation: $E \int {}^* = R \int [E_m - R \int]$ ß shows that there is one
   unknown—the measure of risk (beta). It also shows that CAPM required
   the market portfolio to be on the Efficient frontier.

   APT equation: $APTE^* = R_J + \sum_{J=1}^{m} R_i P_j bi J$

   In this equation, there are several independent variables that factor betas
   (risk factor sensitivities), corresponding to the unspecified number of
   undefined risk factors measures. Also, this equation shows that APT does
   not require the market portfolio to be on the Efficient frontier. In other
   words, APT does not require the restrictive assumptions of the market
   portfolio. It follows from the APT equation that to determine the specific
   APT required return equation we need "risk-free rate $(R \int)$" and anticipated market return.

   Both CAPM and APT indicate that the required expected equilibrium, or
   the required expected return, is a linear function. Nevertheless, the key
   difference between CAPM and APT is that CAPM is derived using an
   equilibrium argument, and APT is based on an arbitrage argument. The
   arbitrage argument, in essence, shows that an asset whose price is
   unknown can be determined by combining other assets whose prices are
   known in such a way as to replicate the future payoff stream of the
   unknown asset. Furthermore, because the unknown asset and the combination of assets have the same future payoffs, they must have the same
   price; otherwise, arbitrageurs would buy the cheap asset, sell the expensive one, and collect the difference. Options theory requires perfect market conditions with no transaction costs.

OPTIONS THEORY

As previously mentioned, options theory is based on an arbitrage argument, which assumes that investors have a single period time horizon and are risk averse, the market is perfectly competitive, arbitrage causes the market to be in equilibrium, and actual return for an investment is a linear function of its expected return and an unspecified number of undefined risk factor measures.[2]

Furthermore, there are theoretical difficulties in applying options, such as deciding how to model the random prices that determine the underlying asset value if the futures price is unknown. The only way to price flexibility is to characterize this unknown future by the stochastic process[3] that assigns probabilities to possible future events over time. There are a variety of "random walks" that can be used. These random walks, or random processes, can be thought of as an "event" tree that branches out over time, the simplest tree being a binomial model in which there are two future possibilities for every current possibility at any point in time. Figure 9.1 is a simple binomial expression with a 20 percent volatility. Other processes modify this binomial approach.

---

2 "Risk-free arbitrage opportunity" arises only when an investor can construct a zero investment portfolio that will yield a sure profit. A zero investment portfolio means that the investor need not use any of his or her own money. If actual security prices temporarily allow for risk-free arbitrage, trades should quickly occur to take advantage of the risk-free arbitrage opportunity. The result will be strong pressure on the security prices to eliminate the risk-free arbitrage. In a well-functioning market, such opportunities cannot exist.

3 A stochastic process is one subject to a random walk, most often a time-related series. The stochastic equation describes the correlation between two or more variables, testing it with actual data. In this process, all the variables are independent and normally distributed. In the market, other types of random walks are frequently taken into consideration, such as the so-called mean reverting markets or jump process which would always revert to a mean in random markets. These are characteristic of the oil market—in short periods of time, prices in the oil markets tend to follow a random walk, but over a long period of time, they tend to follow the jump process.

FIGURE 9.1

Example of an Event Tree from the Electricity
Market

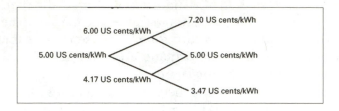

"Integrating Financial Theory and Method in Electricity Resource Paning" by F. A. Felder from *Energy Policy*, Volume 24, Number 2.

HISTORIC EVOLUTION OF OPTIONS
AND OPTIONS BASICS

In the 1960s, options were available, but not used. Options began to be considered legitimate financial instruments from the building of Black-Scholes options pricing model in 1973. From this date, and particularly after the acceptance of modern portfolio theory (which was developed by Harry Markowitz in the 1950s), the science of financial engineering became widely accepted in the financial industry.

Nevertheless, during this period of time (1973–1990), both computational power and computer technology were lagging behind theory, and there was insufficient technology to compute complex equations. During the same period of time, the abolition of the gold standard during the Bretton Woods conference in 1973 caused enormous FX volatility and high increases in interest rates. This exposed the serious limitations of the "tried and true" model and created a demand for new instruments such as swaps and caps. The demand for academics and financial engineers was growing. There was increasing interest in what financial engineering could do to provide better explanations and tools to produce better "mousetraps." It became acceptable for students to study the Black-Scholes formula.

Today, on the contrary, there is a lag between academic modeling and industry implementation. Many models are now first developed in industry. The leading role in financial engineering is changing hands from academia to the financial industry. The number of useful, readily available options pricing models (which have been benchmarked using the Monte Carlo Simulation technique[4]) is now so large as to strain the reserves of the "taxonomists."

OPTIONS BASICS

To understand options, we assume perfect market conditions: no risk-free arbitrage, no taxes, no transaction costs, and no distractions of any kind. Under these perfect market conditions, an option essentially works like an insurance policy.

One party, the holder (or buyer) of an option, has the right, but not the obligation, to exercise his or her option. Another party, the seller (or writer) of an option, has an obligation to perform if called upon to do so. There are two basic types of options: calls and puts (there is also a spread options contract called the "crack spread," which we examine later in this chapter). A call gives the holder of the option the right to buy the underlying futures contract. A put gives the holder of the option the right to sell the underlying futures contract.

---

4 The Monte Carlo Simulation (MCS) technique uses scenario testing and simulates the terminal payoff of an option. Furthermore, the MCS technique provides a statistical description of the risk for key inputs through an artificial probability distribution, identification, and statistical description of any relationship (covariance). The most significant feature of MCS is that the accuracy of the estimates of the parameter depends on the sample size, not on the number of inputs. Since the MCS's answers arrive from random observations, they are uncertain, but they serve a useful purpose by making uncertainty manageable.

OPTION'S PRICE, ALSO FREQUENTLY CALLED OPTION' S PREMIUM

Option buyers pay option sellers a premium over the price to receive rights without obligations. The major factors affecting the premium or price of an option are:

- The underlying futures price relative to option strike price; hence the correlation between the underlying price and the exercise price of the option. The exercise price or strike price is the price at which the underlying futures contract may be bought or sold prior to the expiration date. Therefore, we can generalize that an option is always worth at least its intrinsic value before expiration date.

- The volatility of underlying futures prices.

- The time remaining before option expiration, which is called the "time value" of the option. In the commercial sense, time value is the amount buyers are willing to pay for the option above its intrinsic value in the expectation that, at some time before expiration, it will move into the money. Premiums on out-of-the-money options are fully based on time value. As the option becomes deeply in or out of the money, the time premium shrinks substantially. The time premium for the in-the-money option is the amount that exceeds the option's intrinsic value and reflects the possibility that the option may move deeper into the money. The time value of the option necessarily shrinks as the expiration day approaches. The reason is that there is less time for a major change in the market's behavior and a decreasing likelihood that the option will increase in value.

- Interest rates are considered to have the least effect on options premiums.

STRIKE PRICE VERSUS FUTURES PRICE

To understand the relationship between strike prices and the price of the underlying financial instrument, we examine the concept of moneyness. *Moneyness* is an options concept which refers to the potential profit/loss from the immediate exercise of an option. An option can be at the money (ATM), in the money (ITM), or out of the money (OTM):

- ATM option: An option is at the money when the strike price equals the price of the underlying futures contract.
- ITM option: An option is in the money when the price of the futures contract is above a call's strike price or when the futures price is below a put's strike price.
- OTM: A call is out of the money when the futures price is less than the option strike price. A put is out of the money when the underlying futures price is higher than the put's strike price.

Intrinsic value is the most important relationship between the underlying instrument (contract) and the strike price of the option. The intrinsic value can never be a negative number. We can conclude that option price = intrinsic value + time value. It then follows that:

- Out-of-the-money and at-the-money options have *only* time value.
- In-the-money options have *both* time and intrinsic value.
- At expiry, all options must have a value equal to their intrinsic value.
- Time value decays with time; therefore, options are wasting or declining assets.

The following two examples illustrate the interactions between intrinsic value and time value:

EXAMPLE 9.1 [5]

Short Natural Gas Call Option

Futures Price	Options Premium	Intrinsic Value	Time Value
2.50	0.08	0.00	0.08
2.50	0.14	—	0.14
2.65	0.25	—	0.25
2.90	0.39	0.25	0.14
3.15	0.58	0.25	0.18

· EXAMPLE 9.2

Short Natural Gas Put Option

Futures Price	Options Premium	Intrinsic Value	Time Value
2.50	0.23	0.15	0.08
2.40	0.39	0.25	0.14
2.65	0.25	—	0.25
2.70	0.14	—	0.14
3.00	0.08	—	0.18

At expiry, what is the value of the insurance policy in:

- Case 1: The probability that the commodity price is below X?
- Case 2: The expected loss (i.e., the average $S - X$) for all cases when the commodity price is below X?

In Case 1, $S > X$. Therefore, it is an in-the-money call. The greater the option is in the money, the less likely it is to fall below X, and the cheaper the insurance policy. For in-the-money options, time value is inversely related to the degree to which the option is in the money.

In Case 2, $S < X$. Therefore, it is an out-of-money call. The value of the insurance policy is given by: amount out of money + expected additional loses.

---

5 Natural gas strike prices are listed in increments of 5c per million British thermal units. There are at least 11 strike prices listed for these contracts, one nearest to the previous day's close of the underlying futures contract, and five each at 5c intervals above and below that price. Strike price boundaries are adjusted according to the futures price movements.

If a Call Option Is Used as Insurance, How Can We Determine the Expected Losses?

To estimate the expected losses, we must assume something about the probability distribution of commodity prices through time. The assumption is made that commodity returns (rather than commodity prices) are normally distributed. Normal distribution is the classic bell shape, which is symmetric about its mean. The width of the bell is related to the standard deviation of the distribution of returns. This is called the volatility of the commodity returns and hence the volatility of the commodity prices.

The following two examples show that commodity returns distribution = options prices distributed around the mean.

Example 9.3: The current price of a security is 100. You believe that in 1 year's time the distribution of the security's prices will be:

Price	Probability, %
70	5
80	10
90	20
100	30
110	20
120	10
130	5

What would you charge for insuring the owner against a fall below 100 in 1 year's time? The cost of the insurance is equal to the expected payout (discounted to reflect the fact that the payout will not occur until 1 year's time).

The expected payout is given by: $(100 - 90) \times 20\% + (100 - 80) \times 10\% + (100 - 70) \times 5\% = 5.50$.

The value of the insurance is the present value of 5.50. Note that the expected value of the security in 1 year's time is 100. Hence, the expected value of the payout (5.50) is greater than the value of the expected payout (0).

Example 9.4: The current price of a security is 100. You believe that in 1 year's time the distribution of the security's prices will be:

Price	Probability, %
70	2
80	7
90	21
100	40
110	21
120	7
130	2

What would you charge for insuring the owner against a fall below 100 in 1 year's time? The expected payout is given by: $(100 - 90) \times 21\% + (100 - 80) \times 7\% + (100 - 70) \times 2\% = 4.10$.

Hence, the value of the insurance is the present value of 4.10. This value is less than in Example 9.3 because the volatility of the price distribution is smaller. Note that the expected value of the security in 1 year's time remains at 100. According to this analog, we can say that price distribution affects call options premium in the same way.

PRICE VERSUS YIELD VOLATILITY

There are three different types of volatility: historic, expected, and implied.[6] When pricing options, the volatility of asset

---

6 Historic volatility is calculated from the past movements of natural gas prices over a specified time period. Technically, historic volatility is the standard deviation of the log of change in the futures prices, expressed in percentage terms annualized. For example, 50 percent volatility means that there is a 68.3 percent chance (one standard deviation) that 1 year from now prices will be 50 percent higher or lower. We can estimate future volatility on the basis of historic volatility. This means that we can estimate the expected volatility of the underlying commodity or security between the option's purchase and its expiry. Implied volatility is implied in the price of an option and represents the market forecast of futures volatility. Other types of volatilities have been introduced recently, but these are beyond the scope of this chapter.

returns is volatility based on asset prices. However, it is common market practice to quote the volatility of 3-month interest rate futures contracts on a yield basis. Yield-based volatilities are greater than price-based volatilities by about a factor of 10.

Typical Volatility Ranges	
3-month interest rate futures	12–20% (yield based)
Medium/long government bond futures	6–12%
Equity index	15–25%

The expected volatility of a futures contract should correlate strongly with the initial margin for that contract.

Using Volatility

Example 9.5: The expected volatility of a bond futures contract is 10 percent. If the price of the contract is 100, what is the expected daily range?

The daily volatility,[7] assuming a 250-day return, is given by:

$$\frac{10\%}{\sqrt{250}} = 0.63\%$$

This is the average deviation of the returns about the 1-day forward price. The expected daily range (95 percent confidence) is given approximately by two standard deviation.

OTHER FACTORS THAT AFFECT OPTIONS PRICES

Now that we have examined the most significant price factor affecting options–volatility–we demonstrate how other pricing factors affect options premium.

---

7 The expected volatility is always the annualized volatility. Therefore, to find the daily volatility, we divide the annualized volatility over 250 days.

Time value is determined by:

- the "true intrinsic value," that is, F and X.
- the volatility, that is, $\sigma\sqrt{t}$, where σ = the volatility expressed in annual terms and t = the time to maturity of the option in years.

Premium paid options are functions of the interest rate because the expected payoffs are discounted to give present values. Interest rate volatility affects options premium according to the Black-Scholes options pricing model. As this rate increases, the cost of the option does so as well over any given time frame. We have to mention that, because it is an expression of a factor which is unaffected by either the futures or the over-the-counter (OTC) markets, this rate is generally not negotiable in specific transactions.

PUT/CALL PARITY

Calls and puts of the same exercise price have the same

$$C - P = (F - X) \times D$$

amount of time value. This is expressed by:

where C = the call option price
P = the put option price
F = the forward of futures price
X = the exercise price
D = the discount factor (=1 margined options)

This means that the difference between the call and the put is equal to the present value of the difference between the underlying futures price and the strike price. The put/call parity relationship also indicates that calls and puts of the same exercise price have the same amount of time value.

The importance of this relationship lies in the ability to substitute positions within defined price zones for specific purposes. For example, a long call position and a short put position both constitute a long position at initiation, but their profit profiles are quite different.

Options Style

This factor takes into consideration the construction of the option. The elements used in the construction of the timing of exercise rights for the option buyer change the probability that the option will be exercised. For instance, an American option can be exercised at any time prior to the expiration, while European options can be exercised only at expiration. If all other factors were held constant, the premium of the American option would be slightly higher based on the fact that it has a higher probability of being exercised. The Black-Scholes options pricing model is derived for European-style options.

BLACK-SCHOLES MODEL

Fischer Black and Myron Scholes developed their options pricing model using the assumptions that asset prices adjust to prevent arbitrage, that stock prices change continuously, and that securities follow log normal distribution. The model was also based on European stock options with no dividends.[8] The mathematics used to derive the formula are stochastic and calculus. The form of the Black-Scholes model is very close to binomial distribution.

The following is the original equation of the Black-Scholes pricing model for a call option:

$$C_1 = S_1 N(d_1) - X_e^{\sigma(T-1)} N(d_2)$$

where $N(.)$ = the cumulative normal distribution function.

$$d_1 = \frac{1N\frac{S_t}{x} + (\sigma + 0.5\sigma^2)(T-1)}{\sigma\sqrt{T-1}}$$

$$d_2 = d_1 - \sigma\sqrt{T-1}$$

This model has the general form we have previously considered—the value of a call must equal or exceed the stock price minus the present value of the exercise price:

---

8 European options can be exercised only at maturity, whereas American options can be exercised at any time before maturity.

$$C_1 \geq S_1 - X_e^{\sigma(T-1)7}$$

$N(d_1)$ and $N(d_2)$ are risk-adjusted factors. These risk-adjusted factors are, in essence, the continuous time equivalent of the binomial model.

From the original Black-Scholes formula, scholars and industry practitioners have developed a number of options pricing models suited for the different needs of the financial commodity industry. One pricing model, which is a simplified approach but analogous to Black-Scholes, is expressed as follows:

$$C = [FN(d_1) - XN(d_2) \times D$$

where F = the forward or futures price
X = the exercise price
D = the discount factor
$N(.)$ = the area under the normal curve

$$d_1 = \frac{In(F/X) + 1/2\sigma^2 t}{\sigma\sqrt{T}}$$
$$d_2 = d_1 - \sigma\sqrt{t}$$

As we can see, this simplified options pricing model still maintains the main assumption, which originated in the Black-Scholes pricing model. The latter is widely used in the energy options futures market and in most exchange-traded options. Recently, scholars have developed more precise options pricing models for commodity futures evaluation by using the stochastic convenience yield.[9] Under the stochastic convenience yield, the volatility of futures price is shown to be dependent on time but independent of the convenience yield and the spot price levels. The detailed presentation of this evaluation method for options

---

9 This formula occurs in the single period call pricing model (see binomial single pricing model) and shows that the value of a call option equals a long position in the stock, plus some borrowing at the risk-free rate.

on futures is beyond the scope of this chapter.[10] However, this method also shows that we cannot use an estimate of spot price volatility as a proxy for future price volatility, as the Black-Scholes formula does. The stochastic convenience yield method shows that the futures price formula depends on the term structure of the volatility of the futures price, while the Black-Scholes formula assumes that the term structure is flat. This method is analogous to Black-Sholes in that the same basic assumptions are being made, but even though we assume flat term structure for the volatilities of the spot price and convenience yield, we obtained futures volatility, which varied with time. Furthermore, this method demonstrates that the volatility of futures prices can be different from the volatility of spot prices, but at the maturity of the futures contract, the volatility of the futures price equals the volatility of the spot price, since spot price equals futures price at maturity.[11]

The foregoing demonstrates that there has been much interest in developing sophisticated futures options pricing models which would more precisely price options on futures. Nevertheless, the earlier conventional futures options pricing formula still dominates the energy futures industry.

---

10 Fischer Black and Myron Scholes used the binomial approach for their options pricing model. The single period binomial call pricing model holds for a call option expiring in one period when stock prices will rise by a known percentage or fall by a known percentage. The model shows that the value of a call option equals a long position in the stock, plus some borrowing at the risk-free rate. The single period binomial model can be extended to a multiperiod binomial model, applying the same principle. In the multiperiod binomial model, we consider two or more time period horizons. We can analyze an option expiring in n periods.

11 In a broad sense, the convenience yield can be treated analogously to the dividend yield. The *convenience yield* of a commodity is defined as the flow of services which accrues to the owner of physical inventory but not to the owner of a contract for future delivery. Most recently, there has been evidence that convenience yield can be approximated by a well-defined stochastic process. The two-state pricing model is based on spot prices and a mean-reverting convenience yield.

ASSUMPTIONS OF THE
BLACK-SCHOLES MODEL

- Log normal distribution
- No continuity in price movements
- Constant volatility
- No transaction costs

The same basic assumptions apply for evaluating options on energy futures (see formula on page 146). These assumptions show that the exercise price and the time until expiration can be known with certainty. We want to consider how to obtain estimates for the underlying contract.

Estimates of the risk-free rate are widely available and are usually quite reliable. We need to select the correct rate. Since the Black-Scholes model uses a risk-free rate, we can use the US Treasury bill rate as a good estimate. (The quotes for T-bills are expressed as discount rates, so we need to convert these to regular rates and express them as continuously compounded rates. In addition, we should select that T-bill whose maturity is closest to the options' expiration.)

PROBLEMS WITH OPTIONS PRICING MODELS

The problem with options pricing models is that we always have to make some type of assumptions, such as assumptions about futures distribution of the forward price, assumptions about the way security prices move with time, assumptions about the correlation between forward rates and interest rates, or assumptions about the normal distribution of option prices. Most of the time, these assumptions are offtrack and lead to mispricing options. For example, the use of the Black-Sholes options pricing model over time has repeatedly confirmed that this model undervalues call options and overvalues put options, respectively. If we knew the amount by which these premiums were under/overvalued, we could resolve the problem quickly by adding or subtracting the appropriate amounts. The real problem is that we cannot quantify this difference.

This particular handicap of the Black-Scholes model arises from the fact that expected volatility remains unknown, even if we accept all the other assumptions of the model. As a result, a number of extensions of the Black-Scholes pricing model have followed since 1973 which use two different pricing methods: (1) variations of the Black-Scholes pricing model and (2) the binomial model (Cox Ross Rubinstein, 1976, or variations). Nevertheless, scholars still have not found a perfect options pricing model that eliminates the original problem of not being able to estimate the volatility.

There are two basic approaches to estimating the volatility. The first approach is to use historic volatility to estimate the expected volatility. The second approach is to use fresh data from the options market itself. The second method uses options prices to find the option market's estimate of the underlying commodity price's standard deviation. An estimate of the underlying commodity price's standard deviation that is drawn from the option market is called an "implied volatility."

USES OF OPTION PRICING MODELS

The most important application of options pricing models is to estimate fair value[12] prices in illiquid markets. Second, these models estimate implied volatility in liquid markets. And last, they estimate price changes given a change in one or more of the pricing inputs.

OPTION SENSITIVITIES (OPTIONS RISK MEASURES) ARE EXPRESSED BY THE "GREEKS"

Delta reflects the expected change in the option premium given a small change in the price of the underlying instru-

---

12 A study on the valuation of futures options with the stochastic convenience yield has recently been developed by the University of Georgia, Athens, and was presented at the fifth annual meeting of The International Organization of Financial Engineers in New York on October 17, 1996.

ment and all other variables held constant. For example, if we have bought a call and the delta is 50 and the underlying price changes by $1, our position will change in value by 50 cents. When the underlying futures contract moves up, our call becomes more valuable. When the underlying contract moves down, our call becomes less valuable. Our underlying futures contract hedging position offsets much of the risk of our long call position. As we gain value on the call when the futures contract goes up, we lose value on our short futures position. As we lose value on our call when the futures contract moves down, we gain value on our short futures position.

In other words, delta is a measure of price risk. It is our first option risk parameter. Delta shows how the option price moves when the underlying price moves. It also shows how to hedge our position when we buy or sell an option. Delta varies from 0 to +1.0 in the case of long calls and from 0 to –1.0 in the case of long puts. Delta is frequently used in delta-hedging a position. *Convexity* means that delta underestimates option price increases and overestimates price decreases.

Another important options risk measure is gamma, which demonstrates how quickly a position becomes unhedged when the underlying price changes. Gamma is the measurement of the change in delta in response to a one-point change in the underlying price. In other words, it is the "delta of the delta," which leads to the conclusion that gamma is a measure of convexity.

Theta is the relationship of options value to time. It reflects the expected change in the option premium given a small change in the option's term to expiration with all other variables held constant. In other words, the remaining life of an option declines. This means that, as time goes by, if nothing else happens—if volatility does not change, if interest rates do not change, if the spot price does not move —both the call and the put will be worth less. Correspondingly, short option positions become more profitable with the passage of time if everything else is constant.

Vega is the measurement of exposure to changes in volatility. Accordingly, vega is frequently used to measure the sensitivity of the option premium to shifting volatility levels, all other variables held constant.

Examples of Each

Delta

A call option had a delta of 0.40. What will the change in the option price be if the underlying price moves from 100 to 110? How many call options are equivalent in price movement terms to 1 unit of the underlying price?

$$\Delta C = \delta \times \Delta P = 0.40 \times (110 - 100) = 4$$

The total number of call option equivalents is given by:

$$\frac{1}{\delta} = \frac{1}{0.40} = 2.5$$

You require 2.5 call options to produce the same price change that would be produced by 1 unit of the underlying price. 2.5 call options will hedge 1 unit of the underlying price.

Gamma

Current underlying price	= 95
Current call option price	= 0.38
Option delta	= +0.16
Option gamma	= +0.05

Estimate the new option price if the underlying price rises to 100.

Price change in underlying price = 5.00
New option price (change)   = 1.98 (1.60)
Price change from delta only   = 5 x 0.16 = 0.80
Additional change from gamma = 0.5 x 0.05 x 5^2 = 0.62
Estimated new option price   = 0.38 + 0.80 + 0.62 = 1.80

Vega

Underlying price   = 100
100 put option price   = 1.98
Option volatility   = 10%
Time to maturity   = 90 days
Option vega   = 0.20

I am long the 100 put option because I think that the
price of the underlying price will fall. What is my loss
if the underlying price is unchanged, but volatility
falls by 2 percent (in a short time)?

Change in put option price = –0.20 x 2 = –0.40
New put option price =1.58

Vega is the measurement of exposure to changes in
volatility. Accordingly, vega is frequently used to
measure the sensitivity of the option premium to
shifting volatility levels, all other variables held
constant.

Some Typical Values

Premium Paid, American Style, Futures-Based Calls
Exercise price   = 100
Volatility   = 10%

Options Prices

	–5 OTM	ATM	+5 ITM
90 days	0.38	1.98	5.44
60 days	0.19	1.62	5.24
30 days	0.04	1.15	5.07
15 days	0.00	0.81	5.01

ATM Option

	Delta	Gamma	Vega*	Theta**
90 days	0.51	0.08	0.20	0.01
60 days	0.51	0.10	0.16	0.01
30 days	0.51	0.14	0.11	0.02
15 days	0.51	0.20	0.08	0.03

* Expressed as the change in option price for a 1 percent absolute change in volatility.

** Expressed as the change in option price for a 1-day change in time to maturity.

OPTIONS APPLICATIONS

Both over-the-counter (OTC) and exchange-traded options have wide popularity in the energy markets. They serve commercial purpose by being a flexible risk management tool, offering flexibility about the market view of the energy trader. By using options traders do not need to be certain about the direction of the market. For example, buying a call option allows hedgers to obtain protection against price increase while still participating in price declines. Crude oil buyers who have entered into a fixed price purchase contract can use put options to participate in price decline should their market view change after they have entered into the fixed purchase agreement.

HEDGING WITH OPTIONS

There are a variety of ways to use options for hedging purposes: long hedge, short hedge, or using synthetic positions, which in essence are buying and selling puts and calls simultaneously.

> Example 9.5: A synthetic long crude oil futures = short crude oil put, long crude oil call.
>
> A synthetic short crude oil futures = long crude oil put, short crude oil call.
>
> Options are used most frequently in delta hedging (or to achieve delta neutrality) of a particular energy portfolio. In order to do that first, we have to know the net delta exposure of the portfolio.

Example 9.6: We have an existing natural gas
portfolio consisting of:

Position	Delta
long 20 futures	+ 20
short 10 ATM calls (delta −0.5)	− 5
long 12 ITM puts (delta −1)	− 12
Net delta	+3

Once the trader knows the net delta exposure of his or
her option (or underlying) position, it is possible to hedge
the price risk by taking an equal and opposite position in
the underlying (or option) market. In this particular example, the trader needs to sell three futures contracts (or the
equivalent) to achieve delta neutrality.

This hedging technique (delta neutrality) enables a
trader who has no opinion about the direction of the market to exploit the implied volatility in the options market. (If
a trader observes that the natural gas market is currently
trading at 28 percent volatility, and thinks that this is too
low and that volatility is going to increase, the trader would
buy calls or puts. The trader will buy volatility, which in
essence means that both premiums from the put and from
the call will appreciate, given the rise in volatility.)
Simultaneously covering any +/− delta position would
then be completed in the underlying futures market.
Assuming that the volatility will rise, the trader would sell
back the option positions and simultaneously close out the
futures position.

A common type of hedging widely used in the energy
industry is synthetic hedging. In this case, the trader uses
synthetic positions to hedge his or her position (already
illustrated in this chapter). Another common type of hedging used for hedging energy portfolios is static hedging.

CONCLUSION

There are a number of risk management strategies frequently used in the energy markets today, without which

the complex possibilities on the large range of flexibility that options are offering as a risk management tool would not be possible. In this chapter, we gave a brief application of the options framework in the energy industry (particularly in the energy futures industry). There are other uses of energy options that go beyond the scope of the energy markets. For example, the "crack spread" option, which we mentioned earlier in this chapter, serves as a portfolio diversification tool for fund managers,[13] since this option allows the use energy's low correlation with the rest of the financial instruments in a portfolio.

As we already demonstrated, the use of options and options framework goes beyond risk management purposes to meet the variety of needs in the evolution of the energy markets into the financial markets. Options are unique and versatile financial products which can be employed in a variety of ways to limit risk, earn income, and pursue trading opportunities because they reflect both market and the passage of time.

---

13 See the study on the valuation of futures developed by the University of Georgia.

CHAPTER 10

Value at Risk for Power Markets

By Kenneth Leong and Riaz Siddiqi

WHY IS VaR RELEVANT?

The electric power industry is at the juncture today where the banking industry was at about 15 years ago. Ongoing deregulation of the electricity market is creating unprecedented uncertainty for the industry's decision makers. Deregulation means the influx of aggressive new players, intensification of competition, widening of customer choice, downward pressure on profit margins, and increase in the volatility of earnings. All these are familiar themes for those who have lived through the banking deregulation of the 1970s. There are also parallels on the product side. There are a myriad of new products in the power markets and an increased usage of derivative instruments as hedging or trading tools. These new developments mean that the business environment is much riskier than it used to be. As a result, the development of sophisticated risk management tools and techniques becomes imperative.

Managers in the power industry are fortunate because many generic risk management tools have already been developed by their counterparts in the banking industry.

Substantial knowledge and technology transfer from the banking industry to the utilities industry has occurred. For one thing, several progressive energy trading firms and forward-thinking utilities have acquired derivatives and financial engineering talent from Wall Street and the energy trading complex. Also, a few prominent consulting firms and software developers who have a long and successful track record of serving the financial community are adapting their skills and repackaging their products to capitalize on the new opportunities available in the power industry. As deregulation in the power market escalates, expectations are that there will be cross-fertilization between the banking and energy fields.

One of the key risk management concepts that has received much attention in the banking industry is called "value at risk" (VaR). Several earlier developments help to put value at risk in the limelight. In July 1993, the Global Derivatives Study Group, a task force sponsored by the Group of Thirty, published a list of 20 "good practice" recommendations for derivative dealers and end users. One of these states that "market risk is best measured as 'value at risk' using probability analysis based upon a common confidence interval and time horizon." In April 1995, the Basel Committee of Banking Supervision issued a proposal that lays out the technical details for measuring value at risk. In December 1995, the SEC released for comment several proposed amendments to clarify and expand the risk disclosure requirement of registered companies, with a special emphasis on quantitative risk measurements. Among the three alternatives for quantifying risk exposure is the value at risk approach.[1] Undoubtedly, value at risk has become a focal point of corporate risk management and a new standard for risk reporting and disclosure. In fact, many financial institutions and a handful of leading industrial corporations are already reporting to their shareholders their market risk

---

1 The other two risk disclosure methods are tabulation and sensitivity analysis.

exposure using a value-at-risk methodology. Among these companies are J.P. Morgan, Statoil, and Enron.

A complete discussion of value at risk would require book-length treatment. The objective in this chapter is simply to provide a general introduction to this new concept and work out some practical examples to illustrate how value-at-risk can be an invaluable tool to decision makers in the power industry. More specifically, we illustrate how the value-at-risk methodology can be used for making trading and portfolio management decisions and how it can serve as a guide for performance benchmarking and capital allocation purposes. Although we do attempt to share with you our insights derived from developing and implementing the value at risk methodology at Cinergy Corp., what we present in this chapter is generic in nature and does not necessarily reflect the current state of Cinergy's risk management framework.

WHAT IS VALUE AT RISK?

The Global Derivatives Study Group defines *value at risk* as "the expected loss for an adverse market movement with a specified probability over a particular period of time." Essentially, it is a scientific estimate of a portfolio's potential for loss (or gain) due to market movements, using standard statistical techniques.

This concept may be understood intuitively by looking at the empirical frequency distribution of the gains or losses of a given portfolio of assets and liabilities over a specific time interval (daily, weekly, etc.). For example, the 1994 annual report of J.P. Morgan presents a histogram of the daily combined trading revenue for that year. Exhibit 1 of the report shows that, 95 percent of the time, daily trading revenue ranged from a loss of $11 million to a gain of $21 million, a deviation of approximately $15 million from the average daily revenue of $5.8 million. This deviation of $15 million can be viewed as a kind of maximum expected loss. Thus, one way to understand value at risk is to view it as a statistical worst-case scenario in association with some degree of confidence.

CASE FOR VaR AS A RISK MEASURE

Those who grew up in the world of trading and risk management are probably familiar with a myriad of well-established risk measures. For example, in the fixed-income market, sensitivity measures such as duration and basis point value are common. (*Duration* measures, in relative terms, the sensitivity of bond price to interest rate change. This interest rate sensitivity is expressed relative to the current bond price. *Basis point value* also measures the sensitivity to interest rate movements, but in absolute terms.) Modern option traders live and breathe the "Greeks"—deltas, gammas, vegas, and thetas—representing the sensitivities of option value to change in the price of the underlying instrument, change in volatility level and the elapse of time, and so forth. Financial managers at major energy companies also perform sensitivity studies or stress tests to find out how vulnerable their companies' bottom lines are to adverse changes in oil price, gas price, and so forth. All these risk measures have something in common: they are deterministic in nature, provide a stand-alone risk view without properly accounting for portfolio effects, and make no probabilistic statement about the likelihood of a potential loss.

The primary strength of value at risk lies in the fact that it is a holistic risk measure. In a sense, all traditional risk measures are "wrong" in that they provide only a partial view of risk. One key lesson for a risk manager to learn is that risk is amorphous and context dependent. The risk associated with a particular trade or a particular instrument is not an absolute number that can be determined out of context. The incremental risk of adding a new position to a portfolio, for example, depends on the interaction between the risk of that new position and the risk of other portfolio components. When the correlation between the risk of the new position and that of the rest of the portfolio is low or negative, we can expect little incremental risk. Value at risk is a powerful aggregate risk measure in that it captures all relevant portfolio effects in a summary manner.

The second major advantage of using the VaR methodology is that it utilizes certain key statistical information, whereas traditional risk measures don't. For example, in quantifying the risk of holding a bond, we may say the bond has a basis point value of $3000. This means that a 10 basis point move in interest rates will incur a profit or loss in the bond's value of around $30,000. But how likely is a 10 basis point move in interest rates? The basis point value measure offers no clue. As we shall see, a VaR measure can offer some insight by incorporating the historic volatilities of portfolio components into the risk calculation. Similarly, consider the risk associated with a portfolio of 100 power contracts, of varied maturities, and associated counterparty credit quality. We understand intuitively that portfolio risk will be reduced through diversification. But how strong is the tendency for asset prices to move in tandem and how big is the diversification effect? The incorporation of correlation statistics into the VaR analysis allows companies to quantify these.

The third major advantage of VaR as a risk measure is its simplicity. A corporation is often exposed to a multitude of risk factors. Cinergy Corp., for example, has exposure to electricity prices, gas prices, coal prices, interest rates, and exchange rate movements. In terms of reporting to the corporation's board or shareholders, it would greatly simplify the matter if all these risk exposures could be summarized in one single number rather than as a set of separate sensitivities. For instance, it is relatively easy for a shareholder to understand that within a 95 percent confidence level the daily fluctuation in the value of Cinergy's trading portfolio, including exposure to all relevant commodity risks, will not exceed, for example, $20 million.

The fourth major advantage of VaR is the potential of using it as the basis of integrating risk management. A commodity trading firm may simultaneously trade oil, natural gas, power, and other commodities. One way to manage trading risk is to divide the risk positions into separate portfolios so that there is an oil book, a gas book, a power book, and so on, and have each book managed on a stand-alone basis. However, since there are substantial correlations between commodity prices, the overall commodity risk to the firm should be much less than the direct summation of the risks associated with each book. Therefore, there is a case for integrating risk management and consolidating hedging activities. Another way to illustrate the need for integrated risk management is to look at the profit margin of a deregulated electric utility company. The profit margin is a function of two components: electricity price and fuel cost. We could separately hedge the market risk of electricity price and the market risk of fuel cost. But that would not be an efficient way to hedge. In providing a proper mechanism for netting price risks, the VaR framework can serve as the basis on which we implement integrated risk management and improve hedging efficiency.

QUANTIFYING THE RISK OF A POWER CONTRACT

The VaR framework was originally developed by banks and bank regulators to measure the risk exposure in financial portfolios. To see how it is relevant to players in the power market, let us assume that we are a nonregulated subsidiary of a utility company that owns a portfolio of wholesale power contracts. Further, for simplicity's sake, assume that the portfolio consists purely of forward contracts with no explicit or embedded options in it. The first step is to quantify the risk associated with a single power contract. Assume that we are committed to selling power to another utility for the next N days for h hours per day at a delivery rate of w megawatts per hour. Then, we can calculate the total quantity of electricity on which we have market risk as:

$$q = N \times h \times w$$

To further simplify the risk analysis, the following assumptions are made:

1. There is no time value of money, (i.e., the present value effects are ignored).

2. The day-to-day fluctuation (or changes) in the unit price of electricity for the power contract follows a normal distribution.

3. There is reasonable stability in price volatility so that historic price behavior can be used as a guide for the future.

To the extent that these assumptions are valid, we can express the variance of the daily fluctuation in position value as:

$$\text{VaR @ 95\%} = 1.96 \times q \times P \times \sigma$$

where $\qquad$ X = the value of the power contract
P = the current unit price of electricity underlying the contract
σ = the Black-Scholes volatility of P

The confidence interval for daily position fluctuation can then be computed. We estimate that there is only a 2.5 percent chance that a daily loss in this forward position will exceed the position VaR, which is calculated as:

$$\text{VaR @ 95\%} = 1.96 \times q \times P \times \sigma$$

For those unfamiliar with the option pricing literature, the Black-Scholes volatility is defined as the annualized standard deviation of logarithmic returns, which can be approximated as the standard deviation of the daily price movements expressed in percentage terms. In other words:

$$\sigma = \sqrt{\text{VaR}(\Delta P / P)}$$

A formal derivation of the VaR formula is provided in the notes at the end of this chapter entitled " 1. Value at Risk for a Single Power Contract." To illustrate with a life example, assume that Cinergy enters into a 5-year power purchase agreement with another utility. The contract calls for around-the-clock (ATC) delivery at a rate of 25 MW/h. If the current unit price of electricity for a 5-year power contract is $27/MWh and the daily price volatility is 2 percent, what is the daily value at risk, at 95 percent confidence, of this contract?

To calculate the VaR for this power purchase contract, we can directly apply the formula for position VaR. Two inputs to that formula are:

$$q = 25 \times 365 \times 5 \times 24 \text{ MWh} = 1{,}095{,}000 \text{ MWh}$$
$$P = \$27/\text{MWh}$$

The daily position VaR can then be computed as:

$$\text{VaR} = 1.96 \times 1.095 \times 10^6 \times \$27 \times 0.02 = \$1.16 \text{ million}$$

If we plot the histogram for the daily changes in position value for this power contract, we can expect that, in 95 percent of the cases, the change in contract value will not exceed $1.16 million.

Note that the value at risk of a power contract is a function of the following variables:

- the tenor of the power contract
- the type of the contract (on-peak, off-peak, or around-the-clock)
- the delivery rate (MW/h)
- the current unit price of the contract
- the volatility of unit price fluctuation

We observe that the value at risk is not dependent on the original contractual price at which the deal was transacted. The sensitivity of VaR to each of the relevant variables can be easily deduced. For example, position VaR is directly proportional to deal tenor. If the tenor of the contract is shortened by one half, we expect that the VaR will also decrease by one half. Since VaR is also directly proportional to h, which is the number of hours per day in which power is deliverable, it is obvious that all else being equal, the VaR for an ATC contract should be bigger than that of a peak-hour contract, which in turn should be bigger than that of an off-peak contract. The formula for position VaR also shows that it is sensitive to the current market level. Should the unit price of electricity decline by 5 percent, we expect that the VaR will decline by a corresponding 5 percent. Conversely, position VaR increases as the price of electricity rises.

QUANTIFYING THE RISK OF A POWER PORTFOLIO

The path-breaking work on modern portfolio theory was done by Harry Markowitz, co-winner of the 1990 Nobel Prize in Economics. Since the advent of modern portfolio theory, professional money managers have used the theory extensively in managing the risk and return of equity portfolios. Recently, J.P. Morgan generalized the analytical framework to analyze the risk associated with various asset classes—bonds, swaps, equities, foreign exchange, etc. Here, we show how modern portfolio theory can be adapted to analyze the risk associated with a portfolio of power contracts.

To simplify the risk analysis, let us assume that our portfolio consists only of forward contracts. In addition, we make the following simplifying assumptions:

1. There is no time value of money.
2. The daily fluctuations of the unit price of electricity underlying each contract in the portfolio are normally distributed.
3. There is structural stability in the variance-covariance matrix—the volatility of the unit price for each underlying contract and the pairwise correlation between the unit prices of any pair of power contracts are stable over time.

To the extent that these assumptions are valid, we can express the variance of the daily fluctuations in portfolio value as:

$$\mathrm{Var}(\Delta W) = \Sigma q_i^2 P_i^2 \sigma_i^2 + 2 \cdot \Sigma\Sigma_{i>j} q_i q_j \rho_{ij}(P_i\sigma_i)(P_j\sigma_j)$$

where:

ΔW = the change in value of the portfolio

qi = the total number of MWh remaining in the ith contract

Pi = current unit price of electricity for the ith contract

$\sigma i2$ = Black-Scholes volatility for the unit price underlying the ith contract

ρij = $\rho(\Delta Pi, \Delta Pj)$

The derivation of this formula is presented in the notes section of this chapter under the title "2. Value at Risk for the Wholesale Book." Note that the formula for portfolio variance is quite similar to that for position variance. The main difference is the presence of the "cross-terms" symbolized as $qi\ qj\ \rho ij\ (Pi\ \sigma i)\ (Pj\sigma j)$.

The portfolio VaR at the 95 percent confidence interval is given by:

$$\text{VaR @ 95\%} = 1.96\ \sigma_p$$
$$\text{where } \sigma_p = \sqrt{\text{Var}(\Delta W)}$$

From the formula, it is obvious that portfolio VaR is a function of the individual asset volatilities and the correlations between assets. Each interasset correlation can range from -1.0 to $+1.0$. In general, assuming that all positions are either long or short (but not both), the higher the correlations, the bigger will be the portfolio VaR. Conversely, the lower the correlations, the smaller will be the portfolio VaR. Note again that the contractual price of electricity is not a factor.

To illustrate how the portfolio VaR formula works, let us assume that there are only two power contracts in an electricity portfolio. Assume further that both are for around-the-clock delivery and at a rate of 25 MW/h. The first contract has 2 years of life remaining. The second contract has 5 years remaining. If the applicable unit price for a 2-year power contract is currently at \$30/MWh and the applicable unit price for a 5-year power contract is currently at \$32/MWh, what is the weekly value at risk for the portfolio, assuming that the volatilities for 2-year and 5-year electricity are 32 percent and 20 percent, respectively, and the correlation between 2-year and 5-year electricity is 50 percent?

The relevant portfolio information is summarized in the notes section of this chapter under the title "3. Portfolio Analysis." Applying the formula for portfolio variance, we can calculate the variance of this two-asset portfolio as:

$$\text{Var}(\Delta W) = q_1^2 P_1^2 \sigma_1^2 + q_2^2 P_2^2 \sigma_2^2 + 2q_1 q_2 \rho_{12}(P_1\sigma_1)(P_2\sigma_2)$$

Since $q_1 = 438,000, P_1 \cdot \sigma_1 = 1.33, q_2 = 1,095,000,$
$P_2 \cdot \sigma_2 = 0.89, \rho_{12} = 0.50,$ we get:

$$\text{Var}(\Delta W) = (438,000 \times 1.33)^2 + (1,095,000 \times .89)^2$$
$$+ 2 \times 438,000 \times 1,095,000 \times .5 \times 1.33 \times .89$$
$$= 1.8512 \cdot 10^{12}$$

Since the distribution for price movement is supposed to be normal, we can compute the weekly value at risk at the 95 percent confidence interval as:

$$\text{VaR}_p \ @ \ 95\% = \$1.96 \cdot \sqrt{(1.8512 \cdot 10^{12}} = \$2.667 \text{ million}$$

The portfolio VaR depends critically on the individual asset volatilities and the correlation coefficient. But while the relationship between asset volatility and VaR is a linear one, the relationship between portfolio VaR and the correlation coefficient is not. The notes section of this chapter entitled "4. Benefit of Diversification" illustrates how the portfolio VaR varies as a function of the correlation level. In general, portfolio VaR decreases as the correlation weakens. But the rate of decrease accelerates as the correlation coefficient declines. The graph shows that the minimum is reached when $\rho = -1.0$. The corresponding portfolio VaR is $761,918.

The benefit of diversification is apparent if we compare the portfolio VaR with the stand-alone VaRs of each portfolio asset. When $= \rho$ 1.0, there is no diversification effect and the VaRs of the two assets in the portfolio are additive. The portfolio VaR is $3.048 million, which is equal to the summation of the two individual VaRs of $1.143 million and $1.905 million, respectively. However, as long as the correlation is less than 1.0, there will be diversification benefit, and the portfolio VaR will be less than the direct summation of the individual asset VaRs. As the correlation turns negative, the two assets become hedges to each other, and the portfolio VaR is substantially reduced. In many cases, the net VaR is less than either of the individual VaRs. However, even when the correlation becomes –1.0, the portfolio VaR does not drop to zero. This is because the individual VaRs of the two assets are not equal.

PUTTING VaR TO WORK

How can the VaR framework be applied to assist business decisions in the power industry? We illustrate it with the following case studies as illustrations.

Evaluating a Deal

One direct application of VaR is in portfolio management. Assuming that you are the portfolio manager for the power marketing and trading arm of a utility company and that your weekly VaR is currently at $23 million, one of your traders would like to do a 5-year, 25-MW deal. The trader anticipates that the profit on the deal will be $2 million. Should the deal be made?

Let us evaluate this deal from the perspective of risk-return tradeoff. From the previous section, we know that the daily VaR for a 5-year, 25-MW deal is $1.16 million. Making some simplifying assumptions, this translates into a weekly VaR of $3.07 million. This means that, evaluating this deal on a stand-alone basis, the risk-return ratio is about 3:2—not a very attractive proposition. However, to the extent that the correlation between this deal and the existing portfolio is less than perfect, there are certain diversification effects that can be expected, which means that the marginal increase in portfolio risk due to this deal will be less than $3.07 million. By incorporating the deal into the portfolio and recalculating the portfolio VaR, we can quantify the margin impact of adding the deal. Suppose the analytical results are as follows:

Original portfolio VaR	$23 million
New portfolio VaR	$24 million
VaR increment	$ 1 million

Note that the change in VaR due to adding this deal is only $1 million, which is less than one third of the deal's stand-alone VaR. This brings the risk-return ratio down to 1:2, which is a much more attractive number.

Setting of Risk Limits

The VaR framework can be used for setting up risk limits. Traditionally, trading limits are set using parameters that are not associated with the statistical measurement of risk. In the case of power trading, for example, the trading manager may set up limits to restrict the total number of megawatts traded, the maximum tenor of a deal, the net amount long or short, and so on. A trader of electricity futures may have a limit in terms of the total number of contracts he or she can leave uncovered. Somewhat more sophisticated are the risk limits based of sensitivities. For example, a trader's limit can be defined in terms of the maximum profit or loss allowed for a given amount of market movement. There are several common problems with these risk limits—they do not incorporate portfolio effects and they provide no probabilistic measure of loss. As a result, this may lead to wrong trading decisions. A deal may be rejected because it carries substantial megawatt hour exposure. However, as was shown before, depending on the correlation between this deal and the rest of the portfolio, it may or may not introduce substantial marginal risk.

Trading limits based on VaR can overcome these limitations. Incorporating asset volatilities and correlations, VaR-based trading limits enable power traders to have better risk control and make better trading decisions. At Cinergy, the power marketing and trading group is assigned an overall VaR limit, which is delegated downward to the trader level. Note that, because of portfolio effects, the summation of all traders' risk limits will exceed the overall trading limit. By taking into account the risk chemistry between traders, portfolios, and regions, the VaR framework provides a solid basis for integrated risk management on a firm-wide level.

Evaluating the Benefit of Geographic Diversity

The synergy of geographic diversity is often a mysterious number that is difficult to quantify. However, from the perspective of risk management, it is not difficult to get a rough estimate of the benefit of geographic diversification. For example, assume that a power marketing and trading entity trades in two different geographic locations. The first region has a total position of 20,000 MW and an average utilization ratio of 75 percent. The spot price of electricity in its region is currently at $25/MWh, with an annualized volatility of 150 percent. The second region has a total position of 15,000 MW and an average utilization ratio of 90 percent. The spot price of electricity in the second utility's region is currently at $20/MWh, with an annualized volatility of 175 percent. What kind of diversification benefit is there?

Using the methodology we established before and focusing only on the on-peak production of 1 day, we analyzed the VaRs of these two regional positions. The results are presented in the notes section of this chapter entitled "5. Geographic Diversity Analyses." We find that the two regions have a daily production VaR of $923,320 and $775,589, respectively. The undiversified VaR is therefore $1,698,908. If we assume that their spot prices have a 50 percent correlation, we can estimate the diversification benefit using the portfolio VaR formula as follows:

Undiversified VaR	$1,698,908
Diversified VaR	$1,473,151
Risk reduction	$225,757
VaR/MV	14.27%

Thus, we find that the risk due to electricity price movement is reduced by 13 percent from $1,698,908 to $1,473,151. The VaR to market value ratio (VaR/ MV) of the combined portfolio is 14.27 percent, whereas the same ratios for the two regions are 15.39 percent and 17.95 percent, respectively. The benefit of diversification is quite apparent.

Challenge of Implementing VaR

The versatility of VaR in business management is obvious. However, its implementation is not as easy as it may seem. In the previous two sections of this chapter, we mentioned some of the simplifying assumptions that we have to make to implement VaR. As a reminder, these assumptions include the facts that price movements are normally distributed and that price volatilities and correlations are stable over time. In reality, price movements are never exactly normal, and volatilities and correlations are never very stable. The VaR number is therefore more a rough guide as to the magnitude of portfolio risk and a framework to perform scenario analysis than a precise risk measure. In particular, the normality assumption implies that asset prices will have a symmetric distribution, which is definitely not true when option instruments are involved. While more sophisticated mathematical methods can be used to calculate VaR when things deviate from the simplifying assumptions, they also tend to substantially increase complexity and computation time.

There are also problems that are specific to the nascent power industry. The portfolio VaR formula requires asset prices as inputs. In mature financial markets, asset prices can be readily observed. In the power market, however, prices for electricity with a delivery date that extends beyond 1 year are still difficult to observe. This creates more uncertainty on the VaR number. Even more difficult is the quantification of asset volatilities and correlations. Often, what is needed are the volatilities and correlations of forward prices. While volatilities and correlations on spot prices are readily observable, they are not that useful because spot prices of electricity exhibit strong seasonality and hour-to-hour variations. To conduct the VaR analysis properly, we need volatility and correlation data on the relevant forward prices. However, historic data on forward prices are very scarce, making the computation of these statistics very difficult.

Finally, there are organization challenges. VaR is still a foreign concept to many business managers and executives.

However, the effective use of VaR requires cooperation at all corporate levels. One prerequisite for implementing VaR is therefore extensive corporate education and training. Board members and corporate executives have to learn how VaR can be used as a tool to fulfill their fiduciary duties and shield them from certain liabilities without imposing excessive managerial burdens. Once the limit structure based on VaR is established, there is no need to micromanage. Traders and originators have to understand that VaR is not just a part of a control process which limits their freedom. They have to come to see that it is also an empowerment tool that creates a certain safe haven within which risk can legitimately be taken and creativity exercised. VaR is also a system-intensive venture. Proper implementation of VaR requires commitment of significant corporate resources, and both human and financial capital, to be successful. Management in the utility business has to understand why VaR is vital to its company's survival in this rapidly transforming industry and be willing to do what is necessary.

All in all, the implementation of VaR in the power industry faces many hurdles and requires much effort. Our experience, however, is that it is well worth it. In fact, the president of Cinergy's Energy Commodity Business Unit, J. Wayne Leonard, often remarks that he cannot see running this business without this system. As Mr. Leonard stated, "The only choice left is to exit the business."

NOTES

1. Value at Risk for a Single Power Contract

Let q = number of megawatt hours remaining in the power contract

        θ = the original unit price of electricity as specified in the power contract

        P = the current unit price of electricity for the contract

If we ignore the time value of money, the value of a power contract X can be expressed as follows:

$$X = q \cdot (P - \theta) \tag{10.1}$$

where q is positive for a long position and negative for a short position.

Taking the differential on both sides, we have:

$$\Delta X = q \cdot \Delta P \tag{10.2}$$

Taking the variance on both sides of the equation:

$$\mathrm{Var}(\Delta X) = q^2 \cdot \mathrm{Var}(\Delta P) \tag{10.3}$$

Note that $\mathrm{Var}(\Delta P)$ can either be directly calculated from a historic time series or derived from a Black-Scholes volatility. The following is the approximate relationship between absolute variance and relative variance:

$$\mathrm{Var}(\Delta P / P) \approx P^{-2} \cdot \mathrm{Var}(\Delta P) \tag{10.4}$$

From Equations 10.3 and 10.4, we derive:

$$\mathrm{Var}(\Delta X) = P^2 \cdot q^2 \cdot \mathrm{Var}(\Delta P / P) \tag{10.5}$$

The standard deviation of the portfolio value can then be expressed as:

$$\sigma(\Delta X) = q \cdot P \cdot \sigma \tag{10.6}$$

where σ = $\mathrm{Var}(\Delta P / P)$ = Black-Scholes volatility of the unit price.

Since we assume that ΔP is normally distributed, we can assert:

$$\Pr\left[-1.96 \le \left(\Delta X - m\right) / \gamma \le +1.96\right] = 95\% \tag{10.7}$$

where $m = E(\Delta X)$ and $\gamma = \sigma(\Delta X)$.

Assuming that $m = 0$, the value at risk for the power contract at a 95 percent confidence interval can be expressed as:

$$VaR = 1.96 \cdot \gamma \qquad (10.8)$$

Substituting Equation 10.6, we can express the value at risk of the power contract at 95 percent confidence as:

$$VaR = 1.96 \cdot q \cdot P \cdot \sigma \qquad (10.9)$$

Let:
N = # days remaining in the power contract
h = # h/day
w = # MW/h
Then, q can be expressed as:

$$q = N \cdot h \cdot w \qquad (10.10)$$

2. Value at Risk for the Wholesale Book

Assume that the wholesale book is composed entirely of forward contracts. The market value of such a portfolio can be expressed as:

$$W = \Sigma_n X_i \qquad (10.11)$$

where Xi = market value of the ith contract
n = total number of contracts in the portfolio

From Equation 10.1, we can express the market value of each power contract as:
where:

$$X_i = q_i \cdot (P_i - \theta_i) \qquad (10.12)$$

qi = the total number of megawatt hours remaining in the ith contract
Pi = current unit price of electricity for the ith contract
θ_i = contractual unit price of electricity for the ith contract

From Equations 10.11 and 10.12, we deduce:

$$\Delta W = \sum{}_n q_i(\Delta P_i) \qquad (10.13)$$

If the ΔP_i's are normally distributed, then ΔW will also be normally distributed, with a variance expressed as:

$$\text{Var}(\Delta W) = \sum q_i^2 \, \text{Var}(\Delta P_i) + 2 \cdot \sum\sum{}_{i>j} q_i \cdot q_j \cdot \rho(\Delta P_i, \Delta P_j) \cdot \sigma(\Delta P_i) \cdot \sigma(\Delta P_j) \quad (10.14)$$

Define:
$u_i = \sigma(\Delta P_i)$
$\rho_{ij} = \rho(\Delta P_i, \Delta P_j)$
Then, Equation 10.14 can be rewritten as:

$$\text{Var}(\Delta W) = \sum q_i^2 u_i^2 + 2 \cdot \sum\sum{}_{i>j} q_i q_j \rho_{ij} u_i u_j \qquad (10.15)$$

From Equation 10.5, we deduce:

$$u_i = \sigma(\Delta P_i) \approx P_i \cdot \sigma(\Delta P_i / P_i) \qquad (10.16)$$

Substituting Equation 10.16 into Equation 10.15:

$$\text{Var}(\Delta W) = \sum q_i^2 P_i^2 \sigma_i^2 + 2 \cdot \sum\sum{}_{i>j} q_i q_j \rho_{ij} P_i \sigma_i P_j \sigma_j \quad (10.17)$$

Since we assume that ΔW is normally distributed, we can write the 95 percent confidence interval for ΔW as:

$$Pr[\, -1.96 \le (\Delta W - \mu_p)/\sigma_p \le +1.96 \,] = 95\% \quad (10.18)$$

where $\sigma_p = \sqrt{\text{Var}(\Delta W)}$

If we assume that there is no drift in the change in portfolio value, (i.e., $\rho = 0$), then we can express the portfolio VaR at 95 percent confidence as:

$$\text{VaR} = 1.96\sigma_p \qquad (10.19)$$

Considering the case in which there are only two assets in the portfolio, Equation 10.17 will be simplified as:

$$\text{Var}(\Delta W) = q_1^2 P_1^2 \sigma_1^2 + q_2^2 P_2^2 \sigma_2^2 + 2q_1 q_2 \rho_{12}(P_1\sigma_1)(P_2\sigma_2) \quad (10.20)$$

The portfolio variance is a function of the correlation between the portfolio components. Let us explore three correlation scenarios:

1. Perfect Correlation ($\rho_{12} = 1.0$)

$$\text{Var}(\Delta W) = q_1^2 P_1^2 \sigma_1^2 + q_2^2 P_2^2 \sigma_2^2 + 2q_1 q_2 (P_1 \sigma_1)(P_2 \sigma_2)$$

This can be simplified as:

$$\text{Var}(\Delta W) = [q_1(P_1\sigma_1) + q_2(P_2\sigma_2)]^2$$

From Equation 10.6, we deduce:

$$\sigma_p = \sigma(\Delta X_1) + \sigma(\Delta X_2)$$

Here, we see that in the case of two perfectly correlated assets the risks are directly additive. The portfolio does not benefit from any diversification effect. In the case where the two assets are not perfectly correlated ($\rho_{12} < 1.0$), there will be some diversification, and the risk of the portfolio will be less than the direct sum of the risks of the two individual assets.

2. No Correlation ($\rho_{12} = 0.0$)

$$\text{Var}(\Delta W) = q_1^2 P_1^2 \sigma_1^2 + q_2^2 P_2^2 \sigma_2^2 \leq [q_1(P_1\sigma_1) + q_2(P_2\sigma_2)]^2$$

If all positions are in the same direction (i.e., either all long or all short), then:

$$\text{Var}(\Delta W) = a_1^2 P_1^2 \sigma_1^2 + q_2^2 P_2^2 \sigma_2^2$$

Therefore, we can write the following inequality for portfolio risk:

$$\sigma_p \leq \sigma(\Delta X_1) + \sigma(\Delta X_2)$$

Note that this inequality applies to all cases in which the correlation is less than perfect ($\rho_{12} \leq 1.0$). The inequality signifies the diversification effect.

3. Perfectly Negative Correlation (ρ_{12}=-1.0)

$$\text{Var}(\Delta W) = q_1^2 P_1^2 \sigma_1^2 + q_2^2 P_2^2 \sigma_2^2 - 2q_1 q_2 (P_1 \sigma_1)(P_2 \sigma_2)$$

After factoring, we can rewrite the equation as:

$$\text{Var}(\Delta W) = [q_1(P_1 \sigma_1) - q_2(P_2 \sigma_2)]^2$$

Alternatively, we can express the portfolio risk as:

$$\sigma_p = \text{Abs}[\sigma(\Delta X_1) - \sigma(\Delta X_2)]$$

In the case where $\sigma(X_1) \neq \sigma(X_2)$, we can write:

$$\sigma_p \leq \text{Min}[\sigma(\Delta X_1), \sigma(\Delta X_2)]$$

When $\sigma(\Delta X_1) = \sigma(\Delta X_2)$, we have the case of perfect hedging, and the variance of the portfolio value is zero.

3. Portfolio Analysis

	Contract 1	Contract 2
# MW/h	25	25
Remaining term (yrs)	2	5
# Days	730	1825
Contract type	ATC	ATC
Total # hr.	17,520	43,800
# MWh(Q)	438,000	1,095,000
Applicable unit price	$30.00	$32.00
Price volatility (annualized)	32%	20%
Price volatility (weekly)	0.044376016	0.02773501
Vol x Price	$1.33	$0.89
Individual VaR	$1,142,878	$1,904,796

4. Benefit of Diversification

FIGURE 10.1

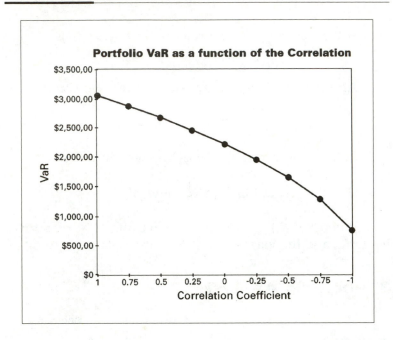

Portfolio VaR as a function of the Correlation

5. Geographic Diversity Analysis

	Region 1	Region 2	Combined Portfolio
Total Capacity (MW)	20,000	15,000	35,000
Capacity Utilization	75%	90%	
Number of Hours/Day	16	16	
Total MWh/Day	240,000	216,000	456,000
Current Price ($/MWh)	25	20	
Volatility (annual)	150%	175%	
Daily Volatility	7.85%	9.16%	
Price x Volume	1.9628397	1.831983729	
Position Variance	2.219E+11	1.56585E +11	
VaR @ 95%	$923,320	$775,589	$1,689,908
Market Value	$6,000,000	$4,320,000	$10,320,000
VaR/MV	15.39%	17.95%	16.46%

CHAPTER 11

Technical Analysis in Energy Trading

By Henry Lichtenstein

INTRODUCTION

While it is an article of faith within the commodity futures trading industry that technical analysis is a required tool for successful trading and for optimizing risk management and hedging programs, every industry that has been drawn into hedging by the advent of new markets has initially viewed technical analysis as a seemingly irrational or unnecessary requirement.

Industry professionals sincerely believe that their understanding of the fundamentals of their own industry is so comprehensive that their knowledge and experience are all they need to effectively manage their risks with fledgling futures contracts. Let it be stated at the forefront: Technicians are not suggesting that hedgers cease analyzing their markets fundamentally, nor are they advocating that hedgers abandon their professional knowledge of supply and demand factors that affect the prices of the commodity inputs and outputs used in their industry. What is being suggested is that trading without integrating technical analysis will put them at a disadvantage vis-à-vis more enlightened and open-minded competitors.

Commercial traders of new types of futures contracts, such as financial instruments, petroleum, and natural gas, have been highly skeptical, if not downright hostile, toward technicians, speculators, and "locals" (exchange members trading on the floor for their own account) who participate in the determination of the price of "their" commodity and even to the idea that price is determined so transparently and widely disseminated. This has certainly been the case with the recent introduction of electricity futures on the New York Mercantile Exchange. In this environment of change and clashing perceptions, no issue is more disconcerting to uninitiated commercial interests than the commodity futures industry's conviction that all markets can be successfully interpreted with technical analysis. It takes a good deal of practical experience to understand that technical analysis does not contradict the fundamentals, but is actually complementary.

Generally, what is referred to as technical analysis is the analysis of past price behavior of a market in order to make probability predictions of future price behavior of that market. The techniques are well known in the securities industry, but the case can be made that they are used more universally in the futures industry because they are so effective. Although very complicated models and techniques do exist, for the purpose of this essay we are strong adherents of the KISS (Keep It Simple, Stupid) principle, and we reference only the most basic (and effective) concepts of trend analysis and pattern identification of price data charted as high/low/settle bar charts.

The reasons that technical analysis is effective are varied. Understanding why it is effective requires a large measure of common sense and an open mind with a strong bent to empiricism and a lack of bias. In addition, it requires some understanding of human nature and of the structure of participation within a liquid futures market.

Under the heading of common sense let us first say that a picture is worth a thousand words. The graphical representation of price history is a picture that only a fool of a hedger could believe has no value. Moreover, this graphical representation should be consistent with what other traders are looking at, not some unique representation that somebody has represented as some kind of a secret to the universe. That brings us to the next commonsense item. There is no secret to the universe, or least there is no such secret that anybody has discovered, and most important, there is no such secret that anybody is willing to "share" for a few hundred dollars, more or less. The absolute proof that no such secret for successful trading exists is that, if it did, the possessors of the secret would already own the world and everything in it. This is not to say that technical traders and technical trading systems cannot be successful and profitable or that technical analysis cannot help hedgers optimize and help time their hedges. It is to say that there are logical limits to what the tool can accomplish.

Technical analysis is a game of guesstimated probabilities. Even if a future event has a high probability that it will happen in the near future, this probability is less than 100 percent because technical analysts cannot see the future and are not predicting the future. They are not fortunetellers or tea leaf readers, nor are they using ancient esoteric divination methods of the exotic Orient. What they are doing, or should be doing, is producing a probability array for all possible outcomes and grouping bullish and bearish scenarios. Unfortunately, the actual probability of each price scenario is subjectively guesstimated, based on the experience and skill of the technician, and is not mathematically arrived at.

If the probability of bullish scenarios is guesstimated at 70 percent, it follows that the probability of the not bullish (neutral and bearish) scenarios is 30 percent. As anybody who has fooled around with probability will attest, probabilities come home to roost. So every time technicians suggest that a market is likely to move in a certain direction and in a certain manner, the technicians know that, if they have done their job and analyzed the market properly, then they are going to be right only a certain percentage of the

time. This is a serious limitation and must be clearly understood to utilize technical input effectively. However, the
value comes in realizing that professional technical analysis
can identify high-probability events accurately and that this
identification will be beneficial not in any one single use but
in many uses over time.

TREND ANALYSIS

The underlying assumption of trend analysis is that, once a
price trend is set in motion, it will tend to stay in motion,
more or less indefinitely. The corollary to this assumption is
equally important: all trends break. The most effective model
of a trend is the simplest, the equation of a straight line, $Y =
mX + b$, where m is the slope of a trendline. What a technician
is primarily concerned with is the sign of m. An uptrend line
has a positive slope, and a downtrend has a negative slope.
Uptrends are drawn along lows, and downtrends are drawn
along highs. An uptrend is defined as a series of higher highs
and higher lows, and a downtrend is defined as a series of
lower lows and lower highs. This means that an uptrend
exists on a chart if a market has made a discernible low, rallies to a discernible high, and then dips lower but stays above
the earlier low. When the market then rallies above the first
high, it creates the series of higher highs and higher lows
required for an uptrend line, which is drawn by connecting
the lows and extending the line into the future. Downtrends
are analogously created and drawn along the highs. A bar
chart has many points, and any two connected points form a
line. However, there are only a few currently valid and functioning trendlines that meet the criteria of the required series
of highs on a contract chart or longer-term chart at any point
in time. Trendlines may exist over different terms, from near
to long term, but the definitions of short and long term are a
bit slippery and dependent on whether a daily, weekly, or
monthly bar chart is being discussed. Even a casual examination of a variety of actual commodity futures life of contract price charts from various markets over any period of
time will offer compelling visual evidence of the price trend-
ing tendency of markets.

A technical trader's most basic trading strategy is to either buy a dip to an uptrend line or sell a rally to a downtrend line. Based on the assumption that any uptrend is likely to hold the market and not be broken, then the trendline is likely to provide support, and the market will bounce to new highs. If the market does not bounce and in fact the trendline breaks as we know all trendlines eventually do, then the technical trader is "stopped" out of the trade with a small loss. The object is to make opportunistic trades where the market is likely to hold trend and thus produce a big profit, and even if the trendline does not hold the market and is broken, only a small loss would result. Thus, the most basic technical technique using trend analysis can produce a high probability of a successful trade that also has a high ratio of reward to risk. Wall Street traditionally expresses the usefulness of trends as "the trend is your friend."

The concepts of support and resistance are critical. Support and resistance are generated in several ways. The market would have support from an uptrend and resistance at a downtrend as discussed in the previous paragraph. Since trendlines by definition are linear, they have a constant slope, so we can easily project where the trendline will be at any date in the future. Trendlines are only broken on a close basis; intraday penetrations not confirmed by the close are only nicks. Another major generator of support and resistance is lateral support and resistance based on previous market tops and bottoms. Any price level that has held the market in the past from either direction is capable of holding a future market move in either direction. In other words, when resistance is broken by a market eventually moving above the resistance, the former resistance level will then immediately be converted into a support level. Moreover, a later break under this support will reconvert the price level into resistance.

The interchangeability of lateral support and resistance is based on human nature. For example, imagine becoming the owner by inheritance of a security, XYZ Inc., which is priced at $60. XYZ rallies and you happily watch it trade higher over time until it reaches $100. Then XYZ sells off quickly under $90 and keeps working lower down to $80 before the sell-off runs out of steam. You soon realize that the reason the stock sold off was that many owners had instructed their brokers to sell XYZ if it ever got to $100. Now a bit wiser and more experienced, you like many others would tell yourself that if XYZ ever got back near $100, then you were going to take profits and sell. Eventually, XYZ rallies again and trades back to the high 90s, and you sell your shares at $98, just before the market tops out at $98 1/2 as other stockholders also sell just in front of $100.

This demonstrates the importance of big even numbers to markets and how resistance and support are ultimately a function of human nature. Returning to the hypothetical market for XYZ, we can imagine that the resistance at $100 turned the second rally back and that the people who were hoping that the market would be able to make new highs (because it takes all kinds of people to make a market) are becoming increasingly worried that they have missed the boat once again. As they sell into a declining market, XYZ approaches $80 again. This level had stopped the previous sell-off; thus, it can be identified as support and would generate some bargain hunting buying as it approached $80. However, a break under $80 would result in another wave of selling as the bargain hunters realized they acted prematurely and other holders become increasingly troubled by XYZ's still declining price. They become so troubled that some will sell their shares into the declining market.

This illustrates a technical pattern called a "double top" (see Figure 11.4 for an illustration). This occurs when a market rallies to a new high, dips to an intermediate low, and then rallies to test the high. If the market cannot trade significantly above the old high and the market sells off to test the intermediate low, this price action becomes a potential double top. Potential patterns are not tradable because they are not predictable as to a probability of completion. A double top is completed if and only if the market closes below the intermediate low. Of great importance is the fact that completed double tops usually result in a downside move after completion where the downside move is equal to the vertical distance between the higher of the two highs and the intermediate low. Thus, if XYZ were to close under $80, technicians would project that the market would continue trending lower with a highly likely downside swing objective of $60. They would also indicate that, if the market were to close back over $80, the top pattern would no longer be functional, and the $60 swing objective would be canceled. If one swing objective has been achieved, then a second equal swing objective becomes the target. Likewise, after the second swing objective is achieved, a third equal swing objective becomes likely.

Patterns do not project reliably beyond three swings, and any market that moves further than three swings is governed by trend analysis best expressed in a slightly different context by the immortal New York Yankee legend, Yogi Berra, as "It ain't over till it's over." Other patterns that have similar predictable swing objectives are head and shoulders, tops and bottoms, and triple tops and bottoms. Returning to the market for XYZ one more time, any sustained move above $100 resistance would be bullish, and the market would now have major support at $100. If a double top was not completed and instead the market rallied from $81 off of the test of $80 support above $100, then the market would form a completed double bottom with an upside swing objective of $120, the vertical distance between the lower of the two lows and the intermediate high.

COMMODITY FUTURES TRADING

Now, instead of a security, which at best can be leveraged 2 to 1, consider the case of commodity futures trading where speculators can easily be leveraged 20 to 1. Moreover, given the generally greater volatility of commodity futures prices, it becomes readily apparent that fear and greed are the primary emotions that motivate speculators. In addition, speculators cannot logically hope to understand the fundamentals of a specific commodity market as well as commercial hedgers. Since they still are ready, willing, and able to assume the risks of speculative positions, we must conclude that the use of technical analysis plays a key role in their continued presence in the marketplace. Locals are a specialized version of speculators who generally operate with an incredibly short-term outlook and a very high degree of awareness of short-term technical factors.

Technicians can prepare hedgers, in advance, to be ready for the very large upside potential of certain bull markets as well as the very large downside potential of certain bear markets. Commercial hedgers trained before the advent of futures inevitably think in archaic terms of "unrealistic" or "too high" and "too low" prices and look for some kind of equilibrium. But the futures markets can be very dynamic. By virtue of inevitable substantial speculative participation in liquid markets, large positions are held by financial interests who are by no means indifferent to price movement because they have no cash position moving in an equal and opposite direction. While the leverage of futures makes futures trading so attractive to speculators, the leverage can also lead to economic distress. A bad position can be allowed to become catastrophic, and eventually, an order can be given that is more time sensitive than price sensitive.

In general, futures can overreact to the upside and downside and go further and faster toward major technical targets than hedgers would consider possible. In addition, rogue hedge traders can have unwarranted positions, and the inevitable plug pulling can result in eye-opening but technically viable price action. Moreover, any last day of trading can have wild price movements, and seemingly outrageous technical targets can be achieved if entities unable to make or take delivery overstay their welcome in the expiring contract.

As we have seen, technical analysis is easily utilized by speculators. They have no bias (or should not have a bias) to buying or selling futures, and they have a great need for technical analysis to impose some discipline in their trading decisions, as well as to help level the playing field with locals and hedgers. However, the usefulness of technical analysis is not limited to speculators. At the very least, for commercial hedgers to understand the technical situation and how speculative technical traders will approach a given market and react to changes is a matter of being forewarned, and thus forearmed. In addition, use of technical signals and awareness of supports and resistances are important optimizing tools on a macro- and microbasis.

On a microbasis, even when hedges are established without consideration of whether the market is bullish or bearish, short hedges can be sold opportunistically on rallies to resistance, just as long hedgers may be able to concentrate their buying on dips to support. Patient waiting for relatively small market moves on an intraday basis can be a function of understanding both the immediate short-term technical outlook as well as the longer-term technical picture. In situations where a hedger needs to buy contracts and the market is trading under a significant resistance level, the choice might be made to risk the market going above resistance and then having to quickly buy in a rising market because the odds favor getting a better price in the near term. This type of optimization is common, yet its effectiveness can be judged only by averaging the results of many such attempts.

On a macrobasis, if the market is technically bullish, a long hedger may want to immediately enter the market to put on a hedge. A technical bearish market would strongly suggest that long hedges should be gently layered in over time, with buying conducted just above technical supports. Short hedging can be similarly influenced by the technical outlook. Optimum results would be produced in bear markets by immediate execution of short hedges and by delaying long hedges and clustering buying just in front of technical support zones.

Another primary benefit of technical analysis to commercial users is based on the fact that futures prices reflect all the knowledge of all market participants. While large commercial hedgers may possess all relevant knowledge and be the first to know and realize the importance of some new information for altering the fundamental outlook for the market and thus change the price trend, it would be foolish arrogance for commercials to assume that they always will have the best information first. A careful analysis of the technicals will guarantee that when they are not the first to get trend-changing information, at least they will not be the last.

In situations where the technical outlook is strongly divergent from the fundamentals as the commercial understands them, caution is required. Fundamental information may be carefully reconsidered, and if the analysis remains the same, then the commercial can and should act. However, the technical situation may warrant slower and more advantageous timing to the execution of necessary hedges.

Other interesting situations can be envisioned. A company may suddenly become aware of conditions within the company that have major implications for risk management and likely to seriously influence the price of a commodity. This type of information may actually be inside information as far as the securities markets and regulators are concerned, limiting insiders' ability to legally buy or sell certain securities. However, the concept of inside information does not exist in commodity futures trading in this context. In fact, it would only be ordinary and necessary or even vital business practice to immediately react to the changed realities by going to the futures markets to lift hedges previously required, which now are in need of adjustment or elimination, and to enter into required new hedges as swiftly and anonymously as possible. Moreover, sophisticated hedgers will tend to enter into larger futures positions than strictly required to reap some additional economic benefit when the news reaches the marketplace by liquidating these "extra" long (or short) positions into the ensuing rally. In such situations, it will be quite instructive to keep track of the technical developments in relationship to the release of news to better understand Wall Street's traditional wisdom of "buy the rumor, sell the news."

Technicians will of course be unaware of any "news" before it is released and may not care about any rumors. What they will eventually become aware of is a market that either confirms a top or bottom which they will proclaim upon confirmation. They will realize that some important news will soon be released, but they have probably become used to their fate of never being aware of trend-changing information before their clients, just that it is coming.

The unprecedented major bull market in natural gas futures in late 1996 and the subsequent major bear market which more than retraced the entire bull market provide a case in point. On the natural gas weekly high/low/settle chart (Figure 11.1), which encompasses the entire trading history of the NYMEX natural gas contract, we can see the precursors of this market in the 1995 major bull market. As the market came off the then record high of $3.720 by the January 1996 contract, on its last day of trading on December 21, 1995, the market created major resistance at the $3.100 level. By January 22, 1996, the weekly chart registers a $1.856 low by the March 1996 contract (which was being tracked on the weekly chart along with the February 1996 because it was a roll week). Several bull markets were contained under $3.000 in 1996, which can also be seen on the rolled-over-daily (R-O-D) chart (Figure 11.2). After the October 1996 contract bottomed for the year on the R-O-D at $1.735 on September 5, 1996, the market signaled a bullish breakout by the November 1996, contract rolling into the spot position on September 25, 1996, trading above $2.100 resistance with an upside roll gap. The November 1996 contract rallied all the way to $2.650 on its last day of trading on October 25, 1996. Next, the December 1996 contract climbed above $3.100 major resistance on November 19, 1996, and then rocketed all the way to a new life of trading high of $4.050 just 2 days later on its last day of trading on November 21, 1996. The January 1997 contract (Figure 11.3) dipped to $3.110, on December 3, 1996, where it held just above what is now major support on the R-O-D at $3.100, and it then exploded up to another new record high of $4.600 on December 17, 1996. After some wide swinging action between $4.600 and $3.900, the January 1997 contract expired, trading back down to $3.910 on its last day of trading on December 24, 1996.

FIGURE 11.1

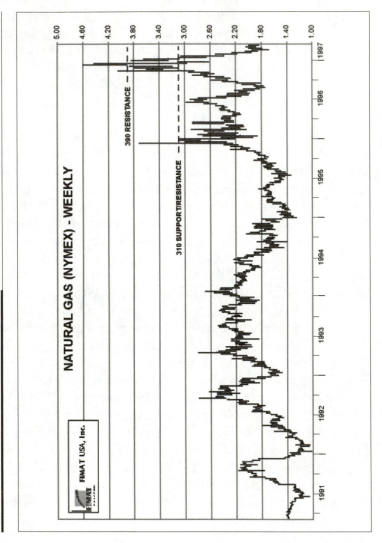

NATURAL GAS (NYMEX) - WEEKLY

390 RESISTANCE

310 SUPPORT/RESISTANCE

FIMAT USA, Inc.

FIGURE 11.2

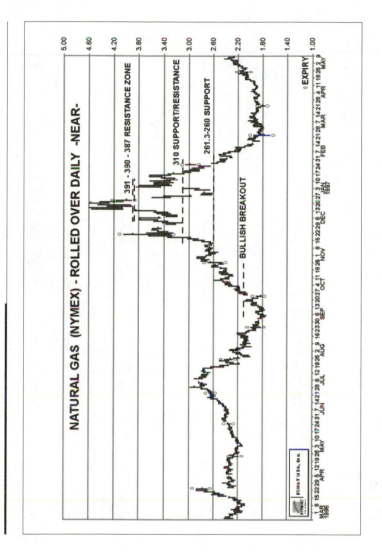

NATURAL GAS (NYMEX) - ROLLED OVER DAILY -NEAR-

391 - 390 - 387 RESISTANCE ZONE

310 SUPPORT/RESISTANCE

261.3-260 SUPPORT

BULLISH BREAKOUT

EXPIRY

FIGURE 11.3

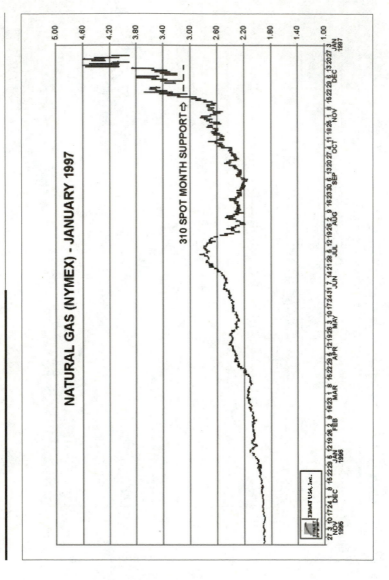

NATURAL GAS (NYMEX) - JANUARY 1997

310 SPOT MONTH SUPPORT ⇦

The roll effect from January 1997 to February 1997 left massive overhead resistance at $3.870–$3.900–$3.910, and the February 1997 contract fell precipitously from a $3.750 high on December 24, 1996, to a $3.595 high on its first day as the spot month the next trading day on December 26, 1996, then all the way down to $2.613 on December 31, 1996. A spectacular bounce reached $3.840 on January 6, 1997, but could not overcome the $3.870–$3.9000–$3.910 major resistance zone, and the February 1997 contract worked back to $2.655 on January 24, 1997, the day before it expired. The March 1997 contract became spot by breaking under potential support on the R-O-D at $2.613–$2.600 and then worked lower. Eventually, the March 1997 chart (Figure 11.4) displayed a major bearish (even if slightly fudged) massive $3.340/$3.400 double top from December 17, 1996/January 6, 1996, with an intermediate low of $2.350 and an enormous downside swing objective of $1.050 below the $2.350 intermediate low down to $1.300. Even though the March 1997 contract could not swing all the way to $1.300, it expired on February 24, 1997, under heavy selling pressure, trading down to a new contract low and a 17-month low basis the nearby of $1.680 on the final bell.

Potential hedgers should note that the January 1997 contract (Figure 11.3), which traded up to a frenzied record high of $4.600 on two different days, was quietly trading below $2.000 for months prior to January 1996.

CONCLUSION

As we have demonstrated, technical analysis is not in opposition to fundamental analysis, but a potentially critical adjunct that goes hand in hand with traditional economic analysis. While a strict technician can look at a long-term chart and point to the various technical signals and how reliable the signals were, a fundamentalist can look at the same long-term chart and put arrows and labels at various tops and bottoms and, in retrospect, detail the major fundamental factors and events that turned the market at those particular times. It's just a question of who knew what, and when, and how helpful either type of analysis was in real time. It's also a question of whether any hedger can afford not to take technical analysis into account.

FIGURE 11.4

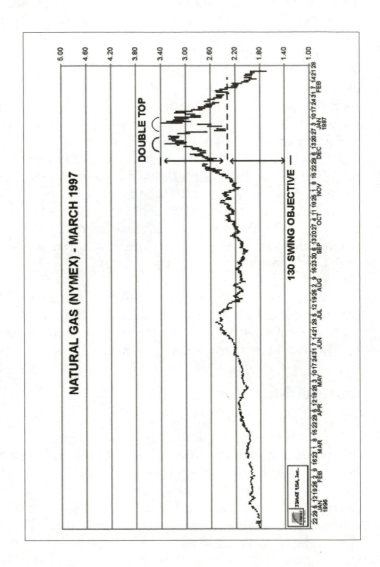

NATURAL GAS (NYMEX) - MARCH 1997

CHAPTER 12

Credit Issues and Counterparty Risk

By Robert Maxant and George Travers

INTRODUCTION

With more opportunities and more market participants in the power and energy industry, electric utilities can expect to face significantly increased credit exposure in the near future. Credit exposures will increase as wholesale transaction volume increases and utilities market to a myriad of relatively unknown, unrated counterparties who are facing competition within their own service territories—regions that were once under their monopoly control.

In today's new competitive market, customers may default on a power contract with one utility and enter into another contract with a company willing to deal with tainted credit in exchange for market share.

In this chapter, we comment on credit risk as it relates to electric utilities. In particular, we discuss:

- Nature of credit risk
- Market participants
- Credit scoring
- Monitoring counterparty creditworthiness

- Estimating credit losses and determining reserves
- Credit spread pricing
- Credit enhancements
- Portfolio effects and concentration ratios
- Active versus passive credit risk decisions
- Credit risk reporting
- Additional observations

NATURE OF CREDIT RISK

Credit risk is the risk that a counterparty will fail to perform on its contractual obligations. Credit risk includes current exposure, which can be measured as the replacement cost of the position or portfolio, and potential exposure from an instrument or portfolio, which may arise over time as a result of market dynamics. Virtually all capital markets and trading transactions involve credit exposure. Over-the-counter transactions such as swaps and options can involve large and very dynamic credit exposures due to market fluctuations.

Current Exposure

Credit judgments affect the pricing, tenor, and terms and ultimate acceptance of most over-the-counter transactions. Customers with low credit ratings often face large bid-offer spreads and find few counterparties willing to engage in transactions, especially those of a longer term. Some market participants will deal only with counterparties with strong credit ratings and may choose to limit their population of potential counterparties based on internal or external credit ratings.

Credit exposure exists whenever the contract valued at replacement costs has a positive value to an entity and (usually) negative value to the counterparty. The current replacement cost of the contract is its mark-to-market value (i.e., the value of a position at current market prices). If the counterparty defaults on the transaction before maturity or expiration of the deal, the entity on the other side of the transaction has an immediate exposure to fill. If the contact is in the money (i.e., has a positive fair value, representing a utility receivable) for the nondefaulting party, then the non-defaulting counterparty has suffered a loss. Thus, all deals with a positive mark-to-market value represent actual credit exposure.

Example

Transacting strategies that a utility could use to reduce market risk may actually increase credit risk (see, for example, Figure 12.1). On October 1, the utility:

- enters into a contract with counterparty A to purchase 100 MWh of electricity at $20/MWh for each weekday from November 1 to January 31 for the hour starting at 7 A.M. and ending at 10 P.M. (peak hours)
- simultaneously, it enters into a contract to sell 100 MW to counterparty B in which all terms are the same, but the per megawatt hour price is $21.

In this scenario, the utility is hedged against market risk: The margin is $1/MWh regardless of an increase or decrease in market rates. However, suppose the market price rises to $25/MWh.

FIGURE 12.1

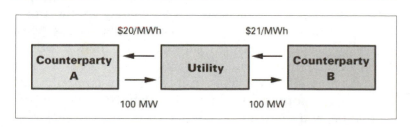

In this instance, the utility is exposed to credit risk. The contract with counterparty B is out of the money because the utility is receiving $21/MWh power in a market in which it could sell power for $25/MWh. The utility's contract with counterparty A is in the money because it is paying $20/MWh in a market in which it would have to buy power for $25/MWh which, if counterparty A were to default, would require it to replace that contract with one that would cost $25/MWh.

Any fixed price commitments related to nuclear fuel, coal, natural gas, or electricity could be subject to such market fluctuations that could cause the contract to be in the money or out of the money at any point throughout the life of the contract.

Netting Provisions

A utility can have different power contracts with different counterparties made at different times. In assessing credit risk on a portfolio of contracts, an organization should measure current exposure on a contract-by-contract basis. If a utility has more than one open transaction with a counterparty, and if default netting provisions are included, then all contracts with that counterparty should be aggregated and netted for purposes of determining current credit exposure.

Potential Exposure

Potential exposure is an estimate of credit exposure in the event of a future change in market price of the underlying commodity. Unlike the credit exposure of a loan, the exposure of a derivative transaction can change as the price, index, or rate of the underlying instrument changes. Most derivative transactions are transacted at market prices; therefore, the mark-to-market value at inception is near zero. As a result, derivatives involving firm commitments (i.e., swaps or forwards), which initially have a zero net present value, and therefore no credit exposure. However, participants in such transactions face credit exposure as market prices of the underlying commodity change during the life of the contract.

Determining the potential exposure on a power or energy contract is more complex than calculating the current exposure; determining the potential exposure on a portfolio of contracts is even more complex. The maximum exposure on an individual contract is a function of several factors: diffusion, mean reversion, and amortization. The *diffusion* effect describes price movement away from the original contract price. Longer contracts tenors and greater volatilities (electricity has the highest daily volatility of any commodity) allow for more significant price movement or "drifting" from the original contract price. Mean reversion and amortization effects are inversely correlated to the diffusion effect. The *mean reversion* effect describes the tendency for electricity (and other commodity) prices to revert to a level commensurate with their cost of generation (production). The *amortization* effect refers to the decrease in exposure over time due to the decreasing time remaining to maturity of the transaction.

For an electricity forward swap, the estimated maximum credit exposure, depending on a number of factors and assumptions, occurs at a period which is approximately 20-40 percent through the term of the transaction (see Figure 12.2).

FIGURE   12.2

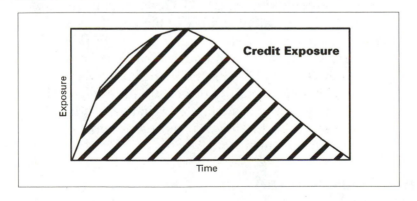

Maximum credit exposure to a utility occurs at different points and would be different in magnitude depending on whether the utility were purchasing or selling electricity at a fixed price.

MARKET PARTICIPANTS

To ensure a certain level of credit quality, instruments traded on an exchange are subject to requirements such as counterparty margins. The exchange also assumes settlement risk. In the near term, the primary contractual instruments are over-the-counter and bilateral contracts, but more exchange-traded market instruments are expected to be developed.

Before entering a bilateral agreement with a counterparty, it is important to understand the counterparty's credit risk and the influences which affect creditworthiness. The participants involved in the market and the issues surrounding their credit risk include:

- **Utilities** are accustomed to dealing with counterparties they know well. However, with competition—new market participants and less stable earnings—utilities need to consider the implications of increased credit exposure to a larger pool of counterparties. Utilities' credit ratings are usually between A and BB.
- **Power marketers** are legally permitted to buy and sell electricity at market prices, and these activities can involve significant risk. Today, many are subsidiaries of parents with varying credit, though the support a parent will give if a credit problem arises is unclear. Many power marketers are thinly capitalized and on a stand-alone basis. Many, whether creditworthy or not, are unrated. Marketers may not have adequate capital to weather losses, which might occur during periods of market volatility.

- **Municipalities**, for the most part, have little to no experience with power and energy markets. Others have been active for some time. Those municipalities with no experience will not be able to actively manage market and credit risk. It is therefore important to consider municipalities' creditworthiness, along with the risks their strategy may imply.

- **Commercial and investment banks** functions may include activities in wholesale marketing, power operations, fuel supply, and financial risk management. Such entities are generally experienced in transacting and in managing market and credit risk. These institutions also possess large capital bases and have established credit ratings that are usually single A or better.

- **Independent power producers (IPPs)** are electricity producers that are not traditional, vertically integrated utilities. They are under different contractual agreements with respect to generation, transmission, and distribution. These entities' earnings may be subject to greater levels of volatility than current regulated monopoly utilities. The capital bases and creditworthiness of these entities vary significantly.

- **Energy-dependent and nonenergy-dependent corporations** (large industrial and commercial electricity users) will be able to purchase electricity from several different competing sources in the near future. The larger of these counterparties may be rated and may issue certified financial statements. It will be more difficult to discern the creditworthiness of smaller participants.

- **Brokers** are legally obligated or restricted from transactions with certain parties, and these requirements must be understood, as must the relative creditworthiness of the counterparties. Brokers' degrees of credit risk depend on the availability of capital, their past history with power and energy, and their lines of credit. While many brokers are affiliated with well-known banks, and therefore gain credibility, others are not.

CREDIT SCORING

A counterparty's creditworthiness is based on the probability that it will default on its contractual obligations. Therefore, credit classification is perceived as the creditworthiness of a counterparty in general or with respect to financial obligations. While organizations like Standard & Poor's, Moody's, and Fitch provide ratings for many large companies, many medium and small potential electricity counterparties are not currently rated by these agencies. In many cases, utilities will be required to perform their own credit analysis and perhaps establish internal rating criteria. Classifications must be based solely on the fundamentals of the potential customer's creditworthiness relative to the returns that may be earned by transacting with that customer.

Ratings

Rating agencies often provide general guidelines on ratings criteria for various industry categories. Single utilities should focus on the key industries they serve and develop ratio ranges for different credit levels in those industries. Issues to consider in evaluating general industrial clients include:

Business Risk	Financial Risk
Industry characteristics	Financial characteristics
Competitive position, such as:	Financial policy
- Marketing	Profitability
- Technology	Capital structure
- Efficiency	Cash flow protection
Management	Financial flexibility

Source: Standard & Poor's Corporate Ratings Criteria.

Power marketers and brokers are an important counterparty type for which limited information on ratings criteria is available. These potential counterparties may have high credit risk due to:

- limited physical assets or steady cash flows to fall back on
- significant net market positions (on an overall commodity market, in particular locations, and/or at various points on the forward curve)
- inadequate capitalization
- lack of credit risk analysis for contracts they are already involved with

In determining the credit quality of power marketers, possible factors to consider power include those in Table 12.1.

We observe that a solid parent (or other party) guarantee would give the power marketer the same credit rating as the parent (net of consideration of power marketing cash flow effect on parent). To the extent the relationship seems less protective, ratings should rely more on the fundamental business aspects of the power marketer alone.

TABLE 12.1

Business Performance and Profitability size	Financial strategy, practicality of business objectives, reputation and scale
Corporate Structure and Capital and	Key operating and financial plans, ownership, subsidiary relation degree of support from parent
Risk Management Policies and Internal Controls	Cash flow protection, financial flexibility, means by which company manages price risk, basis risk, physical/delivery risk, etc.
Management and Staff	Management polices, reputation of officers, link of corporate

A utility may create an internal rating system based on certain attributes that are deemed to be the most correlated to the credit quality of the counterparty. Such a rating system would be determined by the extent to which the counterparty meets certain criteria. Based on our experience, an AAA to A+ rated company would have the characteristics shown in Table 12.2, and companies with less strong characteristics would have lower ratings.

Similar classifications could be developed for other groups of customers. To develop these ratios and credit classifications, access to relevant information and documents is required. At times, one utility may have a competitive advantage in access to that information (for certain customers and/or markets). At other times, that utility may not. Documents and information that may be required on a potential counterparty include the following:

TABLE 12.2

- Past market experience in the derivatives markets including participation in the evolution of energy markets (i.e., crude oil, refined products, and natural gas);
- Large amounts of capital; and
- Strong lines of credit:
- Adequate cash flow;
- History of consistently stable profits;
- No past history of defaults. Increasing revenues and earnings;
- Reputable managers, strong corporate structure, strong corporate leadership
- The company has the necessary resources to manage its own risks;
- Well-designed pricing system;
- Well-documented company;
- An obligor for which any bank of finance company would approve the deal. Very low level of debt.
- Diversified and flexible, i.e., able to deal with market volatility through diversification. Flexible company structure which allows company to mitigate risks.

- Credit reports
- Financial statements
- Understanding of degree of financial and operating leverage
- Knowledge of debt covenants; other information on debt performance
- Business/marketing plans
- Information on lines of credit
- Cash flow management strategies and performance
- Quality of controls, results of audits

- Lease information
- Accounts payable characteristics
- Information on company performance/sales results
- Information on stability of large customers and markets
- Industry economic trends
- Information on employee turnover
- Risk management strategies and management of net exposures (sensitivity to market volatility)
- Legal information

As appropriate, portions or all of these documents should be updated throughout the life of the contract.

Credit classification (sometimes referred to as "bucketing" is a process that groups similar counterparties and arrives at generalized default probabilities and recovery rates. Rather than estimating these for each individual customer or counterparty, looking at those with similar ratios, capital structure, growth rate, and so forth, may be an efficient way to understand credit risk in a large-volume setting. If default rates within a given credit classification show wide dispersion and volatility, or do not develop trends and characteristics different from other classes, then the process of classification should be done on a more granular basis. In a developing market with large groups of customers unrated by any rating agency, it will be important to "backtest" internal ratings assigned in order to assess and adjust the credit classification model.

MONITORING COUNTERPARTY CREDITWORTHINESS

Monitoring a counterparty's creditworthiness involves understanding industry-specific trends and reviewing the financial performance of firms, that are similar to the counterparty. Generally, companies should perform periodic formal reviews of counterparties for which lines of credit have been granted. The depth and frequency of such periodic reviews will vary. Counterparties which are less creditworthy, which have larger exposures, or for which there is less publicly available information should be reviewed more frequently. A company should also have the capability to perform ad hoc reviews as it becomes aware of specific issues regarding a counterparty's creditworthiness.

Estimating Credit Losses and Determining Reserves

Estimates of expected losses can be determined through observation of marketplace credit spreads or through theoretical calculation. Observed marketplace credit spreads embed within them the consensus market expectation of estimated credit losses. If credit-adjusted price curves are used for portfolio valuation, then additional credit reserves need be made only for credit counterparties and/or specific situations. If, as is much more likely, credit-adjusted price curves are not available, then estimates of expected credit losses must be theoretically calculated.

Calculating estimates of expected credit losses can be complex. Generally, the estimate of expected credit losses can be determined by multiplying current and potential exposures by credit-weighted default factors. The resultant expected loss is further reduced by expected recoveries. These historically average approximately 40 percent across all counterparties. The calculation of expected loss may be described as follows:

> This calculation should be performed on a transaction-by-transaction basis or, if default netting is permitted, by aggregating all transactions for each counterparty.
>
> Estimates of expected credit losses are complex to determine and are influenced by the judgment and assumptions underlying the calculations:
>
> - The calculation of potential exposure is determined through a value-at-risk calculation, which is significantly influenced by the confidence interval, the holding period chosen, and other assumptions.
> - Credit-weighted default probabilities are based on historic averages. Publicly available default probability

estimates represent averages across many industries, which do not reflect the specific default probabilities of the power and energy industries.

- Default probabilities also represent averages across time. These averages may be higher or lower at different points in the business cycle.
- Calculating expected losses for a portfolio generally assumes that the portfolio is large and diversified.
- Failure to appropriately consider credit "migration" or "drift" may cause estimates of expected losses to be understated.

CREDIT SPREAD PRICING

The total commodity price charged by a utility should be based partially on the counterparty's credit after consideration of any credit enhancements offered by it. The following is a hypothetical example to show how there are a number of similar ways to arrive at a price that embeds credit risk:

1. A utility could start from a risk-free price curve. Credit spreads would then be added to the risk-free curve. As shown in Figure 12.3, a high-quality

FIGURE 12.3

Credit-Adjusted Price Curves (Ask or Sell Prices from One Utility's Viewpoint) Forward Prices from Power Markets Weekly

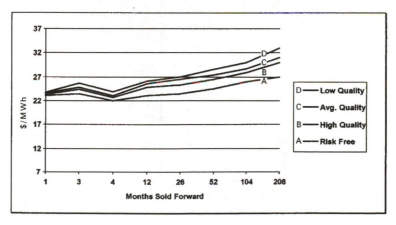

credit would have the amount from point A to B added to the no credit price. A low-quality credit would have the amount from A to D added.

2. Beginning from midmarket or average credit price (with a credit charge for average quality already embedded), dollar amounts could be added for low-quality credit (C to D) and subtracted for high-quality credit (C to B). This average rating would be similar to a Standard & Poor's rating of A or A−.

3. If counterparty credit was homogeneous, for certain counterparty segments or in total, a single price average-quality curve price (point C) could be used.

A few points bear mentioning:

1. These curves represent what the utility would sell power for (i.e., the ask or offer price). The bid/ask structure is described further below.

2. Alternative A may be impractical due to the limited number of high credits in the marketplace. The futures contract at Palo Verde and COB essentially represent a risk-free price. However, all other delivery points will have basis risk to both COB and Palo Verde. In addition, because an east coast

FIGURE 12.4

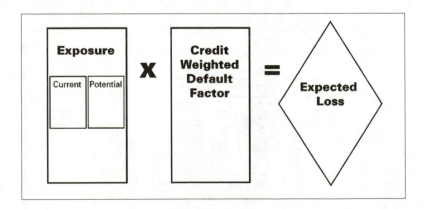

contract does not exist and eastern grid electricity prices are not perfectly correlated to the aforementioned futures contracts, "risk free" does not hold for east coast delivery.

3. The credit spread should generally be more than the actual expected dollar amount of credit loss to reflect a profit on the taking of credit risk. Apart from the marketing of power, the taking of credit risk implies certain costs, uncertainty, and expected profit based. To account for credit risk, a participant could book a reserve for each contract to represent the expected loss. Taking an example, if the midmarket price for power in 7 days is $22, and we have a low-quality credit, we may add a spread of 18 cents. At the same,time we may book a reserve against the deal for 13 cents to reflect the actual credit risk. In the same way the $22 amount reflects a profit on electricity (sale price less cost to buy or produce), the 18 cents reflects a profit on the taking of credit risk (sale price less cost to buy credit protection).

4. Each credit curve is subject to a bid/ask spread. This is true even for the risk-free price curve because the bid/ask spread also reflects the fact that we are transacting in what may be an illiquid market. Even if it was liquid, as with Treasuries, we would still have a small bid/ask spread. Regardless of liquidity, marketers impose a spread because, at a minimum, they have workers to pay and computers to buy in order to be present to buy and sell.

In reality, the amount for which the utility would buy power (bid price) from an average-quality credit would not be higher than that paid to a high-quality credit. Hence, the bid curve in Figure 12.3 may actually be lower. In this way, the actual bid/ask curves for high-, average-, and low-quality credits would actually have a nested structure. Low-quality credits would be charged the highest price to buy power and receive the lowest price for supplying power (assuming there is credit risk for the counterparty in both cases). Because of this structure, in certain cases midcurve prices may be inappropriate for marking to market deals. In all cases, valuing deals by specific bid and ask curves results in increased precision above the midvalue convention.

CREDIT ENHANCEMENTS

Credit enhancements may be classified into two categories: those done by the counterparty and those done by the utility.

When credit enhancements are executed by the counterparty, the counterparty may agree to various contractual provisions, guarantees, or collateral agreements. If the counterparty enters into these, it is the one paying for them. The credit risk spread charged by the utility would then be decreased to reflect the "all-in" credit quality including consideration of the credit enhancement. Types of provisions or agreements include: *default netting provisions* (require that all contracts with a counter-party be netted and aggregated in the event of a default); *credit termination provisions* (require that a contract be terminated and cash settled in the event of the counterparty's credit downgrade); *credit guarantee* (enhances credit through an affiliate or third-party guarantee or letter of credit, and this provision can also take the form of a credit put, if legal restrictions otherwise exist); *unilateral* or *reciprocal collateral arrangement* (requires that one or either counterparty provide collateral to the counterparty that is in the money).

All of these provisions may result in risk mitigation. Whether implicit or explicit, most provide for the payment of some type of certain dollar amount today in exchange for the laying off of credit risk. These provisions represent options and are similar to traditional insurance contracts. If a guarantor determined that the probability of default was high, the price of the guarantee would be expensive and approach the actual present value of the dollar amount the guarantor expects to pay. If guarantor action is highly unlikely, the price of the guarantee may be extremely low. As an analogy, earthquake insurance is certainly cheaper in Columbus than it is in San Francisco. By the same analogy, guaranteeing the credit of a stable company may be less expensive than guaranteeing that of an unstable one.

Other provisions mentioned, such as collateral arrangements, are equivalent to margin calls in financial markets. These are not options and, if reciprocal, may not require an upfront payment.

The second category of credit enhancement may occur when a utility performs contracts with third parties to increase the credit quality of all or parts of its portfolio. In the extreme case, a utility may desensitize itself from all credit risk. Potential enhancements include credit guarantees provided by third parties and paid for by the utility or credit derivatives.

In cases where a utility is paying for the credit enhancement, the credit spread charged would not be adjusted for it. In addition, we would expect a positive amount in the difference between the amount charged to the customer and the amount paid by the utility to eliminate the risk. In this case, although the utility is not taking the credit risk, the counterparty found the utility and made the deal. A credit marketer may extract a fee or profit over and above that earned for the energy sale.

It is important to note that credit risk management can be part of a company's competitive strategy. It may make sense to underprice credit risk for periods of time, for example, to protect or expand market share. Again, this is a decision of risk versus return. Return may come in any form that furthers the company's objectives, including profits, increased market share, and so on. A company may therefore underprice credit risk, knowing that legal bills and cash flow volatility will increase. Of course, judging the value of potential return is extremely subjective, a further factor to consider in the decision. In cases where the return comes in the form of things other than money, this uncertainty may be exacerbated. Other market conditions may lead to decisions to overprice credit risk or pay premium amounts for credit enhancement.

PORTFOLIO EFFECTS AND CONCENTRATION RATIOS

The concentration ratio for the portfolio is the weighted average of the concentration ratio for each industry. Each industry has a relative importance in this average that depends on the relative exposure dollar value in the portfolio. The overall portfolio concentration ratio is the sum of the squares of the concentration ratios of the constituent industry exposures. The possible values of the concentration ratio range from near zero for a highly diversified portfolio to 100 percent for a portfolio contracting with only one industry ($100\%^2 = 100\%$).

Tracking this ratio allows a utility to measure trends directionally in industry concentration. Limits may be placed on the total ratio and/or contribution by individual industries.

ACTIVE VERSUS PASSIVE RISK MANAGEMENT DECISION

The decision as to which counterparties to transact with, and how to manage the resultant exposures, is an important one. As with other activities, the objective is to maximize the return per unit of risk. A utility should consider the following in assessing the likelihood and price at which credit risk can be transferred to other market participants or financial institutions:

- *Diversification*: A utility may have natural offsets of correlation among counterparties such that credit risk is mitigated.
- *Credit Concentration*: By the same token, the presence of a high concentration ratio by geo-

graphy or industry may call for the breaking up and laying off of credit risk to various third parties. This reverse synergy may actually save a utility money.

- *Resources*: Organizations with access to people and systems with the ability to properly understand price and manage credit risk may be able to manage much more cheaply compared to external credit market pricing. A utility may therefore choose to significantly develop its credit risk managing capabilities.

- *Comparative Advantage in Information*: As with any option valuation, the less you know, the more uncertain cash flow predictions will be. Greater uncertainty or volatility implies greater option prices. In pricing credit, information is crucial. Utilities should benchmark themselves on these factors. To the extent a comparative advantage exists, a utility may profit from active management.

CREDIT RISK REPORTING

If one were to look at analogous industries that have earlier undergone deregulation, losses often occurred because of suboptimal initial pricing, inappropriate deal structuring, lax credit screening/monitoring, and poor credit risk management reporting. We have thus far discussed pricing and contract provisions as related to credit. Difficulties in continued credit risk monitoring generally occur in part because of poor management reporting. As we have discussed, we believe that the utility industry, in preparing for deregulated competition, is underestimating credit risk.

On a large-volume portfolio, good management reporting is concise, accurate, and meaningfully summarized. The robustness of credit-related management reporting should be designed in accordance with the volume of transactions and the magnitude of exposures. Types of credit risk reports may include:

1. Current and potential exposure concentration by region, credit rating, industry, contract type, contract tenor, or customer.
2. Current exposure exception report—exceptions would wither above some absolute level or outside a given range of an index benchmark (if available). The exception report could be done in total or by the characteristics identified earlier.
3. Potential exposure exception report—similar to that just described.
4. Report on assumptions underlying current and potential exposure calculations, including where possible a comparison of those assumptions to those of the competitive industry and/or market data.
5. Numbers 2 and 3 would presumably be done under normal market conditions, as well as with sensitivity analysis changing underlying assumptions. A stress or worst-case report could be included.
6. Listing of the percentage of portfolio followed by rating agencies versus that rated by the utility through its active credit risk management.
7. Listing of credit changes (upgrades, downgrades) by rating agencies and the utility. This could include a "watch list" for potential rating changes.
8. Credit reserve analysis.
9. Statistics on and analysis of the utility's counterparty default experience.
10. Recoveries/legal update.

In addition, it is important to have the credit reporting system integrated with the transaction processing system. This is generally an extension of the notion that credit risk assessment and reporting should be supported by the normal transaction processing system. The credit system generally should not stand alone or be an add-on with manual interface unless volumes and exposures are low.

ADDITIONAL OBSERVATIONS

Based on our risk management work with various developing industries, including power and energy, we would offer the following additional observations:

- It has been our experience that in developing markets, such as electricity, credit risk is largely underestimated. Credit losses will occur, as demonstrated by past experience in natural gas, financial services, and other industries that have progressed to fuller competition. Recent events in Canada regarding a gas LDC related to Louisville Gas & Electric highlight this situation.

- Credit risk is extremely complex and, in many cases, much less transparent than the energy price or market risk of the actual product or commodity transacted. Other industries have spent significant sums to develop sophisticated systems only after large credit losses have occurred. Electric utilities have an opportunity to be proactive in recognizing this need and to learn from experiences in analogous industry situations, rather than waiting for unfavorable events in the electricity industry itself.

- Vigilant determination of changes in a counterparty's credit quality is key. Most credit losses occur due to improper or slow recognition of changes in a counterparty's credit quality. Being the first to recognize a counterparty's impairment may allow a utility to limit exposures and maximize recoveries. In this regard, traders are often at the front lines of information gathering.

- Transfer pricing and performance measurement remain important to credit risk. For example, a holding company or affiliate should charge a power marketing affiliate for any credit guarantee provided. Similarly, the determination of profit as well as other measures of performance should be adjusted by estimates of expected credit losses.

- Beware of the cutthroat competitor. Whether for legitimate strategic business reasons or in acting as a rogue trader because of some improper performance incentives, the fact that one or more competitors are pricing credit risk at significantly low prices does not mean that the one company's pricing structure is flawed. On the contrary, the competitor may be taking on excessive risk, rightly or wrongly, in terms of alignment with its corporate goals. If those corporate goals are different from those of the original company, both companies' pricing structures may be correct. Upper management insight is normally critical in properly managing credit risk under these circumstances.

Overall, credit management structure as well as controls, reporting, and a framework for developing limits in the credit market are all important for effective risk management.

CHAPTER 13

Future of Energy Price Risk Management

By Peter C. Fusaro

While oil companies and oil traders adapted and utilized paper barrel trading to manage price risk since the 1980s, this ability to transfer that risk has become an essential element of today's energy business. The natural gas industry in North America accepted these same tools as a means to sell gas forward and hedge price risk as well as provide project finance for drilling, transportation, and end use during the 1990s. And now electric power has become a commodity for hedging and risk management applications in North America, Europe, and Australasia. The energy market will continue to evolve, and the use of risk management instruments will change to meet the needs of the industry.

ASIA PACIFIC PARTICIPATION

The Asia Pacific markets have never been at the forefront of trading in the off-exchange markets, but they have had active paper markets for fuel oil, gasoil, naphtha, jet fuel, and Tapis crude oil. In the past, the Dubai forward contract has been actively traded and well accepted by Japanese and

other Asian players, but the Dubai futures contracts on
both the SIMEX and the IPE failed to gain industry acceptance. The launch of identical Dubai futures contracts on
both London's IPE and Singapore's SIMEX during the
summer of 1990 signaled the establishment of an exchange-
traded sour contract, but the timing of its launch was poor
due to the outbreak of the Gulf War. The Dubai futures contract may have provided Asian refiners and Japanese
traders with an important benchmark to hedge off and
potentially write swaps transactions. Instead, Asian oil
traders have turned to Malaysia's crude oil, Tapis, which
has become a popular benchmark to hedge refined products and lock in profits as well as to price off exchange
swap deals, but it is limited by continued liquidity problems in the physical markets. The listing of the IPE Brent
crude oil contract on the SIMEX in June 1995 has only
added some liquidity to the Asian oil markets; however, it
is not an Asian marker, but a North Sea crude.

While there has been considerable interest in the
development of an Asian crude oil marker that would
allow a reference from which derivative product deals
could be priced off, the development of an Asian crude basket does not appear to be forthcoming. An Asian crude
price index would be a boon for the trading of more derivative products, for it would reflect regional consumption
patterns and make price more transparent. In 1989, a proposed Asian crude basket was to include Malaysian Tapis,
Australian Gippsland, Indonesian Minas crudes, or other
acceptable Asian crudes that would provide liquidity to a
market prone to supply squeezes and violent price swings
because of differentials in Asian crude prices. Both these
actions affected Asia Pacific refiners. Moreover, cash settlement would overcome the physical delivery problems that
often occur. Established exchanges could have instituted
this type of contract but instead opted for the failed Dubai
futures contract on the IPE and SIMEX, which really is a
Middle Eastern contract. The creation of an Asian forward
or exchange-traded contract would allow better global

arbitrage between North Sea Brent, Middle Eastern, and US Gulf Coast sour crudes. It is still needed as the physical oil markets in Asia continue to expand, already overtaking Europe and overtaking North America by the year 2000.

Turning to the petroleum products markets, the Far East Oil Price (FEOP) Index was launched in January 1994 to develop paper indicators for oil products in Southeast and Northeast Asia and for Malaysian Tapis crude. The index is constructed by energy trade and includes daily price assessments from international oil companies, state-owned oil companies, investment banks, oil trading companies, and brokers. The index has gained credibility in specific sectors of the Asian oil industry, most conspicuously in jet fuel during 1996–1997. The use of price indexes in oil in Asia, in electricity in North America (Dow Jones COB Index), and in global tanker markets through Reuters and Citibank demonstrates the ability to construct forward pricing indicators for hedging without the benefit or need of energy futures contracts. It is a trend worth noting.

China and India remain the wild cards in Asian oil demand because of their potential for rapid and unpredictable growth, but China seems poised to actively use risk management tools for energy. China's voracious energy needs are immediately apparent as China became a net oil importer in 1994 and will increasingly be heavily dependent on politically volatile Middle Eastern supply. The Chinese appetite for risk already exists, and Chinese oil companies are hedging in London, Hong Kong, and Singapore to a limited degree.

Chinese futures exchanges for energy emerged in 1993 in Nanking and Beijing but were shut down by the government in 1994. The Nanking Petroleum Exchange (NAPEX) was the most liquid. Others include the Beijing Commodity Exchange and Beijing Petroleum Exchange. One problem of these exchanges was the lack of active cash and forward markets in the domestic Chinese market that would add liquidity to the futures contracts. There are also questions over state regulation of the oil industry affecting their

future development. However, energy derivatives markets
in China should become more liquid with Hong Kong's
integration into China.

Nevertheless, the Asia Pacific markets now seem
poised to use energy risk management tools due to the dual
market drivers of deregulation and privatization and the
continuously growing energy demand for oil, gas, and electric power. Project finance will also get a boost as greenfield
projects take shape throughout the region and innovative
financing techniques using energy derivatives increase.

EAST BLOC AND FORMER SOVIET UNION

Futures markets and other creative oil market contracting
procedures are used to reduce financial and price risks
where competition already exists. In the former Soviet
Union and the Eastern European countries, the institutions to promote competition and freer markets are continuing to develop. Barriers concerning uncertainty over
ownership, taxes, and competition are limiting outside
capital from entering the oil trading business, although
countertrade agreements such as wheat or medicine for oil
exist. Moreover, formerly these state-owned oil companies
were dependent on the supply and distribution of oil and
petroleum products at market subsidized prices. The
changing price structure will eventually establish the
mechanisms needed to establish hedge accounts and
access to hard currency through multiple trading organizations, especially as the former state-owned centralized
and monopolistic trading companies are both privatized
and introduced to competition internally. Capital from the
West will also be forthcoming when some of these risks
are resolved and a banking and legal structure evolves. It
is an incremental process.

Industry restructuring continues to take place. When a
workable framework exists to give the proper incentives to
compete, the new market-based institutions will evolve.
These changes would involve, for example, the introduction

of foreign competition in retail gasoline marketing or structured finance for refinery upgrades based on refiner margins that are fixed by the marketplace, not the government.

Most trading, refining, marketing, and related companies are making only limited use of oil price risk management tools, including relatively new procurement practices in the forward cash market. Hungary had plans to move forward with the establishment of the Central European Energy Exchange if it could determine that the exchange is viable to trade Russian Urals crude. Some observers feel that by the end of the century Eastern Europe will be able to function as an active link between East and West with free trade across borders, an integrated oil marketplace, and perhaps natural gas as well.

The former Soviet Union has other problems to overcome, but it remains one of the world's largest oil producers and has a vast resource base in oil and natural gas. In fact, the fragmentation of control, price, and volume uncertainty are driving the former Soviet republics to use risk management tools, particularly since oil and gas provide much of the hard currency needs of the republics. Oil and gas barter deals are proliferating with Eastern and Western Europe and between the Commonwealth of Independent States (CIS) themselves. The development of commodities exchanges that trade physical oil and oil products during the past several years signals that trading forward and futures contracts will eventually become more developed in the former Soviet republics.

As oil prices move toward world market levels from their previous subsidized levels and as internal prices escalate within the CIS republics, the need to manage price risk has rapidly developed. Already, some oil is hedged and escrowed in private deals. Also, some oil analysts feel that the Soviets in the past secretly hedged a portion of their exports with futures. It is felt that the newly emerging private sector firms should become more active players on the oils futures exchanges in London and New York over time as well as on their own evolving commodity exchanges.

IMPACT ON THE ENERGY FUTURES MARKET

The rapid growth and development of over-the-counter energy markets during the 1990s have changed the structure of the energy futures markets. In a very obvious way, this has been signaled by the growth of open interest for both crude oil and petroleum product futures on both the NYMEX and IPE. *Open interest* is the number of futures contracts left open at the end of each trading day and is an indication of futures contract liquidity. Second, contract extension of the WTI crude oil and the Henry Hub natural gas contracts reflect the growth of the OTC markets. It means that swaps providers will not have to roll their positions as often in the back months of trading. However, these are relatively modest steps for the exchanges to try to recapture lost business to the swaps markets. They are now challenged in developing what their future role will be related to OTC energy market developments.

The growth and worldwide acceptance of paper markets, both forward and futures, have increased the liquidity of global oil markets and the North American natural gas market. The development of the off-exchange market is the natural progression in the evolution of oil and natural gas becoming exchangeable securities, that is, money. It is also the natural evolutionary step in the reintegration of oil markets, since the traditional means of reducing uncertainty, the term contract, disappeared. The maturity of North American natural gas is now being followed by the launch of natural gas futures contracts on the IPE in London in 1997 and the future launch of gas futures contracts on the Sidney Futures Exchange. Some analysts see the development of a Southeast Asian gas hub which would lead to gas futures or at least OTC contracts for that region of the world. And electricity derivatives in the United States emerged in late 1993 while the NYMEX contract launch of two western US electricity futures contracts began in March 1996. Already, there are active electricity futures contracts in Scandinavia and New Zealand and a contract launch of two electricity futures contracts for New South Wales and

Victoria on the Sydney Futures Exchange in September 1997. And major energy swaps providers are trading both electricity and electric transmission of capacity forward.

Financial instruments such as swaps and options need a sufficiently liquid benchmark that is traded in the physical market and viable in the futures market in order to develop effective commodity hedging programs. These features are especially important criteria when it comes to counterparty risk issues, since banks often seek to find other counterparties in which to match their position or offset it through an active futures contract. In the energy markets, these criteria are easily met.

FINANCIAL UNCERTAINTIES IN USING NEW RISK MANAGEMENT TOOLS

There are some obvious advantages to using OTC instruments to manage price risk. The use of these instruments can lower borrowing costs and minimize risk by laying it off on a third party. Ironically, the explosive growth of these instruments in the energy markets has raised the specter of counterparty nonperformance and creditworthiness as new risks that swaps providers need to manage, mentioned in the previous chapter. A big issue was the trading losses of the German metals trader Metallgesellschaft, which dropped over a billion dollars on margin calls in oil futures trading through its US subsidiary MG Corp. in 1993. Credit risk is especially true because of less liquidity in the farther dated swaps, over 5 years. It is an emerging risk in electric power markets.

The ability to fix the price of crude oil, refined products, natural gas, or electricity for delivery of up to 10 years is a distinct advantage over the dependence on vagaries of the spot market or volatility of the futures market price fluctuations. Cash settlement of these agreements offers the additional advantage of guaranteeing underlying performance. In addition, the intermediaries writing swaps and OTC options agreements are constructing forward price indicators to some degree.

One disadvantage of these tools is their complexity and cost, although costs have come down due to competition and more liquidity in the OTC markets as they mature; however, using financial instruments requires more active management by third parties. There are tax and accounting uncertainties as they are applied to the energy industry. For example, there is a question as to whether taxes are to be amortized over the life of the hedge or on an after tax basis. These accounting parameters should evolve over time. A rapidly changing market can also affect performance. Moving from backwardation to contango, or vice versa, can make swaps arrangements money losers for the underwriters, since positions must be counterbalanced quickly. MG Corp. learned this lesson the hard way in 1993 and 1994.

GLOBAL INTEGRATION OF MARKETS SHOULD ACCELERATE

New global trading patterns for physical crude oil and petroleum products that have emerged during the past few years signal the further integration of the world energy markets. Physical product flow now moves where price is best, regardless of the distance and the time period, as windows of opportunity open and close in those markets. This was evident during the Gulf War, when unusual cargo movements followed the price signal. The same is even more evident in the paper markets which respond more rapidly to change than the physical markets. While 24-hour electronic futures trading is not yet in place, multinational banks, oil traders, and oil companies already have developed and actively trade worldwide in a 24-hour market in which financial instruments and physical product deals are bought and sold forward up to 10 years.

The NYMEX began its off-hours ACCESS electronic trading system during June 1993. ACCESS allows after-hours trading of crude oil, heating oil, and gasoline and may be a forerunner of other globally accepted electronic trading systems, although ACCESS may introduce new risk questions as well. It has siphoned off some liquidity from cash markets. NYMEX expanded ACCESS to Asia with links to the Sydney Futures Exchange in 1995 and the Hong Kong Futures Exchange in 1997. Other electronic trading systems for natural gas and electricity are already developing liquidity.

The swaps and OTC options markets already provide these global features to the markets. The trends toward internationalization and globalization should progress in newer, more innovative ways with new and continuing realignments of the energy industry.

These intermediaries of energy markets match party and counterparty, run unbalanced books where applicable, assume the risk, and receive some of the upside profits. They create markets where none previously existed and increase liquidity by offering more choices in the types of products available for trading. Financial instruments such as swaps, options, participation hedges, swaptions, and combinations of several of these financial tools are available to individually customize agreements to best suit the client's needs. And these transactions can be structured to include alternate delivery location in order to meet physical market needs.

While no trading arrangement completely eliminates financial risk, swaps, futures, and OTC options manage that risk better than an unhedged position. In fact, when the physical markets rapidly change, the market maker assumes more risk, as his or her trading position must be readjusted. Risk is shifted through these instruments.

Moreover, the markets are not solely centered in the Atlantic Basin, as has been evidenced by the growing demand and greater interest developing in the use of financial instruments in the Asia Pacific region. The establishment of the Wall Street energy traders, multinational banks, and international companies, and the emergence of energy swaps brokers in Singapore and Tokyo signal the greater liquidity of the Far Eastern swaps market. Asia Pacific participation is growing in the use of these price risk tools using Malaysian Tapis crude as the preferred marker crude in swaps agreements. And Chinese futures exchanges and derivatives markets are evolving.

PROJECT FINANCE APPLICATION

Project finance application is a major target for the application of new financial tools to reduce risk and raise capital. The OTC markets become an avenue not only to turn debt management into a profitable activity but also as a means to reduce borrowing costs by reducing uncertainty. Over the next decade, the size of the market for project finance in power generation will be in the hundreds of billions of dollars. Although much of this spending will be self-financed by the industry, borrowing will also be necessary, as industry cash flow remains uncertain and producer capital requirements need to be met. Asia and North America are expected to take the lion's share of new energy project finance in electric power in coming years. The use of swaps agreements in financing will improve the utility's balance sheet and increase its credit because price uncertainty is reduced. Lower borrowing costs result because the lender's risk is, in turn, reduced. Oil and gas are increasingly securitized to raise capital. In the future, generating capacity will be securitized as well.

One source of capital will be energy-backed loans from large multinational banks. Oil-collateralized loans have been used in the past, with the Petrobonds of Mexico in the 1970s and Standard Oil (now British Petroleum) bonds in the 1980s. And Mexico's surprisingly large hedge position of over 100 million barrels during the Gulf War showed that oil producers are becoming more inclined to use these tools as a means of stabilizing income. The Standard Oil bonds tied the price of crude to interest rates. Oil producers sold a portion of their future revenue potential to raise capital. In future lending, the extraction of revenue from a portion of oil and gas assets that are still in the ground will be a growing trend as oil and gas become more monetized. The concept is simply to extract the present value of the energy asset from its projected cash flows. Until now, future oil production was an underutilized asset; now that resource can be used as cash. Natural gas can be used as collateral, and an efficient mechanism to bank future gas production will probably be sold to the retail side in the future. Electric power assets will probably follow a similar evolution into securitization for generating capacity.

While finding and development costs in exploration and production for oil and gas are now more efficient than in the past, expectations are that the vast capital requirements for new production for the next decade may dwarf previous outlays for the industry. Because most of the world's cheap oil reserves have been found, future exploration and production will be more expensive to develop and will include offshore oil, enhanced recovery, and unconventional oil development. Although much of this new spending will be self-financed by the industry, greater borrowing will be forthcoming over the next few years as the cash flow of the industry remains uncertain to some degree and producer capital requirements need to be met. The need for financing is particularly evident in the US market as oil and gas asset sales continue. The development of new reserves based on this form of financing will improve the producer's balance sheet and increase its credit because price uncertainty is reduced by the swap agreement. Already, oil and gas are increasingly becoming securitized as a means to raise the capital needed for future industry investment.

Although exploration and production of crude oil and natural gas reserves have historically been the principal source of total capital expenditures, the effects of deferred capital spending following the 1986 price collapse will lead to increased borrowing in the refining, marketing, and transportation sectors during the first decade of the 21st century. Refiners, in particular, will need major upgrading to producer lighter, cleaner products from a heavier, more sour crude slate while meeting more stringent environmental standards for products. Tanker spending for both crude and petroleum products will also be significant as consuming nations' imports continue to grow and the worldwide fleet is replaced. Increased spending is also beginning to occur in the capital intensive liquefied natural gas (LNG) sector with its need for tankers, gasification, and regasification facilities as well as for increased natural gas drilling and production.

Oil-Indexed Loans

Oil-indexed loans should be an area of major growth for bank lending for the next decade. Capital-starved producers need money to modernize facilities and increase production. These loans allow producers the capability of tapping into their resource base in order to do so.

The Chase-Sonatrach loan was syndicated in May 1990 and may be the precursor of the kind of deals written in the future. The $100 million 7-year placement of Algeria's Sonatrach oil-linked index loan written by the Chase Manhattan Bank has been the most visible project-finance transaction written into a forward swaps-like contract. This deal demonstrated the creativity of the investment community in developing trading vehicles to raise project-finance capital based on oil price swaps. The loan can be considered an advance on the oil-linked bonds previously described. The "oil index credit" tied to this loan allows the borrower to participate in some of the upside potential of the oil price rises with the investor's rate of return fluctuating with oil price changes. This mechanism is not linked to oil sales but is purely financial indexing. Loan repayments are allowed to fluctuate up or down for the first 4 years of the loan with upper and lower price thresholds of $22 and $16 per barrel. Loan payments are locked in after the fourth year. Consequently, if oil prices are lower, the borrower pays a higher interest rate and has lower revenues from which to repay the loan due to these lower prices. The revenues raised from this loan were used for Sonatrach to develop its natural gas and condensate resources.

In the Chase-Sonatrach transaction, a pure price mechanism was established that is not collateralized by a commodity, but allows the oil producer to look at its assets as an income stream and as a means to reduce its borrowing costs. Sonatrach was able to develop a natural hedge in linking its debt security with its future production. This transaction can also be described as an option written on its long covered position, since the producer has possession of the physical assets. In effect, Sonatrach's oil price risk was hedged through Chase's active commodity swaps book. Chase creates an off-exchange position to future crude oil prices and through multiple swaps agreements markets this vehicle to end users. This is common practice in interest rate transactions.

This type of investment is innovative because it shows how the management of price risk is tied to the capacity to protect future revenue streams and tap into that resource base using swaps. The Chase-Sonatrach deal bundles oil price risk and interest rate risk, which are risks that banks manage well. The deal also allows Chase comparative advantage in creating similar deals. While investors' rate of return will fluctuate with oil price changes, the loan remains a worthwhile investment risk, particularly since Algeria is a "good debtor" nation with diversified petroleum exports including crude oil, condensate, LNG, and residual fuel oil.

While this $100 million loan was based on projected oil production, Algeria may not have enough oil production for other large loans based on receivables. On the other hand, countries such as Venezuela or Mexico could easily set up similar oil receivables or oil-indexed loans to raise capital. While natural gas could be used for other countries such as Algeria, Indonesia, or Norway, gas-debt precedents could also be done. The nature of commodity debt transactions seems to be that if one deal is completed others can be replicated using better and more refined techniques. There is no doubt that natural gas, LNG price swaps, or loan receivables can be set up in similar agreements.

SYNTHETIC OIL FIELDS AND OTHER INVESTMENT TOOLS

The development of new off-exchange financial instruments to manage price risk has evolved to the point where these instruments are being used to package deals that private investors can participate in. Synthetic instruments are being developed and are targeted toward allowing investors to become involved in oil price volatility. Both the Phibro Energy Unit Trust and the British Petroleum Prudhoe Bay Royalty Trust are examples of investment vehicles developed to speculate on the future price of oil. The concept also has been proposed to major oil producers so that they can tap into their resources in the ground and raise capital.

One example of a synthetic instrument was developed by Phibro Energy in 1990. Phibro developed an investment vehicle that it called a "synthetic oil field" which was structured to provide a stream of quarterly income payments varying with the price of light, sweet crude oil (WTI) delivered to Cushing, Oklahoma, over a 10-year period. The unit trust was to trade on the NASDAQ over-the-counter stock exchange with each unit initially priced at about $25 per share. Phibro was to sell about 40,000 units of the trust, and the total of the placement would be for approximately $100 million. The trust is a series of 40 prepaid forward contracts that is tied to WTI delivery at Cushing. Volumes of crude delivered will vary with oil prices and will impact on the quarterly payment stream. The unit trust can be described as a bull market play and has not been placed because the market was in contango (lower futures prices in the forward months). Contango markets make forward prices less attractive to users of these instruments. Of course, over the 10-year duration of the unit trust, some of these price anomalies should be worked out, and the trust should produce positive cash flow, although some quarters will generate less income than others.

Phibro felt that the trust can be expected to be more highly correlated with oil price movements than would be the case with a traditional oil sector investment. The Phibro Unit Trust mimics oil field production. As a synthetic oil field, the unit trust signals another in a growing list of derivative financial instruments that are being created in the oil arena by major oil trading and investment firms.

Phibro, however, held off selling the trust to the public and instead brought out a smaller version for a shorter duration which began trading on the American Stock Exchange on August 24, 1990. The Salomon Phibro Unit Trust was established to sell 4 million barrels of oil over 5 years. Each share is equivalent to one quarter of a barrel of oil and was sold for $4.65 per unit. There are 16 million units in all, which raised about $75 million for Phibro. The principal asset of the trust was a prepaid forward contract that provided delivery of light, sweet crude oil (similar to WTI) in September 1995. The Salomon Phibro Oil Trust was paid off in a single cash distribution in November 1995, based on the price of oil at that time. If the price of oil was not well over $20 per barrel at that time, investors would not receive any significant payment for their risk. A heating oil unit trust was also developed. And Enron designed a similar natural gas trust, which it pulled from the market, but could offer in the future.

Another investment vehicle that allows companies to raise capital in innovative ways is the Prudhoe Bay Royalty Trust. In 1989, British Petroleum sold $500 million in a 30-year unit trust that was based on actual Alaskan North Slope (ANS) production. The Prudhoe Bay Royalty Trust allowed BP to sell to the public a portion of its future revenue potential from its oil reserves. The trust makes quarterly payments based on the average of WTI prices over the quarter. WTI prices were chosen because of their higher trading visibility than ANS. ANS and WTI are not similar-quality crudes, because WTI is a sweet crude, and ANS is a sour crude that fetches a lower price in the market. This trust gives investors the opportunity to speculate on the future price of oil backed by actual oil production. The British Petroleum Trust was a pure oil price play, which raised $500 million for BP immediately and which will be paid back with discounted dollars through future oil prices.

More unit trusts backed by real oil production like the BP trust or pure price plays like Phibro's unit trust should be forthcoming as a means to raise ready capital for the industry and also to allow private investors an opportunity to participate in price plays in the volatile oil markets. The development of these investment trusts signifies the willingness of major market makers in both the physical and paper markets to use the financial risk management tools to develop financial products that private and institutional investors can buy. Oil and gas are becoming securitized in this manner. And asset securitization for electric generating capacity will be another area of new business development in the electric power sector.

FINANCIAL INNOVATIONS SHOULD CONTINUE

Oil price swaps developed in the oil markets primarily because of oil consumers' desire to limit their price exposure to higher prices for the longer term. Swaps users wished to hedge their price risk over the longer term, which is something the existing futures exchanges could not do for them because of the lack of liquidity beyond 6 months. The emergence of short-term swaps became acceptable due to the lack of liquidity of certain petroleum products (e.g., fuel oil) and the ability to customize transactions. The rapid evolution of natural gas futures trading and natural gas swaps during the 1990s indicates a time compression in the maturation of this market as well for North American gas producers, marketers, and end users. Another emerging trend is the development of "Btu swaps," and they have been offered by Enron, Coastal, and Louis Dreyfus Energy in the past but failed. However, with electricity deregulation underway, the Btu markets for power are evolving. These deals allow the delivery of the least-cost fuel (diesel fuel, residual fuel oil, or natural gas) each month in fixed price deals to energy end users, such as utilities, cogeneration plants, and industrial customers. They are integrated, cross-commodity products of the "energy industry."

Weather Derivatives and Insurance

While much focus has been drawn to the concept of hedging Btu markets, the reality is that these markets are just evolving. Thus, electric utilities have been approached by commodity providers to hedge their weather risk through derivative products. Typically, weather is the most volatile variable in an electric utility portfolio, and electric utilities run predictive models based on historic demand on weather patterns showing heating and cooling degree days. But there may be an easier way to hedge the weather through insurance products. In effect, this is taking risk management back to its origins for managing risk.

Weather insurance is writing an insurance policy to hedge for unexpected weather conditions using degree days as a reference point. A degree is the reference to 65° Fahrenheit and actual temperature. The insurance policy would typically be written for 5 years and be reset annually following the exchange of cash flows based on weather on utility fuel usage. Both weather insurance and weather derivatives will be used by electric utilities as electricity becomes further commoditized.

Potential for LNG Hedging

Another potential area for the application of risk management tools is in the growing liquefied natural gas trade. LNG growth is projected to rise to 7 percent per year for the next decade globally, and nowhere is the market as robust as in the Asia Pacific region, which consumes the lion's share of LNG production and consumption. This demand is fueled by economics, environmental considerations, and the geographic distribution of gas resources. Japan, Korea, and Taiwan will increase their imports, and new entrants to the consuming market will include China, India, Thailand, and possibly the Philippines. Increased LNG sales should also be driven by rising environmental concerns over air emissions in Asian markets as well as other parts of the world.

Japan already plays an important role in Asian gas markets because it imports about two thirds of world LNG production, 42 million tonnes or over 80 percent of Asian consumption with electricity generation accounting for over 70 percent of usage. LNG suppliers into the Japanese market include Indonesia, Malaysia, Australia, Brunei, Abu Dhabi, and Alaska. LNG import prices are delivered in a range of $3 to $3.50/MMBtu on a CIF basis. These LNG imports, with the exception of imports from Indonesia, are linked to an average price of a basket of Japan's crude oil imports, the so-called crude cocktail delivered on an FOB basis. For Indonesian LNG supplies, the prices are established on the equivalent of spot prices of a basket of Indonesian crude oil exports plus shipping costs. The price formula used for Japanese LNG imports results in a premium paid for LNG over the thermally equivalent crude oil. In effect, the LNG is indexed to oil prices. In Japan, LNG pricing uses the Japanese Customs Clearing Price, or the average price of crude oil imported into Japan each month is a very commonly used index. For example, if the CIF price for crude oil is $18/bbl, then the LNG CIF price would be about $3.50/MMBtu.

Since Japan has the highest electricity costs in the world for all classes of service, there is an incentive to reduce fuel oil input costs. One idea that has been discussed is to hedge LNG using the disaggregation of the crude cocktail components. Moreover, as the LNG industry continues to grow, alternatives to the traditional pricing mechanisms may be needed. Price formulas incorporating risk management features previously used for refined products may start to be used, including price caps, floors, and collars. An analogous situation is in the new generation of US coal contracts which now use indexes, caps and floors, and fixed prices to sell coal production to end users. Typically, LNG is sold under long-term supply contracts of 25 to 30 years.

Another change in global LNG markets is the development of spot and short-term (up to 2 years) markets, which continue to grow. Abu Dhabi and Australia made spot sales of LNG during 1996 to the European, Asian, and US markets. Multiple discharging of LNG cargoes to customers at different locations may also boost spot sales, particularly in Asian power markets. And there is a developing availability of LNG markets for shorter-term sales.

CONCLUSION

As the financial demands of the energy industry continue to become more pronounced, the pace of financial innovation will accelerate because companies will come to value their assets (including those still in the ground) in new ways and will try to capitalize on those assets. By tapping into these new sources of capital, borrowing costs for project finance should come down, and companies should become more competitive and better able to handle change and uncertainty in the markets. One question concerning credit risk could be a potential problem for borrowers due to uncertainty regarding how to value the "reserve life" of oil and gas field reserves, which thus adds another element of risk. Moreover, companies will be better able to handle currency and interest rate risk as well as price risk management by using these tools.

Financial innovation will grow in its application to the natural gas and power industries as these markets move toward convergence on both the physical and financial sides. Electricity deregulation is impacting the development of commodity markets for natural gas and electric power. Already, mergers and acquisitions in the gas and electric industries are under way in the United States because of the close interrelationship of gas and electricity in the physical market. This change is beginning to expand globally. And new financial products for electricity based on gas fuel inputs will be offered all the way down to the retail consumers. The future uncertainty of natural gas prices coupled with the fact that electricity promises to be the most volatile of any commodity due to its multiple commodity fuel mix and the fact that it is a 24-hour-per-day,

7- day-per-week "real time" market augur well for dynamic growth in the application of energy risk management tools for electric power.

Developing countries are large producers and importers of petroleum, and their exposure to price risk is particularly sensitive. State-owned oil companies, which usually control oil supply, refining, and marketing, have a natural need to use these instruments to manage their commodity price risk and ensure income stability. That need is based on the exposure to oil price volatility that is endemic in their budgets.

Retail price protection programs for energy end users, such as heating oil distributors, trucking companies, and railroads, now offer a wide variety of instruments to manage seasonal and annual price risk in the United States and Europe. These fixed price deals use price caps and floors, collars, strips, and other financial tools that can annualize fuel acquisition costs for end users. Strips, for example, offer a structured price swap as a single seasonal average price. Other price protection programs continue to be developed and offered to the oil retail trade.

There should be continued growth in liquidity and proliferation of energy futures contracts on the futures markets, as the established exchanges meet the needs of market makers and new users of futures with new gas and electric contracts. Swaps market makers can use futures prices as an index and as a means to lay off their excess risk. Futures markets need to extend far month contracts and options contracts to meet the longer-term needs of swaps underwriters. The complementary growth of futures and off-exchange instruments should continue with new varieties of instruments and transactions.

A fundamental change seems to be occurring with the construction of more instruments such as paper oil fields and paper reserves. These synthetic oil fields are constructed using forwards, futures, swaps, and options to ensure supply and fix price at a later date, and they represent an alternative to buying proven physical reserves. More of these financial creations should also be forthcoming as oil and gas securitized issues provide needed capital for the energy industry and investment vehicles for institutional investors. Oil warrants are another form of energy securitization.

The market for these investments should continue to grow as private investors see an opportunity to speculate in energy in a purely synthetic capacity (i.e., dealing only with price risk). Insurance companies and investment banks are at the forefront of this latest area of opportunity. These synthetics strip out all but price risk, and that is what institutional investors are betting on. Next, retail-level investment should be forthcoming in oil and particularly natural gas in new derivative structures. All these financial products should minimize, not increase, risk. Those companies that ignore these tools are actually exposed to far greater risks in uncertain and volatile markets.

More important, it seems evident that the real future importance of these instruments will be in the field of project finance to develop new reserves or maintain current production, to upgrade refineries or undertake expansions, and to raise and spend capital for the substantial structural needs of the energy industry. The global energy industry of the future faces ongoing challenges to develop its resource base balanced with environmental considerations in a period of constant price volatility. Besides political upheavals, the volatility of the oil, gas, and electric power markets during the first decade of the 21st century seems assured because of supply imbalances, unpredictable demand, unpredictable weather, and environmental considerations affecting consumption. These variables indicate that there will be an increasing need to use longer-term financial instruments primarily because most energy futures contracts are relatively illiquid beyond 6 months to 1 year. OTC tools offer the additional benefit of being individually tailored in each deal to meet the needs of each company.

The use of swaps, options, futures, and forwards and the continued growth of risk management tools for the energy markets demonstrate that the financial community can meet the specific financial needs of the energy industry.

The selective use of these financial instruments enables producers, refiners, marketers, electric and gas utilities, and end users not only to manage price risk but also to protect cash flow, meet operational needs, service debt obligations, and support project finance. The energy markets will continue to evolve, and new applications of these tools will emerge to meet the challenges of the future. The most innovative oil and gas companies, utility companies, investment houses, and commercial banks, who now act as market makers, will continue to test the limits of financial innovation and market acceptance for these financial products. Energy risk management has finally arrived as a core competence of the energy business.

American Option—An option which can be exercised by the buyer at any time during its life.

Arbitrage—The simultaneous purchase and sale of similar or identical commodities in two markets.

Asian Option—An option which can be exercised only at expiration, based on the difference between the strike price and the average of daily spot prices over the life of the option. Also called *average price options*.

Backwardation—Market situation in which prices are progressively lower in distant delivery months. Opposite of *Contango*.

Basis—The differential that exists at any time between the futures or forward price for a given commodity and the comparable cash or spot price for the commodity. Basis can reflect different time periods, product qualities, or locations.

Basis Risk—The uncertainty as to whether the cash-futures spread will widen to narrow between the time a hedge position is implemented and liquidated.

Bid/Ask—A measure of market liquidity. The *bid* is the price level at which buyers are willing to buy and the *ask* is the price level at which sellers are willing to sell.

Book—The total of all physical, futures, and OTC derivatives positions held by a trader or company (includes documentation).

Broker—In futures, the person who executes the buy and sell orders of a customer in return for a commission or fee. In the OTC markets, the person who introduces counterparties and arranges the transaction, charging a fee for this service. Brokers never take a position in the market.

Calendar Spread—An option position created by selling

one call and buying another with a longer expiration at the same strike price. Also called *time spread*.

Call Option—An option that gives the buyer the right (but not the obligation) to enter into a long futures position at a predetermined strike price, and obligates the seller to enter into a short futures position at that price, should the option be exercised. See *Put Option*.

Cap—A contract between a buyer and seller in which the buyer is assured he or she will have to pay more than a maximum price. See *Floor*.

Carrying Charge—The total of storing a physical commodity including storage, insurance, interest, and opportunity costs.

CFD—A contract for difference, which is basically a price swap and usually applied to the short-term Brent crude oil swaps market.

CIF—Cost, insurance, and freight.

Clearing Members—Members of an exchange who accept responsibility for all trades cleared through them and share secondary responsibility for the liquidity of the exchange's clearing operation. Clearing members must meet minimum capital requirements.

Clearinghouse—An exchange-associated body charged with insuring (guaranteeing) the financial integrity of each trade. Orders are cleared by the clearinghouse acting as a buyer to all sellers and a seller to all buyers. The clearing-house stands behind all trades made on the exchange.

Close—The period at the end of a trading session; also called the *settlement price* of that commodity.

Collar—Options strategy designed to minimize upfront costs of a cap or floor through the sale of a cap or floor.

Contango—Market situation in which prices are progressively higher in succeeding months than in the nearest delivery month. Opposite of *Backwardation*.

Counterparty—The person or institution standing on the opposite side of a transaction.

Credit Risk—The risk of default by either counterparty in a transaction.

Crack Spread—An intermarket spread where futures are bought and sold to mimic the refining of crude oil into petroleum products.

Delivery Month—The month in a given contract for delivery of the physical commodity.

Derivatives—Financial instrument derived from the underlying commodity including forwards, futures, swaps, and options.

ERMA—Energy Risk Managment Association, US-based professional energy organization.

European Option—An option which can be exercised by the buyer only at expiration.

Exotics—A term used to refer to more structured over-the-counter instruments, such as swaps with a range of maturities, volumes, or fixed prices, transactions that incorporate different commodities, or complex combinations of options.

Floor—A contract between a buyer and a seller in which the seller is assured he or she will receive at least a minimum price. See *Cap*.

FOB—Free on Board. A transaction in which the seller provides a commodity at an agreed-upon price, at a specific loading point within a specific period of time. The buyer must arrange for transportation and insurance for delivery.

Forward—Standardized contract for the purchase or sale of a commodity which is traded for future delivery not under the provisions of an established exchange.

Fungibility—Characteristic of products or instruments that can be commingled for trad-

ing, shipment, storage, or consumption. Only fungible goods can be traded as commodities.

Futures—Standardized contract for the purchase or sale of a commodity for future delivery under the provisions of exchange regulations.

GARP—Global Association of Risk Professionals, international professional association.

Hedging—In the futures or OTC markets, a simultaneous initiation of equal and opposite positions in the cash and futures markets. Hedging is employed as a form of financial protection against adverse price moves in the cash market. Opposite of *Speculation*.

In-the-Money—An option which has intrinsic value at expiration. Opposite of *Out-of-the-Money*.

Initial Margin—Margin posted when a futures position is initiated.

Intrinsic Value—The value of an option if it were to expire immediately. Cannot be less than zero.

ISDA—International Swaps Dealers Association. A trade association, primarily of banks, that promotes the use of all derivative instruments. ISDA has its own master swaps agreement that is heavily used by the energy trade.

Liquidity—A characteristic of a market where there is a high level of trading activity.

Local—A commodity or options principal and exchange member who buys and sells for his or her own account on the floor of the exchange.

Long Position—In the futures market, the position of a contract buyer whose purchase obligates him or her to accept delivery unless he or she liquidates his or her contract with an offsetting sale. In the forward market, a long position obligates a buyer to accept delivery unless a book-out agreement is subsequently made.

Margin—Funds or good faith deposits posted during the trading life of a futures contract to guarantee fulfillment of contract obligations.

Mark-to-Market—Daily adjustment of open positions to reflect profits and losses resulting from price movements that occurred during the last trading session.

Market Maker—A dealer who consistently quotes bid and offer prices for a commodity. Can be an energy company.

Moving Average—Technical analysis term which clearly signals any change in the trendline.

Net Position—The difference between an entity's open long contracts and open short positions in any one commodity.

Notional—The underlying principal of either an exchange traded or OTC transaction.

Offer—A motion to sell a futures, forward, physical, or options contract at a specific time.

Offset—A transaction that liquidates or closes out an open contract position.

Open—The period at the beginning of the trading session on a commodities exchange.

Open Interest—The number of futures contracts on an exchange which remain to be settled.

Option—The instrument that gives the holder the right to buy or sell the underlying commodity at a given price or at a specific date.

Out-of-the-Money—An option which has no intrinsic value at expiration. See *In-the-Money*.

OTC (Over-the-Counter)—Purchase and sale of financial instruments not conducted on an organized exchange.

Paper Barrels—Term used to designate nonphysical oil markets including futures, forwards, swaps, and options.

Position Taking—The action of commercial participants who use the futures market as an alternative cash market rather than as a hedging vehicle.

Premium—The price paid by the option buyer to the option seller.

Price Signalling—Advanced publication of prices prior to their effective date for the purpose of encouraging competitors to make similar price changes.

Put Option—An option that gives the buyers the right (but not the obligation) to enter into a short futures position at a predetermined strike price and obligates the seller to assume a long futures position, should the option be exercised. See *Call Option*.

Short Position—In the futures market, the position of a contract seller whose sale obligates him or her to deliver the commodity unless he or she liquidates his or her contract by an offsetting purchase. See *Long Position*.

Speculation—The opposite of hedging in which the speculator holds no offsetting cash market position and deliberately incurs price risk in order to reap potential rewards.

Spot—A one-time open market transaction, where a commodity is purchased "on the spot" at a current market price.

Spot Month—The futures contract held closest to maturity.

Spread—The simultaneous purchase of one futures or forward contract and the sale of a different futures or forward contract. Also refers to a futures/forward contract purchase in one market and a simultaneous sale of the same commodity in some other market.

Straddle—The purchase or sale of both a put or a call having the same strike and expiration date.

Strike Price—The predetermined price level at which the exercise of an option takes place.

Swap—Customized contractual agreement between two parties to exchange interest payments, typically a fixed-rate payment for floating rate payment. No physical commodity exchange takes place.

Swaption—An option on a swap.

Technical Analysis—Examination of patterns of futures price changes, rates of change, and changes in trading volume and open interest, often by charting in order to predict and profit from such trends.

Time Value—Part of the option premium which reflects the excess over intrinsic value.

Trend—Price activity in markets in a particular direction, which is characterized by higher highs and higher lows.

Variation Margin—Margin paid or collected in order to maintain a minimum level based on daily fluctuations in contract value.

Volume—The number of transactions occurring on an exchange during a specified period of time.

INDEX

ACCESS electronic trading system, 224–225

Actual price, vs. benchmark price, 1

Against Actuals (AAs), 80

Agricultural vs. financial futures, 12

Airline industry, caps usage of, 22

Alaskan North Slope (ANS) production, 231–232

Alberta, Canada natural gas market, 15, 77–78, 79

Algeria, future trends in risk management tools, 229

American energy markets (*See* North American energy markets)

ANS (Alaskan North Slope) production, 231–232

Appalachia hub area, 76

Approved Oil Trader (AOT) scheme, 60

Arbitrage, expansion of, 15–16, 48

Arbitrage pricing theory (APT), 134n1, 135

Asia Pacific energy markets: forward naphtha, 61–63

future developments, xiv, 67–69

futures contracts in, 54, 63–67, 222, 226

historical development, 34, 53–56

liquidity trends in, 225–226

liquefied natural gas (LNG), 233–235

options contracts, 26–27, 84

swaps contracts, 56–61, **58**

use of risk management instruments, 217–220

Asset volatilities, in portfolio management, 166–167

At the money (ATM) option, 139

Automated Brokerage Project, 49

Average price options, 26–27, 84

"avoided cost" pricing, 92, 93

Banks:

as capital resource for energy companies, 226

credit risk role, 32, 200

energy market investment, 112, 237

as market makers, 32–33
relationship-style, 34–35
risk management role, 229
swaps agreement role, 18,
    32
unbalanced book usage, 29
value at risk method in,
    157–158
Basel Committee of Banking
    Supervision, 158
Basis point measures, 160, 161
Basis risk:
    Asian forward markets,
        59–60
    definition, 1
    jet fuel market, 27
    and market makers, 32
    natural gas market, 75–78
    swap agreements, 10, 24
Benchmark price:
    vs. actual price, 1
    in Asian market, 218
    in coal futures, 129–130, 131
    for electricity market, 98–99
    in European market, 38–43
    and swaps/options, 223
Bilateral contracts, and credit
    risk, 200–201
Black-Scholes Model, 145–150
Block contracts, European
    electricity, 114–115
Book:
    unbalanced, 19, 29
    wholesale, 174–177
"bookout," 42–43
Brent crude oil:
    Asian market for, 64, 65–66
    as benchmark, 11, 38–39,
        40–43
    European contracts in,
        50–52

as forward market, 10,
    41–42, 49
futures contracts in, 14
options trading in, 15
Bretton Woods conference, 136
British Energy, 109
British Gas Corp., 46
British Petroleum Prudhoe Bay
    Royalty Trust, 230–231
Brokerage firms, risk manage-
    ment role, 33–34,
    200–201, 203
"BTU" swaps, 232
"bucketing," 205

Calendar swaps, 24
California and Oregon border
    (COB) index, 98–99
Calls, option:
    definition, 14, 24, 137
    determining losses for,
        141–142
    in participation hedging, 28
    and put/call parity, 144–145
Canadian natural gas market,
    15, 77–78, 79
Capital generation, 75,
    226–229, 232, 237
Capital market theory
    (CAPM), 134n1
CAPP (Central Appalachia)
    futures contract, 128–129
Caps and floors, 22–23
Cash flow management,
    through hedging, 34
Cash market position vs.
    futures hedges, 2, 28–29
    (See also Paper markets)
Central Appalachia (CAPP)
    futures contract, 128–129

Central Electricity Generating Board, 109
Cfa's (contracts for difference), 111
Chase-Sonatrach loan, 228–229
China, involvement in energy derivatives, 57, 60, 66–67, 219–220, 226
Coal markets, 119–131
COB (California and Oregon border) index, 98–99
Cogenerators, power, 92
Commercial traders vs. speculators, 179–180, 185–187
Commodities markets:
    and commodities as loan collateral, 33
    energy as, 12
    and inside information, 188
    (see Energy markets)
Commodity swap (see Swaps markets)
Commonwealth of Independent States (CIS), 221
Competition:
    in Asian market, 55
    and electric utilities, 90–91, 92, 93, 107–108
    in natural gas distribution, 46–47
    (See also Deregulation; Liberalization, energy market)
Competitive bidding, in electricity market, 93, 110
Computerized trading systems, 38, 101–104, 114, 224–225
Consumers, energy, need for risk management, 9, 12, 20–22, 23

Contracts for difference (cfa's), 111
Convenience yield, stochastic, 147, 147n9–11
Convexity, options, 150–151
Corporations:
    capital generation issues, 75, 226–229, 232, 237
    credit risk role, 200
    deregulation's effect on, 46–47
    and risk management style, 2–4, 7
    (See also Commercial traders)
Correlation coefficient, in portfolio management, 167–168
Counterparty credit risk, 30, 75, 223
    (see Credit risk)
"crack spread," 16, 137
Credit guarantee, 210
Credit risk:
    concentration ratios, 211–212
    and credit classification, 202–205, **203–204**
    current exposure assessment, 196–198, **197**
    definition, 2
    enhancements to credit, 209–211
    estimation of losses, 206–207
    management strategies, 212–213
    and market makers, 31
    market participants' role in, 200–202
    monitoring of creditworthiness, 205–206

in natural gas market, 75
and OTC instruments, 223
overview of, 195–196,
214–216, 235
potential exposure assessment, 198–200, **199**
reporting of, 213–214
spread pricing, 207–209, **208**
and swaps agreements, 18,
32
"crude cocktail," 234
Crude oil markets:
Asian developments, 63–66,
218–219
Dubai, 10, 11, 63–64, 218
options' popularity in,
153–154
swaps agreements in, 22
Tapis, 218, 226
(*See also* Brent crude oil)
Currency markets, financial
tools from, 3

Dated Brent, 42
The Dealer's Book, 28–29
Debt management, 34
Default problems, in swaps
transactions, 29–31
Delta risk measure for options,
150, 151
Denmark, in electricity market, 117
Deregulation:
and Asian market, 55–56,
67, 68–69
and corporate culture,
46–47
of electricity markets, 89–96,
105, 107–109, 121–125,
213, 235–236
of natural gas markets,
71–73, 77, 87

Derivatives, energy, 5–6, 30,
62–63, 100
(*See also* Exchange-traded
instruments; Off-
exchange instruments)
Developing countries, 33, 221,
236
(*See also* Asia Pacific energy
markets)
Diesel fuel market, European,
45
(*See also* Gasoil markets)
Discount price, vs. premium
price, 1
Diversification, 167, 170, **178,**
212
DJ-COB Index, 99
"double top" in technical
analysis, 184–185
Dubai crude oil, 10, 11, 63–64,
218
Duration measures, 160

Eastern European markets,
220–221
Eastern Group, 109
Eastern Power and Energy
Trading, 112
ECAR (East Central Area
Reliability Coordinator),
120–121
Efa's (electricity forward
agreements), 111
EFP (Exchange for Physical),
16–17, 41, 74, 79–81
Electricity markets:
Asian, 69
brokerage role in, 34
and coal market, 119–125,
129
computerized trading,
101–104

credit risk in, 195, 199–203,
214–215
deregulation of, 89–96, 105,
107–109, 121–125, 213,
235–236
development of, 9
European, 47–48, 107–117
and Exchange for Physical,
17
as forward market, 11–12,
111, 171
future trends, xiv, 222–223,
226
futures in, 6, 14–16, 48,
98–99, 113–117
and natural gas market, 45,
72, 85–87, 112, 234,
235–236
power marketers' role,
96–97
price indexes in, 97–101
swaps agreements in, 18, 23,
29–31, 232
technical analysis in, 180
value at risk method,
157–159, 160–162, 171
(*See also* Utilities)
Electronic energy trading system (ETS), 38
Electronic trading systems, 38,
101–104, 114, 224–225
El-Ex, 116
Energy Broker, 104
Energy markets:
competitive nature of, 19
evolution of, 5–6
future trends in, xv–xvii,
217, 235–238
global integration of,
xiii–xiv, 68, 222, 224–225,
232

Environmental regulation, and
coal industry, 119,
126–127
EPACT (US Energy Policy Act
of 1992), 89–90, 94, 96
ETS (electronic energy trading
system), 38
European energy markets:
benchmarking from, 38–43
Eastern Europe, 220–221
electricity, 47–48, 107–117
future developments, 48–52,
50–51
natural gas, 45–47
oil, 38, 40–45, 54, 220–221
options in, 27, 38, **52,** 84, 145
organization of, 37–38
European Union Electricity
Directive, 48
Event tree, 135, **136**
Exchange for Physical (EFP),
16–17, 41, 74, 79–81
Exchanges, commodity:
functions of, 14
interexchange arbitrage,
15–16
KCBT, 15, 78
LIFFE, 49–50
NAPEX, 219
rise of electric, 95–96, 102
SFE, 65, 222–223
SIMEX, 13, 14, 49, 63–64
(*See also* IPE (International
Petroleum Exchange);
NYMEX (New York
Mercantile Exchange))
Exchange-traded instruments:
and Asian market
development, 218–220
and credit risk, 200
in Hungary, 221

importance to energy
markets, 2
vs. off-exchange, 11
options, 15, 82–85, 146–147
performance issues, 30
(*See also* Futures markets)
Exempt wholesale generators
(EWGs), 94
Exercise price, options, 24, 25,
26–27, 83, 138–140,
144–145
Expected volatility, options,
143*n*7

Far Eastern markets (*see* Asia
Pacific energy markets)
FEOP (Far East Oil Price
Index), 219
FERC (Federal Energy
Regulatory Commission),
92, 94–95
15-Day Brent, 42–43
Financial engineering,
133–134, 136–137, 158
Financial institutions (*see*
Banks)
Financial instruments, and risk
management, 9–10, 12
(*See also* Exchange-traded
instruments; Off-
exchange instruments;
Paper markets)
Finnish electricity market,
116–117
Fixed-income market, risk
measures for, 160
Fixed-price contracts, 123–125,
198, 236
Floors and caps, 22–23, 25
Florida Electric Power
Coordinating Group, 104
Forward markets:

Asian developments, 59–60,
219
crude oil, 10, 41–42, 49, 64
Eastern European, 221
electricity, 11–12, 111, 171
function of, 5, 10–12
gasoil, 45
historical role, 53–54
integration with cash
markets, 2
natural gas, 11–12, 71, 72–73
open spec naphtha, 10,
61–63
sulfur, 127
and swaps contracts,
228–229
(*See also* Physical markets)
Fuel oil markets, 56–58, **58,** 63,
64
Fundamental vs. technical
analysis, 179–180, 188,
193–194
Futures markets:
advantages of, 86–87
Asian, 54, 63–67, 218, 222,
226
and cash market position, 2,
28–29
coal, 122, 128–131
crude oil, 14, 40–43, 218
development of, 12–15
electricity, 6, 14–16, 48,
98–99, 113–117
European, 38, 49–50, **50–51,**
113–117
vs. forward markets, 11
future trends in, 222–223,
236
and inventory management,
81–82
natural gas, 6, 14, 15, 46, 71,
73–75, 78–79

vs. off-exchange markets,
6–7, 19–20, 26, 29, 79–80,
82, 84
options pricing models for,
146–147
vs. physical markets, 13,
16–17, 19, 41, 64, 79–81
purpose of, 5
regulation of, 30–31
technical analysis for,
180–181, 185–193

Gamma risk measure for
options, 150–151, 152
Gas futures (*see* Natural gas
markets)
Gas tolling agreements, 112
Gasoil markets, 14, 38–39,
43–45, **50–52**, 56–58, **58**
Gasoline markets, 13–14, 16, 66
Geographic diversity, in port-
folio management, 170,
178
Geography, and natural gas
risk
management, 75–78
Germany:
as gasoil market, 43–44
Metallgesellschaft fiasco, 26,
223
Global Derivatives Study
Group, 158
Globalization of energy mar-
kets, xiii–xvii, 68, 222,
224–225, 232
Gold standard, 136
Gulf Coast unleaded gasoline,
13–14
Gulf War, 42, 60

Heating oil, 12, 13, 14, 16
(*See also* Gasoil)
Hedge vs. speculative
margins, 4–5, 13
Hedging strategies:
and cash flow management,
34
and coal futures, 129
and corporate culture, 3–5,
7
for credit risk, 211, 212–213,
214–215
disincentives for, 54
early energy, 12
for electricity, 111–112
and futures market, 30
and geographic basis risk,
75–76
for options, 14, 27, 28,
82–83, 150–156
and swaps agreements,
18–20, 22
and technical analysis, 179,
187, 193–194
and value at risk method,
162
Henry Hub futures contract,
73, 76, 78–79
Hin Leong, 57
Historic volatility, options,
143n6
HSFO (High Sulphur Fuel Oil)
market, 63, 64
Hungary, exchange developments, 221

In the money (ITM) option,
139, 140
Independent Power Producers
(IPPs), 69, 91–95, 109,
113, 200

Indexed deals, definition, 26
Indexes, price, 17, 18, 97–101,
    219
Information, and credit risk
    issues, 212–213
Inside information, 188
Insurance companies, invest-
    ment in energy markets,
    237
Interconnector pipeline, UK-
    continental, 49
Interest rate risk, 229
Interest rates, and options
    prices, 144
Interexchange arbitrage, 15–16
Intermarket arbitrage, 15–16
International coal markets,
    130–131
International Petroleum
    Exchange (IPE) (*see* IPE
    (International Petroleum
    Exchange))
International Power Exchange
    (IPEX), 102
Internet, and computerized
    trading, 104
Intramarket arbitrage, 15–16
Intrinsic value, options, 25,
    138, 139–140, **140**, 144
Inventory management, 81–82,
    125, 129
IPE Brent, 43
IPE (International Petroleum
    Exchange), 13
  and benchmarking, 39–40
  electricity markets, 47–48,
    113
  future developments, 48–49
  and gasoil market, 44
  management of Brent con-
    tracts, 43

organization of, 37
types of petroleum traded,
    14
IPEX (International Power
    Exchange), 102
IPPs (Independent Power
    Producers), 69, 91–95,
    109, 113, 200
Iroquois pipeline system, 76
ITM (in the money) option,
    139, 140

J. Aron, 11
Japan, and energy markets,
    62–63, 67–68, 69, 234–235
Jet fuel market, 27, 219

Kansas City Board of Trade
    (KCBT), 15, 78
Katy Hub, 76

Less-developed countries
    (LDC), 33, 221, 236
  (*See also* Asia Pacific energy
    markets)
Liberalization, energy market,
    46–47, 67–68
  (*See also* Deregulation)
LIFFE (London International
    Financial Futures and
    Options Exchange),
    49–50
Liquidity issues, 10, 15, 25–26,
    28–29, 225–226
LNG (liquefied natural gas)
    market, 228, 233–235
Location swaps, 24
London International Financial
    Futures and Options
    Exchange (LIFFE), 49–50
Louis Dreyfus Energy, 11

Magnox, 109
Malaysia, and futures market, 218
Margin deposit, 13
Marked-to-market procedure, 13
Market makers, function of, 31–33
Market price, vs. strike price, 25
Market risk (*see* Price risk)
Market sentiment, and options prices, 25
Market-to-market value, 196–197
Markowitz, Harry, 165
MCS (Monte Carlo Simulation) technique, 137n4
Mean reversion effect, 199
Mega NOPR (Notice of Proposed Rulemaking), 94–95
Metallgesellschaft, 26, 223
Mexico, hedging strategy of, 226
Moneyness, 139
Morgan Stanley, 11
Municipalities, credit risk role, 200

NAPEX (Nanking Petroleum Exchange), 219
Naphtha, open spec market for, 10, 61–63
National Balancing Point (NBP), 46
National Grid Company, 110
National Power, 109, 113
Nationalization, 33, 54, 55, 219–221, 236
Natural gas companies, as market makers, 32

Natural gas markets:
Asian, 68–69
banking role in, 34–35
basis risk in, 75–78
computerized trading in, 101, 103
and electricity market, 45, 72, 85–87, 96, 112, 235–236
European, 38, 45–47, 49, **50–52,** 108, 112
as forward market, 11–12, 71, 72–73
futures contracts in, 6, 14, 15, 46, 71, 73–75, 78–79
and growth of paper markets, 222
inventory management, 81–82
liquefied natural gas (LNG), 228, 233–235
options in, 82–85
and physical markets, 17, 72–74, 79–81
risk management adoption, 2
swaps agreements in, 23, 24, 29–31, 33–34, 84–85
and technical analysis, 189, **190–192,** 193, **194**
NBP (National Balancing Point), 46
Negotiated access, 108
NERC (North American Electricity Reliability Coordinator), 120, 121
Netting provisions, 198, 210
New York Harbor unleaded gasoline, 13–14, 16
New York Mercantile Exchange (NYMEX) (*see* NYMEX (New York Mercantile Exchange))

Nonperformance problems, in
swaps transactions,
29–31
Nord Pool, 114, 115
Nordel, 107
Nordic electricity market,
114–117
North American Electricity
Reliability Coordinator
(NERC), 120, 121
North American energy markets:
vs. Asian, 27
coal, 120–131
electricity, 89–105
vs. European, 145
natural gas, 75–87
North Sea oil production, 54
(*See also* Brent crude oil)
Norway-Sweden electricity
market, 114–116
Notice of Proposed
Rulemaking (Mega
NOPR), 94–95
Nuclear power generation,
Swedish phase-out of,
117
NYMEX (New York Mercantile
Exchange), 3, 13–14
coal futures, 128–129
and crack spreads, 16
electricity futures, 98–99
electronic trading system,
224–225
natural gas contracts, 15,
73–74, 78–79
and SIMEX, 65

OASIS (Open Access Same
Time Information
System), 95
Off-exchange instruments:
and credit risk, 200

future trends in, 230–232,
236
and integration of futures
and physical markets,
79–80
market makers' role in,
31–33
and OTC basis for natural
gas, 77–78
performance risks of, 29–31
vs. regulated exchange markets, 11
rise of, 2, 6–7
(*See also* OTC (over-the-
counter)
instruments)
Ofgas, 46
Oil markets:
Asian development of,
54–58, **58,** 60
basis for pricing in, 10
capital requirements,
226–229
European, 38–39, 40–45, 54,
220–221
futures development in, 13
and growth of paper mar-
kets, xiii–xiv, 222
indexed loans for, 228–229
risk management adoption,
2
as soft commodity, 6
synthetic instruments for,
230–232
(*See also* Crude oil markets)
Oil trading companies, market
role of, 10–11, 32
Oil warrants, 237
Oil-collateralized loans, 226
Oil-indexed loans, 228–229
OPEC (Organization of
Petroleum Exporting
Countries), 42

Open Access Same Time
  Information System
  (OASIS), 95
Open interest, 222
Open outcry system, 38, 43, 74
Open specification naphtha
  market, 10, 61–63
OPIC (US Overseas Private
  Investment Corp.), 33
Options:
  as alternative to futures,
    14–15
  crude oil markets, 153–154
  European, 27, 38, **52**, 84, 145
  exchange-traded, 15, 82–85,
    146–147
  over-the-counter (OTC), 2
  advantages of, 4, 6–7
  and benchmarking, 223
  electricity market, 99–101
  elements of, 24–28
  future trends in, 229
  and market makers, 32
Options theory:
  hedging strategies, 154–156
  importance of, 133–137
  option premium factors,
    138–145
  pricing models, 145–150
  risk measures, 150–153
OTC (over-the-counter)
  instruments:
  and credit risk, 196, 200
  in electricity market, 99
  electronic trading in, 225
  vs. futures markets, 75, 79
  global growth of, xvi–xvii,
    222
  for natural gas, 77–78
  and tax basis, 224
  uncertainties in use of,
    223–224

(*See also* Options: over-the-
  counter (OTC); Swaps
  markets)
OTM (out of the money)
  option, 139, 140

Paper markets:
  Asian developments, 34
  Brent market as, 10
  global integration of,
    224–225
  growth of, xiii, 222
  and oil price basis, 10
  vs. physical market, 29
  (*See also* Forward markets;
    Futures markets)
Participation hedge/swap, 28
Performance issues, 10, 29–31
Permian Basin market, 15, 76,
    78, 79
Phibro Energy, 11
Phibro Energy Unit Trust,
    230–231
Physical markets:
  Asian, 59–60, 64, 67,
    218–219
  and dated Brent, 42
  developing areas' prefer-
    ence for, 221
  and electricity markets, 100
  in European gasoil, 44
  vs. futures market, 13,
    16–17, 19, 41, 64, 79–81
  global integration of,
    224–225
  in natural gas, 72–74, 79–81
  and options, 84
  vs. paper markets, xvi, 29
  secrecy in, 43
  vs. synthetic instruments,
    236–237

Platt's published price assessment, 44–45

Pool prices, UK electricity, 110–111

Portfolio management:
and credit risk, 199, 211–212, 213–214
theory of, 136
and value at risk method, 161–162, 165–170, 174–178

Powder River Basin (PRB), 127, 128–129

Power EX Corp., 102

Power market (*see* Electricity market; Independent Power Producers (IPPs))

Power marketers:
credit risk role, 200, 203, **203–204**
Eastern Power and Energy Trading, 112
Florida Electric Power Coordinating Group, 104
growth of, 95–97
Power EX Corp., 102

PowerGen, 109, 113

PPP (pool purchase price), 110

Premium, options, 25–26, 138–145

Premium price, vs. discount price, 1

Price:
options, 24–27, 83, 138–150
spot market, 10, 115–116, 123–125, 147, 171

(*See also* Benchmark price; Volatility, price)

Price discovery, in natural gas, 72
(*See also* Price transparency)

Price indexes, 17, 18, 97–101, 219

Price risk:
Asian lack of, 55
banks' role in, 34
and benchmarking, 40
in coal market, 127–128
vs. credit risk, 197–198
definition, 1
and deregulation movements, 67, 68, 124
and market makers, 31
and retail price protection, 236
and rise of derivatives market, 62–63
swap agreements' role, 10, 19, 20

Price swap (*see* Swaps market)

Price transparency:
in coal, 129
in electricity, 89, 93, 97–98, 99, 100–101, 113
in natural gas, 72, 81–82, 87
need for, 218

Privatization of electricity industry, 109–110
(*See also* Deregulation)

Producers, energy:
advantages of swaps for, 20–22
floors usage of, 22–23
Independent Power Producers (IPPs), 69, 91–95, 109, 113, 200
need for fixed income, 9
need for futures contracts, 12
unbalanced book usage, 19
(*See also* Corporations)

Project finance application, 226–228, 237

Propane, 14
Prudhoe Bay Royalty Trust,
    230–231
PSP (pool selling price), 110
PURPA (US Public Utility
    Regulatory Act of 1978),
    91
Puts, options, 14, 24, 28, 137,
    144–145

Qualifying facilities (QFs),
    91–93

Railroads, and energy trans-
    portation, 125–126
Random walks, 135
Reciprocal collateral
    arrangement, 210
Refiners, capital requirements
    of, 227
Regulated exchange markets
    (see Exchanges, commod-
    ity; Exchange-traded
    instruments)
Regulation, government, role
    in energy markets, 41–42,
    55, 60, 61
    (See also Deregulation)
Relationship banking, 34–35
Renewable resources, 91–92
Reserves, credit, 209
Resistance in technical analy-
    sis, 183–184
Risk, financial, types of, 1–2
Risk limits, and value at risk
    method, 169
Risk management:
    advantages of, 72
    expansion of, xiii–xvii, 2–4
    need for risk capital, 75
    (See also Hedging strategies)

Risk measures, for options,
    150–153
Risk-free arbitrage opportuni-
    ty, 135n2
Risk-return ratio, 168–169

Salomon Phibro Unit Trust,
    230–231
San Juan Basin, 76
Scandinavian electricity
    market, 114–117
Season contracts, European
    electricity, 114
SERC (Southern Reliability
    Coordinator), 120
SFE (Sydney Futures
    Exchange), 65, 222–223
SIMEX (Singapore
    International Monetary
    Exchange), 13, 14, 49,
    63–64
Singapore swaps market,
    56–61
Single-buyer system for elec-
    tricity, 108
Sinochem, 57
SMP (system marginal price),
    110
Sour crude oil, 13–14
Southern Reliability
    Coordinator (SERC), 120
Soviet Union, former,
    prospects for derivative
    instruments in, 221
Spark spread trading, 16, 85,
    113
Speculation, 4–5, 13, 179–180,
    185–187
Spot market prices:
    electricity, 115–116, 171

vs. fixed-price contracts,
123–125
natural gas, 72–73
oil, 10
options prices and, 147
Spread trading:
Brent crude oil market, 43
and credit risk, 207–209,
208, 210, 211
definition, 15–16
electricity market, 16, 85,
113
"stacking and rolling,"
options, 26
State-owned energy compa-
nies, 33, 54, 55, 219–221,
236
Stochastic analysis, 135n3, 147,
147n9–11
Storage, energy (*see* Inventory
management)
Straddles, options, 83–84
Strangles, options, 83–84
Strike price, options, 24, 25,
26–27, 83, 138–140,
144–145
Support in technical analysis,
183–184
Swaps markets:
advantages of, 4, 20–22, 23
in Asia, 54, 56–61
banks' role in, 18, 32
brokerage firms' role, 33–34
in electricity, 18, 23, 99, 100
and forward market, 10,
228–229
functions of, 17–22
future trends, 23–24,
222–223, 226, 232
and futures markets, 6
in gasoil, 45

integration with cash
markets, 2
and market makers, 31–32
in natural gas, 23, 24, 84–85
participation hedge/swap,
28
performance issues, 29–31
Swaptions, 27–28
Sweden-Norway electricity
market, 114–117
Swing swaps, 84–85
Sydney Futures Exchange
(SFE), 65, 222–223
Synthetic instruments,
154–155, 230–231,
236–237
System marginal price (SMP),
110

Tapis crude oil, 218, 226
Tax basis, and OTC instru-
ments, 224
Technical analysis, 179–194
Theta risk measure for
options, 151
Time value, options, 25, 138,
139–140, **140**, 144
Toll processing, 85
Transmission access, electric,
93–95
Transportation issues, 75–77,
125–126, 127
Trend analysis, technical,
182–185
#2 heating oil, 13, 14, 16

UCPTE (Union for the Coordination of Production
and Transmission of
Electricity), 107
UK Electricity Act of 1988, 109

UK-continental interconnector,
47
Unbalanced books, advantages
of, 19, 29
Unilateral collateral
arrangement, 210
Union for the Coordination of
Production and
Transmission of
Electricity (UCPTE), 107
United Kingdom (UK) energy
markets, 45–47, 109–113
United States energy markets
(*see* North American
energy
markets)
Unleaded gasoline futures,
13–14
US Commodity Futures
Trading Commission, 30
US Energy Policy Act (EPACT)
of 1992, 89–90
US Overseas Private
Investment Corp. (OPIC),
33
US Public Utility Regulatory
Act (PURPA) of 1978, 91
Utilities:
and computerized trading,
102, 104
credit risk role, 200, 202,
204, 212–213
deregulation of, 121–125
as market makers, 31
and natural gas resources,
34–35, 85–86
and power marketers, 96–97
risk management adoption
by, 2–3, 4
societal role of, 90

transmission access issue,
94–95
(*See also*Electricity markets;
Natural gas markets)

Value at risk (VaR) method:
contract application,
162–164, 172–174
definition, 159
in electricity markets,
157–159, 160–162
implementation challenges,
171–172
portfolio application,
165–170, 174–178
"variation margin," 13
Vega risk measure for options,
151, 152
Volatility, price:
in coal market, 127–128, 131
in electricity market,
110–111, 116
and evolution of energy
markets, xiv–xv, 5
and options, 25–26, 27,
141–144, 143n6–7, 149
and portfolio management,
166–167

Waha Hub, 78
"Wall Street Refiners," 10–11
Weather derivatives, 233
Week contracts, European elec-
tricity, 115
West Texas Intermediate (WTI)
crude oil, 13, 15, 41, 231
Western Natural Gas Contract,
78
Western Systems Coordinating
Council, 98–99

Western Systems Power Pool
   (WSPP), 89, 98, 102, 103
Western vs. Asian energy
   markets, 53–56, 59–60
Wholesale book, value at risk
   for, 174–177

WSPP (Western Systems Power
   Pool), 89, 98, 102, 103
WTI (West Texas Intermediate)
   crude oil, 13, 15, 41, 231

Yield volatility, 143